the new complete

Portuguese Water Dog

Friendship's Chloe (Ch. Neocles Acabado ex Ch. Neocles Candida), owned by Debra A. Bender, takes to ball playing as she does to water. Chloe's obvious zest for whatever comes her way is typical of the Portuguese Water Dog's love of activity and a heritage from the breed's life on the swelling oceans. Debra A. Bender

the new complete

Portuguese Water Dog

kathryn braund

illustrations by verne foster

HOWELL
BOOK
HOUSE

Howell Book House
Published by Wiley Publishing, Inc., New York, NY

For general information on our other products and services or to obtain technical support please contact our Customer Care Department within the U.S. at 800-762-2974, outside the U.S. at 317-572-3993 or fax 317-572-4002.

Wiley also publishes its books in a variety of electronic formats. Some content that appears in print may not be available in electronic books.

Library of Congress Cataloging-in-Publication Data:

Braund, Kathryn.
The new complete Portuguese water dog/Kathryn Braund : illustrated by Verne Foster.
p. cm.
Rev. and updated ed. of: Complete Portuguese water dog. 1st ed. 1986
Includes bibliographical references.
ISBN 0-87605-261-8
1. Portuguese water dog. I. Braund, Kathryn. Complete Portuguese water dog. II. Title.
SF429.P87B73   1997
636.752—dc21   97–1267
CIP

Manufactured in the United States of America.
10   9   8   7

Book Design: George McKeon
Cover Design: George Berrian

Dedication

To
Deyanne Farrell Miller
(1931–1988)
First Lady of the
Portuguese Water Dog in America
who inspired the modern revival of interest in the breed, assuring it a
permanent place in the world of dogs.
She surely smiles down from Heaven
happy to see her living labor of love thriving.

And to
Cyril J. "Buzz" Braund
hero of World War II and hero of my heart
without whom I would not have the delight of owning
these incredible dogs nor could I have written this book.

And to
Carol B. Oakes
dear friend
who contributed greatly to having the original Portuguese Standard
for the breed translated into English.
And one who, like the rest of us, truly loves the
Portuguese Water Dog.

Today the Portuguese Water Dog fits into a host of popular performance sports. It shines as a show dog, is a natural for Agility and all levels of Obedience competition, can do the breed's work just as its ancestors did and makes an excellent Tracking Dog.

Contents

Foreword

The first edition of *The Complete Portuguese Water Dog,* published in 1986 by Kathryn Braund and Deyanne Farrell Miller, was probably the most helpful tool that every new and experienced Portuguese Water Dog owner had available to assist them in owning, raising and breeding this super-wonderful breed we all like to call "Porties."

This revised and updated version, *The New Complete Portuguese Water Dog,* by Kitty Braund, covers the extraordinary progress that has been made within the breed since the first edition was published. The number of owners of the PWD today is so much greater than it was ten years ago, as is the number of AKC registrations, and all aspects of the breed have been so improved upon, that a revision of the "PWD Bible" was definitely needed. We can all be grateful to Kitty for accepting the responsibility of this tremendous undertaking.

Deyanne Miller, having been a Poodle breeder for many years before she became involved with Portuguese Water Dogs, was well aware of the hereditary and congenital problems that had plagued many breeds. She was determined not to allow this to happen to the PWD if she could help it. Fortunately, the Portuguese Water Dog Club of America's Board of Directors, members and PWD advocates that followed Deyanne (who passed away in July, 1988) have felt the same way. The PWD fancy of today has taken an outstanding leadership role toward discovering, researching and eliminating problems within the breed, under the supervision and guidance of Dr. Jerold S. Bell, the Veterinary Genetic Counselor who has worked closely with the parent club and has added greatly to this book.

The chapters on performance events can teach us all much that is new, and refresh the skills of the more experienced among PWD enthusiasts concerning all aspects of these marvelous activities. The breed, by virtue of its remarkable intelligence, trainability and versatility, has already, in the relatively few short years of official recognition in this country, distinguished itself in all facets of performance competition.

This updated and well-researched history of the breed by Kitty is a must for all Portuguese Water Dog owners. To be knowledgeable of the origins of our breed and its purpose for being is an absolute necessity, if current and future breeders are to maintain the breed's extraordinary integrity and not allow it to go the way of many other breeds. So many breeds have long since lost many of their natural instincts and ability to pursue the purpose for which they were originally bred. This must not happen to our wonderful "Porties."

There is so much more to be learned about the Portuguese Water Dog, which is very young within our culture by comparison to many breeds. It therefore behooves us all to continue to broaden our knowledge and understanding of this extraordinary canine. This book promises to continue not only to be a source of information and enjoyment, but to be a very needed tool for all of us to utilize in our breeding programs.

Bill and Betty Trainor
Farmion
Oxford, Massachusetts

About the Author

Kathryn Braund is a native of Redwood City, California and was brought up in San Francisco. Following an early career in the theater—stage, radio and vaudeville—she married. After raising her two sons, Patrick and Gary, she worked in advertising and public relations. She eventually became a writer and editor of technical publications for aerospace companies. When her sons were almost grown, she began writing professionally about the animals she has always loved—dogs.

Her previous books are *The Uncommon Dog Breeds* (Arco, 1975), *Dog Obedience Training Manual, Volume I* and *Dog Obedience Training Manual, Volume II* (Denlinger's Publishers, 1982 and 1983), and she co-authored, with Deyanne Farrell Miller, *The Complete Portuguese Water Dog* (Howell Book House, 1985).

Along with her writing for several dog magazines—*Front And Finish*, *AKC Gazette*, and *Canine Chronicle*—in 1988 Kathryn took on editorship of *The Courier*, the newsletter of the Portuguese Water Dog Club of America, Inc. She developed the newsletter into an award-winning slick magazine. Under Kathryn's editorship, *The Courier* received, in both 1989 and 1990, a coveted Best Single Breed National Club Magazine nomination by the Dog Writers Association of America (DWAA) and won the Best National Club Publication Maxwell award for 1991, 1992 and 1994—unprecedented wins. Kathryn retired as editor of *The Courier* in the spring of 1993. In May 1994 she was brought back to resume this position.

She has won over two dozen *Best* awards along with over a dozen Certificates of Merit from the DWAA, including, in 1985, Best Breed Book and Best Book of the Year for *The Complete Portuguese Water Dog*, an honor she shared with Mrs. Miller. Her *Obedience Training Manual, Volume II*, was nominated Best Training Book of 1983. She retired in 1983 as Obedience Editor

The author, Kathryn Braund, and one of her Roughrider Portuguese Water Dogs sharing a good game of "Fetch."

of the *Spotter*, the Dalmatian Club of America's quarterly magazine, after ten years in that post.

Another honor of which she is very proud is the Public Service Award (1983) from the DWAA for her article in the *American Kennel Gazette*, "Fire in a Motor Home."

Kathryn has been a member of the Dog Writers Association of America since 1971. She served as its Secretary-Treasurer for three years, 1980 through 1983, and has been its Newsletter Editor since 1980. In 1985, the DWAA honored her with its Outstanding Service Award for her newsletter contributions.

A breeder of both Dalmatians and Portuguese Water Dogs under the Roughrider kennel name, Kathryn's Dalmatian, Ch. Roughrider's Rogue, CDX, was No. 7 in the top-rated *Canine Chronicle* national system and No. 10 in the Dalmatian Club of America show dog ratings in 1985. Her beautiful Dalmatian bitch, Ch. Roughrider Koda's Kid, UD, placed in the Non-Sporting Group many times. Kathryn has personally placed over two dozen obedience titles on her own dogs, including Utility Dog (UD) titles. She has been a member of the Dalmatian Club of America since 1972 and of the Portuguese Water Dog Club of America since 1983.

Kathryn taught obedience classes from 1970 through 1994 throughout the United States. Her "Teen Age Dog Obedience" classes brought her national acclaim from dog trainers such as Edi Munneke. She also conducted classes for military families at several Air Force bases for over twelve years. These include Grand Forks AFB, North Dakota; Whiteman AFB, Missouri; and Malmstrom AFB, Montana.

Kathryn has been a Portuguese Water Dog breeder since 1984. Her Ch. Farmion Geo, UD(Diver), sent to her by Mrs. Miller, was the first male and the third of the breed to earn a Utility Dog title. He was also top-producing sire of champions until mid-1994. Ch. Camcrell's Roughrider Seeley, CDX (Seeley) tops all the records as top-producing dam of champion get with twenty-three. A Best-in-Show–winning homebred is Ch. Rough Seas First Buoy AWD (Stormy Gremlin). Stormy was Best of Breed at the Westminster KC show twice, and in 1994 was second in the Working Group at this prestigious show. Roughrider has at least forty-five obedience-titled PWDs, including five Utility Dogs and several with AKC Tracking degrees PWDCA water titles.

Kathryn and her husband Cyril were married during World War II and make their home near the village of Winlock, Washington. Kathryn still teaches obedience classes occasionally, and when not teaching, writing, showing her dogs, or helping whelp a litter of Portuguese Water Dog puppies, she pursues hobbies such as fishing and gardening.

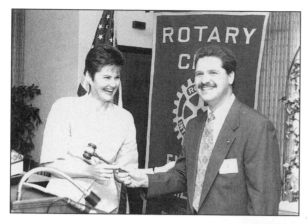

Jerold S. Bell, DVM

Augusto Guimaraes

Verne Foster

Acknowledgments

I thank the Portuguese Water Dog fancy for the submission of stories and photographs of Portuguese Water Dogs.

I am grateful to the following friends for their valuable assistance: Vicki Storrs of Oak Harbor, Washington and Elsa Sell of Taos, New Mexico for their proofreading assistance; and Ranny Green of Seattle, Washington, pet editor of the *Seattle Times*, for his perusal of the copy and suggestions for improving portions of my rough draft.

I thank Augusto Guimaraes of Cascais, Portugal for the information he forwarded from Portugal, and Carol B. Oakes of Potomac, Maryland, for her translations from the Portuguese. She not only had the material translated, she made sure the dictionaries used were compiled during the exact period when the books and articles were written. Due to Mrs. Oakes' diligence for impeccable accuracy, the original Portuguese Standard for the *Cão de Agua* is translated into English as the Portuguese authors would have wished.

Thanks to Michael B. Murphy, DVM, of the Steamboat Animal Hospital, Olympia, Washington for his contribution. We interviewed and thank Gene Rivers DVM, Fellow, Academy of Veterinary Medicine, and veterinary practitioner at the VetSmart Hospital and Health Center, Puyallup, Washington for helping us on the Teeth section of the Health chapter.

I am indebted to Jerold S. Bell, DVM, canine geneticist and small animal veterinary practitioner of the Veterinary Genetic Consulting Clinic of Enfield, Connecticut, who shares his wealth of expertise in the Health chapter.

And last, I thank Verne Foster of Hollis, New Hampshire for her proofreading and suggestions for improvement while creating the drawings and maps seen throughout the text.

Following are brief biographies of three principal contributors—Dr. Jerold S. Bell, Verne Foster and Augusto Guimaraes.

JEROLD S. BELL DVM

Jerold S. Bell, DVM, is the Portuguese Water Dog Club of America's clinical veterinary geneticist. He discusses the four health problems presently found in the breed in our Health chapter.

Dr. Bell was trained in genetics and genetic counseling at Michigan State University, the University of Missouri and the Jackson Laboratory at Bar Harbor, Maine. His Doctorate of Veterinary Medicine is from Cornell University. Dr. Bell is the course director of the Clinical Veterinary Genetics course for the Tufts University School of Veterinary Medicine. He is the national project administrator for numerous genetic disease control programs of purebred dogs. Dr. Bell is a frequent lecturer to all-breed dog and specialty clubs.

VERNE FOSTER

Verne Foster attended Bradford College in Massachusetts, a small liberal arts school with limited art opportunities. Nevertheless, she took every art class the school offered and graduated with honors. Her art experience with animals, Portuguese Water Dogs in particular, is largely self taught. She practices on her two PWDs, who are constantly called upon to pose for her. Artist for the PWDCA's magazine, *The Courier,* for the past ten years, Foster owns *Pawtraits*, a small pet portrait shop specializing in illustrations and cartoons of dogs.

In her spare time Foster is active in showing and training her dogs. Each of her three PWDs have been outstanding performers in obedience competition.

AUGUSTO GUIMARAES

In 1942, at age ten, Augusto Guimaraes of Cascais, Portugal, owned his first dog, a Portuguese Water Dog. In his teens and as a young man he met Vasco Bensaude (Algarbiorum Kennels), Conchita Cintron (Al-Gharb Kennels) and Dr. Antonio Cabral (de Alvalade Kennels) and has remained friends with Ms. Cintron over the years.

A fluent linguist, Guimaraes attended college in England, graduating with a degree in textile engineering. Before his retirement, he was an advertising executive for both Lever Brothers and Lufthauser.

For over fifty years Guimaraes has dedicated his life to stray, abandoned, unregistered and registered dogs. All of them, old and young alike, live in his house in Quinta de Marinha, Cascais. As a serious breeder he has bred countless champions in Portugal and abroad. Today, his attention has turned toward selective breeding of the *Cão de Agua* (Portuguese Water Dog) and the intrinsic study of genetics.

Guimaraes is a founding member of the Club Portugues de Canicultura and the founding member and first president of the Clube Do Cão De

Companhia De Portugal. He was elected in 1993 as Honorary president of the latter. He and the owner of White Tower Kennels, also located in Cascais, organized the first opthamoloscopic (CERF) examination clinic in Portugal in 1994. Dr. James Clinton traveled to Portugal from the United States to conduct it in conjunction with the Portuguese veterinarian Dr. Neiva Rorreia. Democrate De Gifford and Eurico De Gifford—the only two dogs in Portugal to have traveled to the United States to undergo and successfully complete the health tests (GM-1, OFA and ERG)—were owned by Guimaraes.

SYMBOLS DESCRIBING VARIOUS FOREIGN REGISTRIES WITH TITLES

A.D.
Ascendencia Desconhecida (ancestors unknown)

C.B.
Champion in Portugal

FCI
Federation Cynologique Internationale

LOP
Livro de Origens Portugues, the Clube Portugues de Canicultura Stud Book

CPC
Clube Portugues de Canicultura

R.I.
Initial Registration with the Clube Portugues de Canicultura

Eligibility for a LOP number:
Only after three generations will a dog with an R.I. number be eligible to be exported and/or receive a LOP number. In a second generation, if the dog or bitch with an R.I. receives an "Excelente" after being examined by one judge at a Portuguese dog show he will be granted a LOP number. However, until he has three known generations behind him, he will not be accepted in another country (such as in the U.S.).

Championship in Portugal
A dog has to place first, "Excellent," in four shows. One of the shows in which he wins a qualifying point must be held in Lisbon or Oporto. The second city (Oporto) changes yearly. The dog must win under three different judges.

chapter 1

Modern Homeland Setting

The Portuguese Water Dog's history is linked with that of its homeland. Portugal is, like this amazing canine, picture perfect in its beauty. It's a small country, only 345 miles long and 140 miles wide, covering but 35,510 square miles.

The Minho River forms Portugal's northern boundary with Spain. The northern region is indented with mountains, forests of pine, cork and oak trees, plains and vineyards. The highest mountain range, the Serra da Estrela, stretches up to 6,537 feet. One of Portugal's three great rivers, the Douro, flows west and south from its origin in Spain, spilling tributaries into beautiful valleys before it drains into the Atlantic near the city of Porto. The second great river, the Tego (or Tagus), flows (again from Spain) west through the middle highlands and empties itself into a wide bay in the gracious city of Lisbon.

The third is the river Guardiana. It winds south rather than west over southern Portugal. In this region, renowned for its grapes, oranges, tangerines, figs and almonds, the Portuguese Water Dog was sequestered for many centuries. The peaceful tribes who settled along the pleasant ocean shores were loath to have their dogs leave the picturesque garden country, called the Algarve (meaning "water"), except as important gifts or items of trade. Here, where sheep are raised on green, lush ground, where brilliant hues of blue coat the skies and temperamental seas rush grandly against rock cliffs or sweep gently into harbors, the countryside speaks romance. The dog of choice reflects this feeling.

It is essential to gain a concept of what has stamped this dog with its fundamental, high-powered canine character. Certainly the Portuguese Water Dog's ancestry reflects the skills its ancient masters taught it. It seeks the water as a bird does the sky. To get a clearer focus of the modern Portuguese Water Dog, let's examine its worldly background as well as the setting in which it was discovered by modern civilization.

1

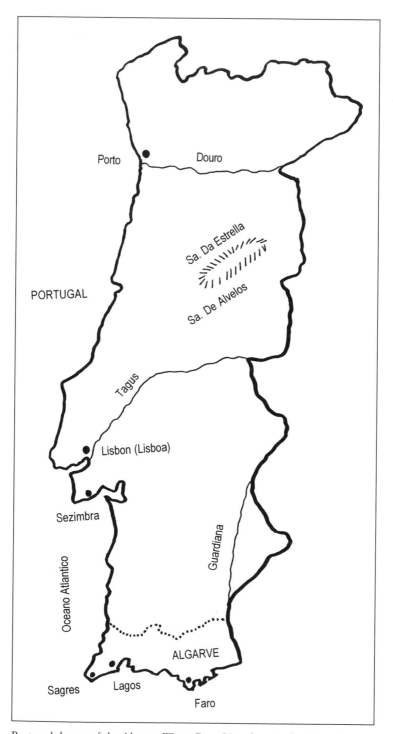

Portugal, home of the Algarve Water Dog. Line drawing by Verne Foster

Early humans were connoisseurs of animals. There wasn't much to distract them from becoming experts in this field. Not only did they have time to study the natural world around them, their survival depended on how they dealt with their immediate surroundings. They observed how animals and plants adapted to their environments; they were cognizant of the animals around them—that the best bred to the best. Even without always recognizing the whys and wherefores, they strove to emulate the animals' impeccable patterns of natural selection in reproduction in their immediate family of plants and animals. In time, small pockets of agrarian society focusing on plant and animal husbandry became known for their art in creating the best maize, the swiftest horses, the most superior beef cattle, the better dogs. The ancient ancestor of the modern Portuguese Water Dog was one of the latter.

THEORIES

Picture the dogs of ancient Asia, the one continent that was in immediate contact with almost every ocean and other continent. Visualize the wild central Asian steppes (the Kirghiz area of Russia). Here, near the Chinese border, were vast, grassy, treeless tracts, with scattered mountains, valleys, lakes and rivers relieving the Spartan landscape. The region is characterized by extreme temperatures. The Tien Shien Highlands, the Pamir Mountains, the Karagiye Depression, the Ural Sea and Lake Balkhash lie here. The terrain and water of the region was guaranteed to nourish ruggedness.

The early peoples who lived here were hunters in the Old Stone Age, or Mesolithic era. They were gatherers in the New Stone Age (Neolithic). They lived off the land, eating wild grains. Eventually, they began raising their own cultivated grain and making their clothing from sheep's wool. Sheep were raised strictly for wool, and cattle for food. Depending upon the territory in which they lived, these people also raised camels or horses.

Archeological findings indicate they reared herding dogs. Isolated from the rest of the world, full of courage and ferocity, their herding dogs were highly interbred within each ancestral clan. Some of these dogs developed into a definite type. The Portuguese Water Dog is a typical example.

The perpetual tugs of wars resulted in frequent migration. The conquered, not waiting to count on miracles from the gods, took their animals and fled the steppes for the far corners of the world. The victors of the conflicts—Cimmerians (700–600 B.C.), Cimbri (100 B.C.) and Goths (100–200 A.D.)—carried away herding dogs, as well as other animals and people, as spoils of war. They spread these in all directions as they pillaged along the early roadways of the world. Before the captives finally settled in their new cultures, some had made incredible migrations.

One theory suggests that some of the dogs left the Asian steppes with the Goths, a confederation of Germanic tribes. The Goths divided. Ostrogoths ventured west, and their dogs became the German Pudel or Pudelin. Visigoths

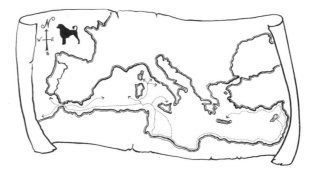

Trade routes along the Mediterranean (Mare Internum) used by Phoenicians and Romans.

traveled south to fight the Romans, with their dogs becoming known as the Lion Dog. Moderns can only guess how the term "Lion Dog" originated. Were the dogs of the ancients shorn in this manner to fashionably image in coat style the strength and boldness of the lion, or were the dogs sheared for cleanliness and serviceability?

Long before Roman times, merchants traversed the continent of Asia on their trade routes. Their ships rode along the edges of the Mediterranean (Mare Internum)—the greatest water route and the center of life in those early times—to seaside ports. Phoenicians, even earlier than 1500 B.C., boldly ventured past the Mediterranean's only opening and sailed on into the Atlantic. Along with the variety of tribes that settled in the area came a variety of dogs, many called by the two common names in use: Canis Leo and Canis Turkus.

Romans also developed settlements in Portugal during their control of the Mediterranean, from about 133 B.C. to 337 A.D. In a technique passed down by the Romans, who developed dog breeding and training to a high art, the dog of the primitive societies that lived along the Algarve was taught to herd fish into a net. It retrieved lost tackle and broken nets, and it served as a courier from boat to boat and from boat to shore.

These tribes "adapted and selected their dogs for fishing and hunting," reported the Portuguese writer Silveira Santana in 1948, "and that semi-natural selection ended up with the Algarve Water Dog."

Santana also said, "Water Dogs are considered the most intelligent dogs of all—[the dog is] robust, a tireless swimmer and resistant to fatigue, a diver like no other...inasmuch as it is not afraid of the temperature and it dives voluntarily into the sea, be it winter or summer, to go in search of a cable, a broken net, or any other object which might have fallen or fish which might have escaped from the net. It also provides good services as a communications agent between the ship and land, even at great distances."

Proof of the Water Dog's intelligence is reflected in the sacred books of the Persians, the Zend-Avesta. In the seventh century, the Water Dog was said to be the most valued of all canines, including even the shepherd dog. The great god Ahura-Mazda gave it the qualities of a saint for its exceptional abilities.

Two plausible theories for the development of the Portuguese Water Dog, both of which accord with the migrations, are these: The Visigoths, Germanic tribes who invaded the Iberian Peninsula in the early fifth century, could logically have carried their Russian Water Dogs, called Pudels (meaning "water"), with them. Alternatively, when the Moslem Arabs and Moors conquered the area in the eighth century, it was they who may have brought to the Algarve the ancestors of what was to become the Portuguese Water Dog.

For canine historical background, however, we rely on many ancient canine legends that were transferred to print by English authorities of the middle centuries. The English, more than any other nationality, explained in glowing and accurate detail the exploits of dog breeds popular in their as well as in ancient times. One such commentator, Gervase Markham, wrote about the Water Dog in 1621:

> Your Dogge may be of any colour and yet excellent...; his head would be round and curled, his ears broad and hanging, his Eye full, lively and quicke, his nose very short; his lippe, Hound-like, side and rough bearded, his Chappes with a full set of strong Teeth, and the general features of his whole countenance being united together would be as Lyon-like as might be, for that shewes fiercenesse and goodnesse: His Necke would bee thicke and short, his Brest like the brest of a Shippe, sharpe and compact, his Shoulders broad, his fore Legs straight, his Chine square, his Buttokes rounde, his ribbes compassed, his belly gaunt, his Thyes brawny, his Cambrels crooked, his Pasterns strong and dewe clawde, and his foure feet spatious, full and round, and closed together to the cley, like a water Ducke, for they being his oares to rowe him in the water, having that shape, will carry his body away faster. And thus you have a description of a perfect Water Dogge...

OTHER THEORIES

Certainly, the intimate knowledge English dog men had of the likeness of the Water Dog gives credence to the theory that Portuguese Water Dogs entered early and mid-century England via trade. Long before the Armada sailed, Galway, Ireland and Bristol, England were ports of call for Portuguese ships carrying goods to Iceland. A treaty in 1353 between the Holder of the Port of Lisbon and the King of England permitted Portuguese fishermen to catch fish in the ports of the kingdom and Britain and other ports of congenial places, paying merely the customary taxes. And in these middle ages, the Portuguese fishermen sailed almost all of the seven seas. Prince Henry of Portugal sent an African lion to Galway in 1429.

Portugal's Famous Legend

A Portuguese legend about the Portuguese Water Dog reaches back to 1297, with a monk's description of the dog that rescued a dying sailor from the sea: "The dog was of black coat, the hair long and rough, cut to the first rib and with a tail tuft. This tuft was white as were the feet and nose."

The Ill-Fated Armada

There's also a popular theory that numbers of the Algarve Water Dog sailed with the Spanish Armada in 1588, serving as messenger dogs between ships. This theory suggests that the Portuguese Water Dogs bequeathed some of their character and looks to such breeds as the Kerry Blue Terrier, Curly-Coated Retriever and Irish Water Spaniel. Portuguese author Margarida Ribeiro wrote that the Portuguese Water Dog was taken from Portugal to Spain during its occupation of Portugal (1580–1640). "As the dogs filtered into Spain," she wrote, "they went to the streets where their robustness was immediately recognized. They were put at the service of the different ships in the invincible Spanish fleet, especially trained as life-saving dogs."

But King Phillip II of Spain had lists drawn up of every statistic of the ill-fated Armada. According to these lists, every one of the 130 mainly unseaworthy ships was crammed full of men and supplies. The average ship carried a complement of 100 sailors, plus convicts and slaves for oarsmen—a minimum of 300 soldiers, along with officers and their servants, gunners and priests. Listed among the inventories were horses and mules for later support for the Spanish "conquerors" on the conquered English soil. But when the battle had been lost and the remnants of the Armada turned to sail home, the Spaniards, "to save water, which was the worst worry of all...threw overboard the horses and mules they had brought for the land artillery.... A merchant ship that crossed the armada's track reported the sea full of animals, still swimming."

Author David Howarth, who wrote *The Voyage of the Armada,* conducted the bulk of his research at the castle of Simancas, Spain, where King Phillip established archives. In all of these surviving documents, there is no suggestion of Caes de Agua (Portuguese Water Dogs) accompanying the Armada. It is inconceivable that dogs, who require both care and food, would be allowed to take up space and time on these crowded ships. The hardships for humans aboard were unbearable, with the fleet doing minimal cleanup. Death from inedible food and undrinkable water, from filth and infectious disease was rampant. Who would care for and clean up after dogs on this disastrous undertaking? Oddly enough, listed in the fleet's statistics were four small Portuguese galleys, oared. So the theory is possible! Still, most of the wild Irish, Scottish and English tribes living along the shorelines who first rescued and then killed many of the scattered human survivors seldom had food enough for themselves. It's unlikely they would have allowed dogs that landed on their shores to remain alive. They would have eaten them.

VARIED FORMS OF THE WATER DOG

So it is logical that the Algarve Water Dog bequeathed traits to English dogs through trade rather than by landing on British soil as an Armada survivor. Varied forms of the Portuguese Water Dog existed in England, Ireland and continental Europe before the Armada fiasco. This is proven by the words of Markham and other Englishmen—and also by Sweden's Carl von Linne, known as Linnaeus (1707–1778). Linnaeus developed a classification system of plants and animals that is named after him. In his listing of dogs, he described both the Great Water Dog ("hair is long and curled like the fleece of a sheep") and the Lesser Water Dog ("of a small size with long curly hair, which about the ears is longer and hangs downward").

Even so, most people in the middle centuries were convinced the Poodle was the ancestor of the "common water-dogges." The reverse is probably true. Sir William Jardine, in his *Naturalist's Library* (published in 1843), alludes to the "water dog or Poodle." He says that "The Water-dog, Canis Aquaticus," was of German origin in its most perfect state, rising into favor first in Germany during the revolutionary wars of the 1870s, then carried by troops into France, and later becoming known in Spain, Britain and the Netherlands. In Jardine's words: "The coarser crisped-haired Water-dog was indeed long known to the middle classes of England, and to fishermen on the north-east coast; he was occasionally brought to the environs of London.... No dog is more intelligent or attached to his master...."

Conversely, *The Sportsman's Cabinet*, Vol. 1 (1803), says, "The Water-dog...an unshaved and rather short-headed Poodle...is of so little general use that the breed is but little promoted, unless upon the sea-coast...these dogs are exceedingly singular in their appearance, and most probably derive their origin from the Greenland dog, blended with some particular race of our own."

The Water Dog, by Reingale, from *The Sportsman's Cabinet* (1803). This drawing has been reproduced in numerous books on a variety of breeds, showing this dog as ancestor of many breeds.

In *Der Pudel Kraus und Pfeffig,* Von Ulrich Maurach says:

The Poodle looked quite different once and with this fact contributes to the dispute about his origin. The French and the Germans claim the creation of this curly dog for themselves; the Barbet and the Cão de Agua belong to his ancestors. The first, a curly Shepherd Dog from North Africa, with a passion for swimming, came through the wars of the Moors to Portugal and Spain. There he crossbred with the Portuguese Water Dog of the local fishermen, the Cão. This dog is a water-loving hunting dog, spirited, obedient and feisty, who looks more like his Poodle descendants than the Barbet. But the mustachioed African gave as his heritage, his woolly coat as well as his alertness, trainability and loyalty. The result of this cross—so it is said—was a dog with a wavy coat who, because of his use in water hunting, was shorn on parts of his body to make swimming easier. On other parts of his body the coat was left at full length to avoid problems with rheumatism. Science gave him the Latin name Canis aquaticus (water dog) without pinpointing the exact time of his existence.

THE CÃO DE AGUA'S LONG HISTORY

Whatever theory or theories prove true, there's no myth about the breed's history. The Portuguese Water Dog has existed for thousands of years. The theory that the PWD is an overgrown Barbet has no truth. The Barbet, Puli and Spanish Water Dog are much shorter than the PWD. Neither do they have the proud, slightly aloof attitude the PWD often expresses.

The fishermen along the Algarve deployed their dogs to help them in their rough, often dangerous work at sea. The fishing fleets swelled through the centuries until, in the early 1900s, there were more than 16,000 Portuguese fishing boats dotting the sea off of Portugal's coast. In this vital industry (quelled by the advent of radio and electronic technology) fleets traveled frequently to Newfoundland, bringing back cod. The Algarve Water Dogs rode in the bobbing trawlers as their masters worked their way to the waters of Iceland and Newfoundland. Imagine, for a minute, the dog standing proudly in the bow, barking during dense fog, alerting other boats of its position.

Like its Portuguese master, who was full of energy and lived life to the fullest, so, too, did the beloved Algarve Water Dog. The happy, cheerful, loving, intelligent yet sensitive PWD of today reflects the gifts the fishermen wove into its genetic spirit as they defined in it the qualities they needed to support their work in the sea.

"Twenty-five men were sailing with two dogs, who earned as much as the men," wrote Portuguese author Raul Brandão in his book *The Fishermen* (Lisbon, 1932). He observed the dogs who worked on the ketches of Olhão: "It was a breed of animals with a lot of fur, one watching each side of the ship and at the fishermen's side. The fish escaped when the lines were pulled in and the dog jumped into the sea and grabbed them in the middle of the water, taking them on board in its mouth."

This historic photo, taken in 1898, in the Atlantic near the village of Cascais, 25 kilometers west of Lisbon, shows an Algarve Water Dog, Segasto, in the traditional clip. The dog belonged to an uncle of Francesco de Costello Branco, husband of Conchita Cintron (Al-Gharb Kennels). Courtesy Conchita Cintron

Maria Ana Marques, another Portuguese writer, quotes from an article about the Portuguese Water Dog written by Dr. Manuel Fernandes Marques in 1938: "Fishermen considered him a member of their crew...having, as any other member, a right to a share of the fish, as rations, a portion approximately equal to that of each man; and more than one-quarter part, in money, of whatever is earned by each member of the crew."

In 1938, when Dr. Marques, a medical veterinary professor, wrote the original Portuguese breed standard, he also wrote about the dog in an article entitled "The Style of Race," published in the journal *Veterinary Medicine*. He wrote:

As far as the origin of this precious animal, nothing can be said for sure. Was it the Phoenicians, the real seamen of old, coming from the Persian Gulf into the Mediterranean and from there radiating out into the Vermillion Sea, the Atlantic, the Baltic oceans, who brought with them the water dog, stopping in the south of Spain, in Cadiz, on the Atlantic coast? Was the original water dog who served there remnants of an older breed of previous times? It is impossible to be certain of this. It is certain though, that his appearance is of old, giving us the impression through literature and old texts, that his existence was noted in various parts of the world without indicating the actual place of origin.

Dr. Marques also said in this article:

Some authors pretend that the water dog actually existing in different countries had to have as his origins Alemanha, Dinamarca, Franca, Italia, Portugal, Russia. Already in the 16th century, there were included, confusedly, by the general denomination of Barbetos, all the dogs of curly hair who entered into the water, some of which were used as bird dogs to chase ducks. Some were known in France as Chiens Caniches. Today the confusion no longer exists. Today the Barbetos, Spaniels and Poodles or the Caiens Canards with only the females called Caniches, are completely separated into different groups. To those authors the proposed Barbetos or Caniche would have originated from various countries in Europe—

Germany, Denmark, Portugal, Russia or from the north east of Africa, like Morocco. As you can see, opinions differ and doubt exists. The great Barbeto, as Dr. Henrique Anacoreta referred to it in his writings on peninsula dogs, published in the journal Caca, around 1901, is that in those times there was found along the coastal provinces, especially in the Algarve, what was with certainly not a show dog but most likely a water dog.

Again, to quote Marques from his article "The Water Dog" (*Magazine of Veterinary Medicine*, Lisbon, 1938):

...Sometimes the dog would see a fish fall from the line and, instead of diving into the sea in search of it as it would habitually do, it would run below deck and hide itself in the ribbing, barking. In cases such as these, sailors never obligated the dogs to obey, because, as they say, the behavior of flight should be interpreted as a signal of the approach of a shark or sharks, whose victim the dog would be if forced to enter the sea; true as it is, some dogs feared being killed by them when caught by surprise in the sea.

The breed is called by several names—Cão de Agua (pronounced Kown-d-Ahgua), *cão* meaning "dog," *de agua,* "of the water"; "Diving Dog," "Portuguese Fishing Dog" and "Algarve Water Dog." Spaniards sometimes call it "Sea Dog"; Americans, "Portuguese Water Dog" and "PWD." Whatever the dog is called, it has retained much of its original skull configuration, conformation and high intelligence.

REGISTRATIONS

"Before 1955," wrote Dr. Maria Marques in 1981, "there appeared registered with the Livro de Origens Portugues (LOP), 100 dogs of the breed name of Algarbiorum. Part belonged to other persons who are not of the Vasco Bensaude family.

"Vasco Bensaude followed the ancient tradition of never selling his dogs, only 'gifting' to other people."

In 1994, the Cão de Agua placed ninth on Portugal's canine popularity poll, with 386 dogs registered. Many Portuguese litters are not registered, and the number of nonregistered dogs in 1994 can be estimated at about 200.

Ana Victoria Ruivo, a resident of Faro in the Algarve, is a forty-year breeder of Portuguese Water Dogs. Her warm relationship with the Cão de Agua goes back to the era when her father, an owner of fishing vessels, used the dogs in various fishing tasks. Until the early 1990s, Senhora Ruivo, who placed many dogs she bred as "family dog gifts" to those she knew, never found the need to register her Caes de Agua. To satisfy those who wanted her to export one or more of her canine family treasures from future litters, she finally opted to get Initial Registrations (R.I.) on each.

Portuguese breeder Ana Victoria Ruivo, president of Faro, with Rolfe and Bianca. Courtesy Augusto Guimaraes

Augusto Guimaraes (De Gifford Kennels), Casa Val De Areal of Cascais, Portugal, is the only breeder in Portugal to have traveled to the United States with his dogs to have them undergo tests for OFA, Storage and PRA disease clearances. "The De Gifford dogs," wrote American Jeanne Rylatt, who exported several puppies from Guimaraes, "are off-square dogs with broad heads, wide muzzles and outgoing temperaments. To see five or six 'native' PWDs on the beach in Portugal is a sight that will stay in our memories. The breed's fascinating history came crashing down in my heart as the surf came crashing on to the rocks. I couldn't help but see in my mind's eye the days of long ago when the fisherman would bring in his catch accompanied by these dogs."

Because of the growing popularity of the breed in its homeland, almost a dozen ocean water trials are held each year, most near Lisbon. They remain almost identical to Bensaude's original tests: a swim, a retrieve and a

Breeder Augusto Guimaraes (De Gifford Kennels) of Cascais, Portugal, with several of his PWDs on Guincho beach, Cascais. Courtesy Yoão Pe Doaso Fernandes

dive. Today, also, at Portuguese dog shows, a fair representative of Caes de Agua are exhibited.

CROSS BREEDING

Not all Caes de Agua in Portugal (or those exported) are purebred, even though they appear to be. As in many countries, unregistered dogs play a large role in supply and demand. Although Vasco Bensaude, the Portuguese founder of the modern breed, would have found it unthinkable to mongrelize the breed with infusion from any other, there is speculation in some quarters of Portugal about cross breeding the Cão de Agua with the Portuguese Sheepdog, the Cão da Serra De Aires, as well as with Labrador Retrievers, Poodles, Bichons, and even Afghans! There is, however, no actual proof of these matings. Through the centuries corrective outcrosses have often been made to improve certain qualities such as temperament, coat or overall structure in a breed.

By not culling incorrect animals, some Portuguese Water Dogs now carry definite brown markings on black coats, long ears, long thin muzzles, long necks, fluffy curls, straight fine hair, hound and otter tails or extremely angulated rear legs; there are also dogs small in structure, long in back and short of leg. Foreigners like to blame the R.I.

Evidence of one such "mistake breeding" is shown by the improperly coated Cao de Agua located in a cage at the Zoo de Lisboa in 1990. It was here, sadly, that Makuti died. Makuti was a dog frequently used at stud— first owned by sr. F. Janeiro (Casabranca Kennels), then by Carla Molinari (do Vale Negro Kennels), and finally sent to the zoo. Carla Molinari describes him in her book *The Portuguese Water Dog* (1993): "Ch. Makuti, extensively used at Vale Negro, transmitted his powerful construction and massive head." Makuti died in a kennel next to the lion cages. This zoo, which used to maintain domestic dogs and cats, does not keep them anymore. It was deactivated in 1994 when it became forbidden by regulations (C.E.E.) to keep pet animals in zoos. "During the years it was the place to send unwanted dogs to die," remarks breeder Guimaraes. "There is now a national kennel in Porto, a handsome establishment, which breeds the Cão de Agua in order to 'save' the breed."

Responsible breeders must watch out for "accidents" (which can happen to anyone) and select and breed carefully, always visualizing the ideal dog in the Standard. Bensaude, savior of the breed, practiced this for twenty-nine years, using each bitch two or three times. Never did he allow his dogs to go to those he suspected would use anything that came along to satisfy their breeding plans or who would falsify breeding charts. Bensaude believed in Leão, who was his Portuguese Water Dog Standard ideal. The Cão de Agua owes much to this impeccably honest man, with his high ideals in breeding.

A possible cross breeding—the Cão de Serra de Aires, an intelligent, hardy herding dog of Portugal. It has a strong head with a pronounced stop, dark eyes and nostrils and a thick, long, rough coat and is colored either red, black and tan or black and tan. Line drawing by Verne Foster

Another possible cross is suggested by this improperly coated puppy, which suggests Afghan Hound ancestry. Although the genes are now blended in a number of strains, use of the probable cross added length of leg and silky texture. Since sighthounds have a higher percentage of red blood cells, this infusion undoubtedly added higher endurance to an inbred strain. Courtesy Kathryn Braund

VASCO BENSAUDE AND LEÃO

Our modern history of the Portuguese Water Dog begins in the 1930s. Vasco Bensaude, a shipping magnate and man of varied interests—gardener, aviculturist, beekeeper, photographer and marine architect—also raised dogs. At one of his homes, Quinta dos Soeiros in Benfica, he raised Irish Wolfhounds, Cocker Spaniels, Clumber Spaniels and, later, Labrador Retrievers.

Eventually, Bensaude became interested in the Water Dog through his friends, Renato Pinto Soares and Manuel F. Marques, both from Sesimbra

Leão, founding sire of the modern Portuguese Water Dog. Courtesy Bensaude Archives

(not too many kilometers south of Lisbon). There, a few Water Dogs still worked on boats. Soares had brought two bitches from Seisimbra in the 1920s—one chestnut and one white. They intrigued Bensaude, but his interest was not aroused until informed by Marques that the breed was threatened with extinction and that there was in Albufeira a magnificent "crew and work dog, named Leao," owned by a retired fisherman. Bensaude then went to the Algarve to see this "magnificent working Cão de Agua."

There are two stories telling how Vasco Bensaude acquired Leão.

In the first version, after Bensaude saw the dog work, he eagerly offered to buy him. The fisherman said, "No, definitely no. He does my work for me. I will never sell him for any price. I will sell him only on the day I leave the earth...in grand style." No matter how much money or what other enticements Bensaude offered, the fisherman refused to give up Leão. Bensaude returned to Lisbon deflated but not defeated. He didn't give up hope that one day he would acquire Leão. The day came sooner than expected. Several weeks later he received a letter from the son of the fisherman. The father had died, and Bensaude could have Leão.

The second version asserts that after Bensaude saw the dog work, he offered to purchase him. The fisherman said, "No, definitely no. He does my work for me. I will never sell him." Finally, weary of Bensaude's continued offers, the fisherman smiled and said, "All right, I'll sell him—but only if and when I win the lottery." Several weeks later, Bensaude received a note from the fisherman's son saying his father had won the lottery and Leão was his.

Whichever account is true, when Bensaude acquired Leão, the renaissance of the Portuguese Water Dog began!

Fausto Pereira dos Santos, Bensaude's kennel master, collected the dog, and Leão quickly adapted to his new life. He enjoyed riding in cars with Bensaude, as well as the attention he received from the two daughters of the house, and he allowed himself to be trained by Fausto. Occasionally, Leao would run away, and each time he was found at the house of his former master.

Finally, Leão settled in for good. Everyone who met him said he was an extraordinary dog. Leão and a Cocker Spaniel lived together in Vasco Bensaude's home in Lisbon. If the door to a bathroom was left open, Leão would walk in, open the water faucet in the tub and lie in the water! Bensaude built pools for his dogs and enjoyed watching Leão dive into them. He would dive even in the winter, retrieving bricks from the bottom of the pools. His favorite water toy, however, was a hard rubber ball that floated when Fausto

Leão in show trim. Courtesy Bensaude Archives

Leão, plunging into one of Vasco Bensaude's pools. Courtesy Bensaude Archives

attached it to a cane. He lived in the kennels too, particularly when Bensaude was traveling. Then Fausto, a proponent of daily conditioning, would release him from his kennels and Leão would go bounding to the big pool where the water lilies grew, first taking a broad jump, then vaulting the back wall and the stone wall before plunging into the pool.

Bensaude socialized Leão readily, and the dog quickly became famous. He was noted for his intelligence, affection and temperamental, almost moody, nature. Some who knew him said he should have been human. The only drawbacks they recognized were his four legs and the fact that he couldn't talk.

Leão (1931–1942) was the founding sire of the modern breed. His first litter of Water Dogs from Bensaude's Algarbiorum Kennels was born on May 1, 1937. The three males and five females were out of a bitch, Dina, whom Bensaude had acquired from the Algarve shortly before he acquired Leão.

Leão sired seven litters. "All other [Algarbiorum] litters were of his descendants," wrote Dr. Maria Ana Marques in 1981. Marques, a veterinarian, inquired about the breed's history upon the urging of the Portuguese Dog Breeders Club. "Some dogs," she wrote in an article, "The Portuguese Water Dog—First Historical Notes," "came from the Algarve, such as Nero and Venesa, but they were always crossed with descendants of Leão such that all Algarbiorum dogs received, to a greater or lesser degree, blood from the dog which served as model for the race."

CONCHITA CINTRON DE COSTELLO BRANCO

Founder of the Portuguese Kennel Club and its Secretary General for years, even after he resigned his membership, Bensaude's passion for the Water Dog never died out. He had brought the Cão de Agua back to life. He had placed dogs with trusted friends. However, there was no one to whom he wished to entrust his dogs in case the unexpected happened to him. He kept his eye out for someone who would care for the dogs as he did.

Recommended to him by his veterinarian was a Perdiguero Portugues (a Portuguese hunting breed) breeder and exhibitor whom he had seen at dog shows, Senhora Conchita Cintron de Costello Branco, the renowned former lady bullfighter and noted horsewoman. Orson Welles had written about her when introducing her bullfighting memoirs: "Women who live by the sword have always been rare to the point of nonexistence...Conchita Cintron, the lady bullfighter, therefore, is a very great rarity indeed. Her record stands as a rebuke to every man of us who have ever maintained that a woman must lose something of her femininity if she seeks to compete with men. Conchita competed. Nobody was ever more perfectly feminine, and she triumphed absolutely in the most flamboyantly masculine of all professions."

When Cintron was introduced to Bensaude, she was theruvian Civil Attaché at the Peruvian Embassy in Lisbon. (Her diplomatic service career with the Peruvian Embassy spanned twenty-seven years.) She and her husband,

Conchita Cintron Castello de Branco of Al-Gharb Kennels in 1995 with Eurico de Gifford, owned and bred by Auguto Guimaraes. Courtesy Augusto Guimaraes

Francisco, were invited to have lunch at the Bensaude home, where they also met his wife and his daughter Patricia (with whom Cintron remained friends). They arrived at one P.M. for lunch and stayed until eight in the evening. When introduced, Bensaude said to Cintron, "You have a better dog than I." She replied that his dog was the better, but hers was better behaved. It was a singular contact. Although they never saw each other again except at dog shows, Bensaude decided that Cintron was the one person he would trust.

Sometime later, at a dog show, among the prizes Cintron won was the "Bensaude Cup." When she asked why the cup carried his name, she was told he had passed away (August 5, 1967). Shortly after that incident, Bensaude's widow contacted Cintron, telling her she had inherited all of Bensaude's dogs. Cintron inherited no money; she inherited four males, ten females and boxes full of detailed archives concerning the dogs! After conferring with her husband, she informed their six children the family now had a large family of dogs to care for. Cintron had kennels built on their eighteen-acre farm south of Lisbon and named them Al-Gharb (an ancient version of Algarve). But after the dogs arrived, they climbed and jumped out of the runs—six feet, six inches high—which she then had to top. She had been told the dogs were difficult to breed and that some were infertile, so it was decided to breed them all. Eighty-nine puppies arrived!

A PRECIOUS LEGACY

Cintron, entrusted with Bensaude's precious legacy, knew she had to place the dogs carefully so the breed would thrive and prosper. As Portugal was a relatively poor country, few fishermen could now maintain dogs, and few workers could afford to care for them. Cintron was sure the breed would never survive in its pure form in Portugal, and Bensaude willed them to her knowing she would make sure none of his beloved Water Dogs would become common street dogs. Well acquainted with the love Americans had for purebred dogs, she decided Portuguese Water Dogs would enjoy a valuable future in the United States. She spent many hours every week writing letters to people in the States telling them about the breed. During a visit to the Portuguese Embassy in Washington in 1970, Cintron fascinated guests with stories about the dogs and her fervent hope that Americans would take this fascinating breed to their hearts.

It was from Cintron, in 1968 and 1971, that Deyanne and Herbert Miller, Jr., of New Canaan, Connecticut, acquired a breeding pair. The Millers' interest was piqued in 1965, and they researched the breed because of its possible kinship to Standard Poodles, which Deyanne raised. They had seen offspring of two English-bred PWDs shipped from England in 1960, from a strain that later died out. Instead of purchasing one of these, as did Sonja and James Santos of Long Island, New York (who later became prominent PWD breeders), Mrs. Miller sent to Portugal for a copy of the breed Standard. Next, she asked a friend, Mrs. Sherman Hoyt, for advice. Mrs. Hoyt, an international dog judge, who imported the first Poodles into America in the 1920s, urged Miller to examine the Portuguese Water Dog in greater detail.

The Millers met with Conchita Cintron in July 1968, saw her dogs (including a one-day-old bitch), and after returning to New Canaan, decided to introduce Portuguese Water Dogs—born in their homeland—to the United States.

chapter 2

The Portuguese Water Dog in America: The Early Years

Introducing a rare breed to the public is a wonderful treat few experience. Certainly, the personality of Deyanne and Herbert Miller's first imported Portuguese Water Dog, Renascenca do Al Gharb, delighted them and a soon-to-be-burgeoning fancy. Whelped July 12, 1968 at Cintron's kennel in Portugal, "Chenze" arrived in the United States on September 16, 1968, as a saucy, insouciant and self-assured youngster. She remained a delightful companion to live with for fifteen years.

It was a heady time for the Millers, to be sure, but some of the offspring of Chenze and other bitches produced offspring with multiple health, temperament and coat problems. Some older puppies were euthanized because of "degenerative neck vertabrae" and "epilepsy—neuro degeneration." Later it was realized they must have been afflicted with Storage disease. Some were overly protective and/or aggressive, reticent with strangers and prone to obesity. Still others had undershot bites.

Consequently, it wasn't easy locating good homes for dogs of this rare breed. Few wanted a pup, no matter how adorable, with a high potential for health problems. Deyanne Miller and others took back dogs. Yet many owners remained determined to resurrect the breed. Portuguese Water Dogs completely altered their lives—not simply because of their rarity, but because most had wonderful character and a comfortably yesteryear shaggy-dog appearance. Sixteen fanciers founded the national club, the Portuguese Water Dog Club of America, in 1972. Deyanne Miller imbued many with dedication. She smiled while she persevered and urged others to do the same when breeding tragedies struck.

Deyanne Farrell Miller with Judge R.E. Beckwith and author Kathryn Braund in Montana at the first PWDCA AKC Sanctioned A match (1986). Courtesy Duncan Bobowiec

One of her first buyers was the late Helen Roosevelt. Roosevelt resided near the Millers in Connecticut, but lived in Florida in the winter of 1971. She saw the Millers' advertisement in her local Connecticut newspaper, which she regularly received in Florida. The ad described a puppy from the "first Water Dog litter born in the U.S." When she contacted Mrs. Miller, she learned that the pup was a six-month-old male out of Chenze and Anzol do Al Gharb, Chenze's half-brother, purchased from Conchita Cintron by the Millers in 1969. The pup had been sold tentatively to the famed mariner Jacques Cousteau and would be living aboard the *Calypso*. Miller explained to Roosevelt, "There are eleven sailors aboard her and he is turning out to be a one-man dog. He'll probably do better with you because you will be a one-dog owner."

Roosevelt replied, "I want a good dog. You say he is. I also want a guard dog. And because I live a block from the ocean, a water dog will do just fine."

Farmion Azinhal (Cristo) arrived in Florida on December 17, 1971. He developed into a very good watch dog. "He was also very gentle," Roosevelt wrote later, "carrying my glasses around in a very soft mouth, bringing me my Lady Danielle cigarette holder or my solitaire playing cards and so forth. He was quite an unusual and different dog, extremely regal in the way he held himself. He's the reason I've always been interested in Algarbiorum. I saw the difference between him and some of the others."

Farmion Azinhal (Anzol do Al Gharb ex Renascenca do Al Gharb) was from the first litter bred in the United States of Portuguese imports. Courtesy Richard Meek

Helen Roosevelt with a grandson of Christo, Ch. Bittersweet Maximillian (Victor's Vencedor ex Zinia de Alvalade), handled by Mark Threllfall. Max was born on July 30, 1984 and was BOB at the Westminster KC in both 1989 and 1990. Courtesy John Ashbey

Barbara and Ed Whitney of Smithtown, New York, staunch breed supporters, also purchased a dog from Chenze's first litter. Ed, who later served as PWDCA vice president and board member and is now an AKC obedience judge and PWDCA Water Trial judge, tells the story:

It seems only yesterday that Barbara and I met Deyanne Miller and were introduced to our first Portuguese Water Dog, Renascenca do Al-Gharb, and her "A" litter. I had a Pearson 30-foot sailboat and was looking for a dog that could go sailing with us. In the summer of 1971 I read an article by Walter Fletcher, in the *New York Times*, about this rare breed. He finished the article with the comment that this breed did not exist here in the States. I turned to the classified ads and found an ad Miller had put in the paper!

I drove up to Farmion and looked at America's first litter. I saw a male that I liked and asked Miller, "How much?" I was told $350. I thought this was a high price to pay for a dog and went home. But I couldn't get that dog out of my mind. Barbara had no interest in a dog since it would tie us down. I had to have him. So I drove back to New Canaan, Connecticut and purchased Farmion Algoz, whom we named Gully.

Gully was a great companion, rather aloof with strangers and a small version of the breed. Barbara and I enjoyed him, and he had a great, if short, life with us. He spent most of his summers sailing on our Pearson 30 and really liked being around us—a real "people" dog. I took him to a couple of obedience classes so he would be better behaved.

One summer day we found ourselves docked in a slip at Essex, Connecticut, and became friendly with a couple next to us. They came aboard and we socialized for some time. Gully was his lovable best, accepting goodies from anyone that was kind enough to offer. Barbara and I then decided to go to dinner and we placed Gully inside the cabin. When we were gone our boat friends ran into some people they knew and wanted to introduce them to this rare breed. When they got aboard the boat Gully's guarding instinct took control. They were amazed that such a friendly dog, when we were around, could turn into such a beast. Gully was a great guard dog.

Miller purchased only the two dogs—Chenze and Anzol—from Cintron. She next went to the Portuguese veterinarian and president of the Clube Portugues de Canicultura (CPC), Dr. Antonio Cabral, for an import. Cabral was also in charge of the Canil da Camara (Lisbon Counsel Kennels). He was responsible for pickup and disposal of all the city's lost and stray dogs.

Cabral's main breeding focus was Smooth Fox Terriers. As a sideline, he undertook breeding all Portuguese breeds, with the idea of preserving and developing those that were facing extinction, but he could not obtain any of Bensaude's Algarbiorums. The first Cão de Agua of his de Alvalade line was an R.I. dog, Silves, registered in 1954. Cabral raised some dogs at the Lisbon Counsel Kennels, close to his apartment. He also sent other dogs he retrieved from the streets and from the Algarve—after giving them R.I.s—to Carla Molinari, who was establishing kennels less than twenty-five miles away. From

1970 to 1978, all the de Alvalades were born at Val Negro (including those known to Americans—Truta, Trovoada and Tordo). It was at her do Vale Negro kennels that Molinari maintained her prize-winning Afghans and Salukis. It was from her kennels that most de Alvalades were exported to America.

From 1965 to 1975, the de Alvalade kennels at Val Negro had only two bitches to breed: sister look-alikes, Truta de Alvalade and Trovoada de Alvalade, born October 19, 1970. When Trovoada was eighteen months old, in 1972, Cabral exported Trovoada to Miller. Lumpi was the only male. Here is the LOP record of Truta's nine litters. Her last two, in 1979 and 1980, were whelped at do Condinho Kennels, owned by Portuguese breeder Sally Starte. Dogs notable in the pedigrees are listed in the column at the far right.

Litter No. 1	February 24, 1973	Lumpi x Truta	Xelim
Litter No. 2	March 7, 1974	Tordo x Truta	Yole
Litter No. 3	March 18, 1975	Taro x Truta	Zum-Zum
Litter No. 4	April 17, 1976	Taro x Truta	Amora
Litter No. 5	October 16, 1976	Taro x Truta	Arriba
Litter No. 6	November 17, 1977	Arriba x Truta	Baluarte
Litter No. 7	May 16, 1978	Taro x Truta	Charlie
Litter No. 8	May 24, 1979	Taro x Truta	Dana (U.K.)
Litter No. 9	May 30, 1980	Ruby x Truta	Farol

The other males of the de Alvalade line were sons of the aforementioned bitches. Ria, Trovoada and Truta's mother, arrived at do Vale for only one litter and disappeared from view. She was not an Al-Gharb descendant (as called out on page 99 of *The Complete Portuguese Water Dog*) of Algarbiorum dogs. Taro, who sired five litters out of Truta, wasn't an Algarbiorum dog in either structure or size. He was a small foundling to whom Cabral gave an R.I.

Following is a letter from Cintron this author received in January 1996. It corrects pedigree inaccuracies in the two breed books, *The Complete Portuguese Water Dog*, by Kathryn Braund and Deyanne Farrell Miller, and *The Portuguese Water Dog*, by Carla Molinari.

Dear Kathryn,

I am including two homemade photos of Al-Gharb adults and juniors spending a while with us at the beach on a cold winter day in 1972. Perhaps they can convey some of the love and care that surrounded their lives.

Taro, a wavy-coated dog, bred to Truta five times, was a small foundling, with ancestors unknown, to whom Dr. Antonio Cabral granted Portuguese registration (R.I.).

Conchita Cintron in a training session with two of her Al-Gharb dogs at the large pool on her beautiful 18-acre farm south of Lisbon. The dog at her lef 's the BIS winner, Rey do Al-Gharb. Courtesy Conchita Cintron

I know this contribution comes into conflict with the phantasy that during 1971 I had put an end to the Al-Gharb kennels. But this is precisely my intention. 'Rey do Al-Gharb' (meaning King) stands out clearly. The previous summer he was Best In Show (BIS) competing with imported foreign animals. It was the first time a Portuguese dog won such an award!

Another misinformation is to be found in your *Complete Portuguese Water Dog* and has to do with errors in pedigrees. On page 95, the female Farrusca, dam of the Alvalade line (Dr. A.B. Cabral), is said to have been born on August 30, 1951 out of C.B. Azinhal Algarbiorum and C.B. Dala Algarbiorum.

Litter No. 27 of Mr. Vasco Bensaude's archives informs us that on August 30, 1951 Azinhal and Dala produced nine (9) puppies, four (4) males and five (5) females.

One female was eliminated (put aside) due to accentuated prognathism (undershot jaw). The puppies' names and registered numbers are as follows:

Nadas	male	5079/51
Narval	male	5080/51
Nodal	male	5081/51
Nese	male	5082/51
Nauta	female	5083/51
Nanja	female	5084/51
Nipa	female	5085/51
Negrela	female	5086/51.

Farrusca, in your book, acquires a LOP No. 7.481 document. I don't know how this was managed but I do know, because Vasco Bensaude has a detailed account of every animal born, acquired or transferred in his Algarbiorum kennels, that Farrusca is not mentioned in any of the archives folders.

Another detail: page 99 in *The Complete Portuguese Water Dog,* Lampreia do Alvalade (female) born 8/20/62 appears as Quito Algarbiorum's offspring. Let us see: Quito Algarbiorum, LOP 776/R2995, born March 27, 1942, died March 15, 1947. This means that Quito Algarbiorum died 15 years before Lampreia do Alvalade was born. Last but not least, page 99. I refuse, as owner of the Al-Gharb kennels, to accept an unknown bitch, called Ria, as an Al-Gharb descendant of Algarbiorum dogs.

Wishing you all the best!

Conchita Cintron.

A copy of the LOP from 1957 (shown here) depicts Farrusca as being born in Bensaude's litter No. 27, yet she does not carry the Algarbiorum kennel name. A copy of the LOP from 1951 is also shown in which the dogs registered in the litter are listed. According to information from Cintron re Bensaude's archives, no bitch of this litter was given away or eventually transferred to the de Alvalade kennels, nor was any renamed and given a new LOP registration number. The pedigrees that list Farrusca should therefore be revised, with her parentage listed as A.D. (ancestors unknown).

In 1977, Molinari returned Truta and Taro to Cabral in Lisbon. Since he had no place to keep dogs, he handed them over to his daughter, Antonia. At the time she lived in a small apartment and could not keep dogs there for long. Portuguese breeder Sally Starte took them from Antonia when she collected her puppy Collette (whelped May 16, 1978). Taro and Truta lived with Starte for the rest of their lives. It was there that Truta whelped her last two litters. Because statistics point out PRA was brought to America by de Alvalade

SECÇÃO DE CANICULTURA

LIVRO PORTUGUÊS DE ORIGENS

VOLUME IV

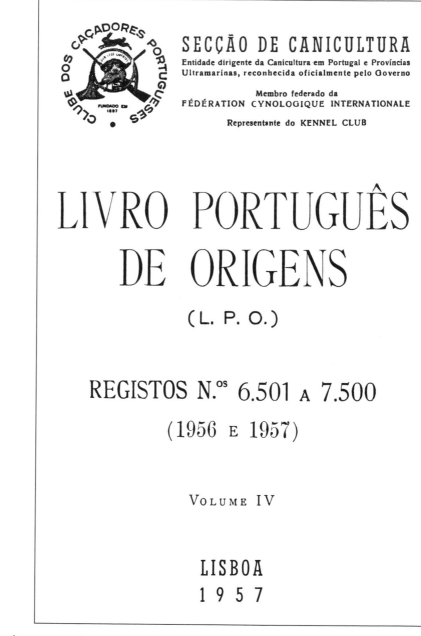

SECÇÃO DE CANICULTURA

Entidade dirigente da Canicultura em Portugal e Províncias
Ultramarinas, reconhecida oficialmente pelo Governo

Membro federado da
FÉDÉRATION CYNOLOGIQUE INTERNATIONALE

Representante do KENNEL CLUB

LIVRO PORTUGUÊS DE ORIGENS

(L. P. O.)

REGISTOS N.ᵒˢ 6.501 A 7.500

(1956 E 1957)

VOLUME IV

LISBOA
1957

Copy of a page in Volume IV, Registos Nos. 6.501 to 7.500 (1956 to 1957) of the LOP,
which lists the name of Farrusca.

— 36 —

CANICHE FRANCÊS GRANDE
Cão

Rex d'Henri Vert — 6.619 e N.H.S.B. 171.498. Preto. Nt. 12-4-55. Por *Mauriceldo* (N.H.S.B. 124.877) e *Casja* (N.H.S.B. 143.631). Cr. H. J. Y. Groen. Pr. D. Hermínia Odete Casimiro.

CÃO DE ÁGUA
Cães

Bandit — 7.483. Preto malhado. Nt. 8-3-57. Por *Silves* (6.318) e *Farrusca* (7.481). Cr. Pierre Teisseire. Pr. Jorge Bares.

Gaúcho — 7.485. Preto mal tinto malhado. *Nin Bandit.* Cr. Pierre Teisseire. Pr. Alvaro Simões.

Pirata — 7.484. Preto malhado. *Nin. Bandit.* Cr. Pierre Teisseire. Pr. D. Cristina Negrão Ferreira.

Cadelas

Farrusca — 7.481. Preto malhado. Nt. 30-8-51. Por *Campeão N.B. Azinhal Algarbiorum* (4.666) e *Campeão N.B. Dala Algarbiorum* (4.022). Cr. Canil Algarbiorum. Pr. Pierre Teisseire.

Galé — 7.487. Preto malhado. *Nin. Bandit.* Cr. Perre Teisseire. Pr. Dr. António Cabral.

Gávea — 7.482. Preto mal tinto malhado. *Nin. Bandit.* Cr. Pierre Teisseire. Pr. Vitor Hugo Esteves de Sousa Marques.

Guiga — 7.486. Preto malhado. *Nin. Bandit.* Cr. Pierre Teisseire. Pr. D. Maria das Mercês Raposo de Oliveira.

dogs, it is important to note that those who saw them report neither Taro nor Truta displayed any night blindness as they aged. It is also interesting that the litter of Taro and Truta in which Collette was whelped included a brown puppy. Charlie de Alvalade's L.O.P. number, 29.288 (shown in the L.O.P. records of 1980), records him as being whelped in this litter. Of all puppies whelped by Taro and Truta, he was the only brown ever recorded.

Cabral closed his de Alvalade "kennels" upon his retirement as CPC president in 1983. His de Alvalade dogs continued, however, to be exported to America.

Following is a list of the Portuguese Water Dogs imported from Portugal in the early 1970s. This listing shows who the dogs were, their sires and dams, their breeders and where they were sent. Interestingly, #9-Xelim arrived shaved down to his skin. His new owners were told he had a skin condition before being exported. When his coat came in, however, it was not a typical Portuguese Water Dog coat. By the time the truth was known, it was too late to do much about it.

1. Renascenca do Al Gharb (b), (Lis x Enga) *Breeder Al Gharb (Conchita Cintron),* July 12, 1968; imported to Deyanne F. Miller, Connecticut

2. Raja do Al Gharb (d), (Lis x Enga) *Breeder Al Gharb,* July 12, 1968; imported to George Wauchope, New York

3. Anzol do Al Gharb (d), (Lis x Espada) *Breeder Al Gharb,* November 2, 1969; imported to Herbert H. Miller, Jr., Connecticut

4. Ancora do Al Gharb (d), (Lis x Espada) *Breeder Al Gharb,* November 2, 1969; imported to Fay Harbach, New York

5. Xino do Al Gharb (d), (Lo x Escuta) *Breeder Al Gharb,* June 5, 1969; imported to Natalie B. Rees, New York

An important import, Ancora do Al Gharb (C.B. Lis Algarbiorum ex C.B. Espada Algarbiorum) arrived in the United States on November 2, 1969. Ancora, a black curly owned by Fay Harbach, became the sire of eleven American litters. Courtesy Petra Schaefer

6. Trovoada de Alvalade (b), (Lumpi x Ria) *Breeder de Alvalade,* October 19, 1970; imported to Deyanne F. Miller, Connecticut

7. Daho do Al Gharb (b), (Lo x Espada) *Breeder Al Gharb,* March 10, 1972; imported to Natalie B. Rees and Virginia M. Stone, New York

8. Febo do Al Gharb (d),(Lo x Espada) *Breeder Al Gharb,* November 17, 1972; imported to John A. Scott, New York

9. Xelim de Alvalade (d), (Lumpi x Truta) *Breeder de Alvalade,* February 24, 1973; imported to Dorothy M. and Eric J. Pearson, Rhode Island

10. Zinia de Alvalade (b), (Taro x Truta) *Breeder de Alvalade,* March 18, 1975; imported to Helen Roosevelt, Connecticut

11. Zingara de Alvalade (b), (Taro x Truta) *Breeder de Alvalade,* March 18, 1975; imported to Mr. and Mrs. James E. Santos, New York

12. Zagaia de Alvalade (b), (Taro x Truta) *Breeder de Alvalade,* March 18, 1975; imported to William M. and Elaine L. Spaller, Connecticut

13. Zaida (b), May 10, 1975, (Taro x Truta) *Breeder Julieta Macedo Vieira,* May 10, 1975; imported to Raymond Burr, California

Those Americans who had received Al Gharb dogs before the Portuguese revolution, which began on April 25, 1974, weren't aware their dogs would be the last survivors of the Algarbiorum line. The *Revolucão De 25 De Abril* was a terrible time in Portugal for many people. Slogans of the military committee, which deposed the old regime and established a new military government, were "*Land* to the land workers!" "*Farms* to the workers!" and "Power to the People!" Banks and insurance companies were nationalized, bank accounts frozen. Farms and holiday houses were grabbed. Many fled. Some hid. Others stayed and waited until the political turmoil quieted.

Cintron, who lived in Lisbon, knew her first priority was to get her children out of the country—and quickly. But she also wanted to preserve Bensaude's dogs, whom she loved and had cared for over a seven-year period. So she hurried to the CPC and offered the dogs as a group, "to be protected." However, they could only take a few. Allowing Bensaude's prized legacy to possibly end up as street dogs or to endure an uncertain life under the new regime would be unthinkable. It would also be undoing the efforts of the Americans who were trying to establish the noble breed there. Cintron had to flee to Mexico with her six children, her husband following. Her beloved dogs were not put out on the street; they were humanely put down according to established custom. And the only dog Cintron kept in her apartment, Rey, died before her husband joined her.

The statements made about Cintron in the Molinari book, *The Portuguese Water Dog* (page 78), should not be taken literally. Cintron preserved the dogs and cared for them as "prized treasures" just as Bensaude knew she would. Neither did she keep them from those she deemed worthwhile. True, she sold them for money, but she also refused to sell or trade to those she felt were interested only in "points of head, body length, or who would not maintain them in a quality environment." During the seven years she maintained them, four males were placed in Portugal, with Cintron following the ancient and established practice that Bensaude adhered to—never selling animal treasures, only gifting them. Neither would this honorable woman risk an American buyer receiving a bad specimen and think it a typical Water Dog. In her Al-Gharb kennels, she could house thirty-eight to forty Water Dogs. She sent twenty-five dogs—the best she had—to America with the fervent trust the breed would be preserved with the genes Bensaude worked so passionately to perpetuate, until her saga with the Cão de Agua had to reach an end in 1974.

In the summer of 1975, after the eighth American litter had been whelped, two PWDCA members—one of them Hermine Munro (due to become the fourth president of the Club in 1977)—journeyed to Massachusetts with four dogs to consult with Rachel Page Elliott. Mrs. Elliott is a famous lecturer on gait and structure in dogs and author of *Dogsteps, Illustrated Gait at a Glance*. She evaluated the four dogs, one an import, and advised members to be more selective in breeding. First and foremost, they had to maintain type. If they didn't, results would not resemble the Portuguese Water Dog that the club wanted to preserve.

That summer, Ed Whitney lost Gully. "On June 17, 1975—his fourth birthday—he was killed in front of me by a car," he said. "Since that incident, all my dogs are trained to come and are seldom off lead.

"We called Miller and conveyed the bad news. Her comment was that 'all things happen for a good reason.' She just had Farmion Alfambra returned. Fambra was not doing well at Farmion. She had gone through Miller's beautiful glass door leading out to her property and had eaten through her kennel."

Fambra had been one of the dogs taken to Elliot for evaluation. Elliott felt Fambra was the most recognizable and possibly the best type of the four shown to her. During the visit, she filmed Fambra in action.

In the fall, when Munro returned to Elliot's home to view the film, it revealed that Fambra threw her rear left hock out when gaiting.

Miller sent Fambra home with Ed and Barbara Whitney on September 3, 1975.

"We didn't know it then, but this was the end of sailing and the start of our dog odyssey," said Ed. "Fambra couldn't have been a more pleasant surprise. She had found a home and was the only dog, just what Fambra had ordered. She had full run of the house and followed Barbara wherever she went."

Whitney bred Fambra to Ancora do Al-Gharb when she came into heat. He also had X-rays taken of her hips. His veterinarian informed Whitney she

Spindrift Kedge (Ancora do Al Gharb ex Farmion Alfambra), one of three in a litter whelped November 16, 1975, bred by Barbara and Ed Whitney.

had Class 4 hip dysplasia after she had already been bred! Three puppies were whelped in this litter on November 16, 1975.

In February of 1976, Carla Molinari attended the PWDCA's annual meeting in the United States. She had been appointed liaison between the CPC and the PWDCA at all meetings regarding the Portuguese Water Dog. During a private meeting with PWDCA president Marjorie L. Ulcickas, Molinari advised that pups that did not meet the Standard requirements of head, coat, tail carriage and type be put down. She also suggested that no puppies be registered until at least three months of age, when they should be examined by the club's breeding committee. Since the club did not have one, she advised that it form one. And since there had been problems with the Trovoada and Xelim litters (Nos. 4 and 5), she suggested that no one should breed a dog to anything with Trovoada or Xelim in the first generation. Later, during the Board meeting discussion, she was asked by Miller if the de Alvalade kennels had any neck problems. Miller told her, "We had to put two puppies down in the G litter." Molinari answered the question this way: "No, but we have had problems with dentition—overshot and undershot. I feel that these should come secondary to breed type."

Molinari explained to the group how tightly the Portuguese Water Dog was inbred, always with the same dog coming up, and that the dogs behind the dogs used—the parents—had not been recognized and had probably been found in the streets. "His grandfather may have been a Poodle, you don't know," she said. She added that breeders must breed until different lines were well established.

"Choose the good ones," Molinari emphasized, "discard the ones that are not true to type...the coat is the most important thing...always try to breed back to the dog that has a good head, good coat, good structure, good tail, and a good body... all of you have been working on numbers. You wanted to have sufficient numbers so that the breed was actually saved from extinction. You've reached that point. You now have numbers—100 dogs. That is a lot to work from."

Hermine Munro, a knowledgeable Kerry Blue Terrier breeder, began evaluating dogs from every litter whelped beginning with Renascensa do Al Gharb's first litter. Accompanying her, taking notes, were the Whitneys.

In April 1976, Ed Whitney wrote to Professor Donald Patterson, chief of genetic counseling at the University of Pennsylvania School of Veterinary Medicine:

We have developed problems which need immediate professional help.... Enclosed please find our records of litters A–N and comments which I hope you might find helpful. I hope this will interest you enough to help us in an advisory capacity. We are willing to do the work required if only we knew how to go about collecting the facts we need and what to do with these facts once we have collected them to produce better dogs and eliminate problems that are now showing up. I am very interested in this breed and feel that if we pay attention to our breeding and receive professional help the Portuguese Water Dog will survive—without it we are helpless and a breed that has tremendous potential will be lost forever to the world.

Patterson answered:

What seems to be occurring in the litters you described is a variety of different defects, some of which may be hereditary. Actually, the situation is not a great deal different from that in many other breeds, where a high proportion of pups die before weaning and structural defects of various kinds are common. There is no simple formula that would eliminate all genetic defects.... What I would recommend is that you attempt to identify specific problems, have them documented by a veterinarian, and then approach us regarding individual entities. Many breed associations have national committees on genetic defects which can organize a collection of information from breeders and make assessments regarding the types of defects that present major problems for the breed.

The PWDCA followed through on Patterson's recommendations. President Ulcickas sent a letter to the membership:

The first stated object in the constitution of the PWDCA is "to encourage and promote the selective breeding of purebred Portuguese Water Dogs"... therefore, the purposes of this committee will be to guide breeders in finding the stud or bitch best suited to their particular animal. ...Enclosed is a fact sheet which is of the utmost importance...in all breeds there are hereditary problems. At this early stage it is most important to locate the problems so that work can be done to eliminate them.

On August 7, 1977, when Carla Molinari judged Portuguese Water Dogs at a PWDCA match, she was pleased with the quality. Most important, she said, was overall compactness—dogs with good depth of chest and heads as described in the Standard. The type she sought and found she described as being a combination of Alvalade and Algarbiorum. Least important was coat type.

More imports continued to enter the United States.

It must be remembered that in those days, dog exhibiting in many European countries, including Portugal, was a very simple affair. Individuals who owned dogs took them to a show to be examined. There was no training of the dogs, no standing and presenting such as has always been done in America. The dogs were simply moved around the ring; some walked nicely, some jumped about. Some were trained only enough for a family member to touch. And many exhibitors and breeders were uncertain what the good and bad points were of the dog they owned.

Here are the remainder of the imports for the 1970s. Not all were bred.

14. Alvorada de Alvalade (b), (Taro x Zulu) *Breeder de Alvalade,* July 16, 1976; imported to Mr. and Mrs. James E. Santos, New York

15. Alvor de Alvalade (d), (Taro x Zulu) *Breeder de Alvalade,* July 16, 1976; imported to Peter Lewis, California

16. Avante de Alvalade (d) (Taro x Truta) *Breeder de Alvalade,* October 16, 1976; imported to Peter Lewis, California

17. CB Baluarte de Alvalade (d), (Arriba x Truta) *Breeder de Alvalade,* November 17, 1977; imported to Mr. and Mrs. James E. Santos, New York

18. Charlie de Alvalade (d), (Taro x Truta) *Breeder de Alvalade,* May 16, 1978; imported to Deyanne F. Miller, Connecticut

19. Duke do Jamor (d), (Fofo x Penny) *Breeder do Jamor,* October 2, 1978; imported to Catherine E. Meisel, New York

20. Tejo (d), *Breeder Henrique José Patricio Simas,* January 9, 1979; imported to Norman C. Vicha and Arlene Summers, Ohio

21. Dolly de Alvalade (b), (Taro x Tamar) *Breeder de Alvalade,* May 4, 1979; imported to Manuel Corte, New Jersey

22. Fe (b), (Tucho x Juca) *Breeder Maria Julia Nobre do Sacramento,* June 22, 1979; imported to Deyanne F. Miller, Connecticut

23. Alianca do Vale Negro (b), (Baluarte x Kira) *Breeder Carla Molinari,* October 19, 1979; imported to Grace M. Meisel, New York

In 1981, Miller sent Cherna Reliant (whelped July 29, 1981, by Farmion V de Gama x Granja Cherna) to Portugal, to reinfuse the country's gene pool.

The dog's influence was carried on by his two sons, Humberto de Alvalade (Cherna x Zari) in the Condinho, Albergaria and Asaumbufa kennels, and Zuba do Val Negro (Cherna x Kira) in the do Vale Negro kennels. Charlie de Alvalade was sent to Miller in exchange. Charlie was to become a famous force in the breed. Cherna Reliant was later returned to Miller.

A breeding accident occurred in Helen Roosevelt's kennel. It was between Cristo (seven years old) and Isobel (a four-year-old import—Zinia de Alvalade). It happened while Roosevelt was in Florida, the dogs in Connecticut. Isobel had been in heat just two months previously; "Who could imagine," Roosevelt exclaimed later, "that she could come back into heat so quickly." But a month after Roosevelt returned, on January 12, 1979, eight puppies were born.

"It would have been nice if the dogs had told me," laughed Roosevelt, "but they did not. The reason I had no thought of breeding the two was because there was much commotion about Isobel looking peculiar. She had a different aspect, caused by her very loose hair. Some of the more dog knowledgeable people criticized her. They also criticized Cristo's hips. They said, 'You should never breed these.' I'm glad Isobel and Cristo took matters into

Deyanne Miller in 1984 with Farmion Nazare (Farmion Azinhal ex Trovoada de Alvalade). Nazare was whelped in the fourteenth litter, June 22, 1976, and was herself the dam of three litters. Courtesy Kathryn Braund

their own hands because I would have held back and felt they shouldn't be bred. As it turned out there were some very lovely, well-dispositioned dogs in the litter.

"You have to understand," continued Roosevelt, "the first breedings in the U.S. were not overseen by anybody whatsoever except Mrs. Miller and her 'breeding privileges.' She used Cristo four times before my accidental litter. Some breedings came out all right and some didn't. Breeding was kind of catch as catch can. Deyanne Miller used to go to the statue of St. Francis (sitting in her garden in the birdbath) and ask who to breed to whom. So I think that God was with us along the way sometimes."

On June 24, 1980, Isobel had two puppies in a second litter, sired again by Cristo. They developed symptoms Roosevelt had seen before. Greatly disturbed by their actions, she sent one of the puppies to Cornell University to be tested. It was diagnosed by Dr. Alexander de Lahunta as having "a disease in the neurons of the cerebellum . . . This kind of disease," he wrote to her on February 23, 1981, "is referred to as a storage disease or lipodystrophy and usually is due to an inherited 'inborn error of metabolism.'"

Storage disease had been discovered in the breed. But when Roosevelt gave the letter to the PWDCA Board of Directors and asked them to investigate, it was not done. There were those who believed parvovirus was the cause of the resultant deaths, others who blamed epilepsy. Previous pups with the same symptoms had been taken to veterinarians. "Degenerative neck," were the practitioners' opinions. The symptoms could mirror each other. So Roosevelt was told it was an individual breeder's problem and would not be taken as a Board issue. Storage disease spread, but it took seven years before it became recognized. Then it emerged as a breed-wide problem.

Storage disease, formally known as GM-1 Gangliosidosis, is a hereditary progressive metabolic fatal disorder in which the pup is deficient in the enzyme Beta-galactosidase. The GM-1 gene is responsible for breaking down and clearing out toxic material from nerve cells. Without the enzyme, the nerve cells accumulate toxic matter, cannot dispose of it and become swollen, and because they can no longer function normally, the afflicted die. Storage disease usually shows up in a puppy between four and seven months of age as an uncoordinated or drunken gait. The dog is not in pain and does not lose its mental faculties, but it loses control of all body functions and dies approximately four months later.

In the winter of 1987, there were six litters with nine confirmed affected puppies. They came from fifteen breedings, bred by thirteen breeders throughout the United States. Chenze, the first import, had carried the gene into America!

A courageous breeder, Jane Harding (Cutwater Kennels), was the second to inquire into Storage disease. She had several puppies examined in the summer of 1987 by a veterinary neurologist, Linda G. Shell. Shell wrote to Harding: "...you have been one of the most helpful clients/breeders that I have ever dealt with, and I am truly grateful for your sincere interest in pursuing the clinical signs that your dogs had. Hopefully with some time and hard work, the researchers will be able to help this breed by detecting the carrier animals."

Harding forwarded Shell's findings to the PWDCA Board. She also sent a complete report to other Portuguese Water Dog owners.

On August 25, 1987, PWDCA President Karen A. Miller wrote to the membership: "Our Board of Directors has asked me to share with you one PWDCA program that has been established to eliminate a form of 'genetic junk' known as 'Storage disease,' which is not widespread at this time, but has serious implications for our breed if it is not addressed immediately...we [need to] stand together without denial, without petty finger pointing, without sweeping the unpleasantness under the rug...the only proof that the 'hidden' gene exists lies in testing....It is hoped that we will refrain from breeding until we have a testing program or at least until the mode of inheritance is clearly established. Dr. Bell will be available for individual pedigree consultations."

Harding introduced the PWDCA to Dr. Jerold S. Bell, a veterinary geneticist. The organization hired him to establish a viable testing program.

Earlier in the year another breeder, Beverly Jorgensen (Sun Joy), bred her bitch Gata to the carefully selected stud dog Kace. Jorgensen helped Gata whelp a litter of six puppies. Unfortunately, one, "wee girl Abbe," had Storage disease.

Jorgensen, a registered nurse, had discussed the shocking discovery of Storage Disease in Portuguese Water Dogs with a veterinarian when her puppies were seven weeks old. Jorgensen truly loved the breed and was deeply concerned for its future. She asked her veterinarian what he thought she could do to help. He told her to get involved with the parent club, since the breed could be in real trouble in ten years if the disease continued.

Jorgensen contacted PWDCA Board members, who thanked her for her concern. A medical friend of Jorgensen's suggested she tell Dr. Joseph Alroy, a neuropathologist at Tufts University, about the problem. He had conducted tests on Storage disease–afflicted English Springer Spaniels who were struck down with a similar disease via a "slightly different pathway." Jorgensen told Alroy what she knew of Storage Disease in the Portuguese Water Dog, but he had never heard of the breed. After correspondence, Alroy replied that he could help. Within a week, the PWDCA acted to meet with Alroy.

Abbe had been taken home as a stud fee puppy by the stud owner, Eleanor Pierce (Regala). In the middle of October, Pierce called Jorgensen. Something about Abbe's actions was frightening her. She would come out of her crate in the morning, half staggering. Jorgensen's heart sank. Could the symptoms Abbe experienced be the same symptoms Harding had described in her report?

Beverly Jorgensen in 1993 with her Sun Joy's Ch. Kalinka do Condinho, CD, TT, CGC (Niquito do Condinho ex Minx do Condinho, bred by Sally Starte of Portugal). Kae was Best of Winners at the Westminster KC in 1990, #1 Brood Bitch at the 1992 PWDCA National Specialty, and #1 Veteran Bitch and Award of Merit at the 1995 PWDCA National Specialty. She has a Best in Show son and many other champion get.

She contacted Dr. Bell, who had now been hired by the PWDCA as the club's geneticist. He put her back in touch with Alroy, who asked that a smear from Abbe be sent to his laboratory. If the smear proved positive for "vacuolated leukocytes in the white blood cell count," Abbe was in trouble. It proved positive.

An examination confirmed the smear diagnosis. Abbe, the adorable stud fee puppy, was afflicted.

"You may take her home to die," Alroy told the two breeders. "However, it would be beneficial to our research if we can conduct some tests. We guarantee she will not suffer. We also guarantee we will put her down within ten days."

It was a terrible decision for both Pierce and Jorgensen to make. But they made it. They left the clinic without Abbe.

They had just returned to Jorgensen's home when Alroy called to ask them to rebreed the two dogs the next time the bitch came into heat. This was not a decision either breeder felt she could make hastily, yet they had to make it immediately. Gata had already come into estrus and was in standing heat!

"It was a traumatic night," Jorgensen said. "We kept seeing the image of Abbe when we left her at the clinic. We kept changing our minds." In the morning they called Alroy and told him their decision. They bred the dogs with tears in their eyes, knowing what lay ahead.

While waiting for Gata to whelp this litter, Jorgensen wrote an open letter to Portuguese Water Dog fanciers:

Apparently eight years have passed since the first diagnosed case but the majority of us [breeders] knew nothing of the disease until this past summer....I know my heart is not made of stone. I have openly grieved for Abbe and fear for the remaining puppies in my "A" litter. There can be no more Abbes. Honesty has to be the only way to tell the Portuguese Water Dog Storage disease story....We breeders need to unify, speak the truth and pray to stop this hideous disease.

Alroy was in close touch with Jorgensen throughout Gata's pregnancy. He asked her to have Gata whelp through a Caesarean section, as he needed to get information not possible to obtain any other way.

On December 29, 1987, Gata was under anesthesia for forty-five minutes while nine puppies were delivered. Samples from each puppy's sac were aspirated, a sample of the amniotic fluid and tissue from the placenta taken and labeled, and the placentas bagged and labeled. The C-section and reviving of the sedated pups went well. Jorgensen took the samples home and kept them in the refrigerator until Alroy came to collect them. When he arrived, he told the breeders that their willingness to help expedite his research "pulled the program two years ahead."

"What you have done," he said, "can only benefit the Portuguese Water Dog breed." He explained they would know the status of each puppy in the litter.

"He wanted me to be able to sell healthy puppies and not put a buyer through what Eleanor Pierce and I (and others before us) had experienced," said Jorgensen.

The test results showed two males positive for Storage Disease, three pups (two females and one male) normal; the other four (one male, three females) carriers. Jorgensen donated the affected puppies to Tufts, where they could be studied. Carriers were sold on a spay-and-neuter contract.

In late 1988, after three pilot studies conducted by Dr. Bell, a blood test for Storage Disease became available.

It seemed a bittersweet victory. While the club could forge ahead full steam with programs, committees and an all-out health effort to protect the breed from any new health threat, it was deep in mourning. Deyanne Farrell Miller had passed away on July 8, 1988. Many feel if she hadn't been the strong, vibrant, dedicated dog woman she was, the breed would not have survived.

PWDCA President Carolyn Meisel, who was in office when Deyanne died, said, "Her devotion to Portuguese Water Dogs is legendary. Mrs. Miller cajoled, prodded and hounded many of us until we successfully raised and distributed dogs throughout the U.S....she courted the American Kennel Club for over fifteen years, setting our course for the admission of our breed first to the Miscellaneous class and then to full recognition in the Working Group. As each goal was achieved, she had another ready for us. She will be sorely missed, but never forgotten."

Seymour N. Weiss, Deyanne Miller's editor at Howell Book House, added: "Hopefully the fancy will always remember what she did—this lady I once nominated as Dog Woman of the Year—for a breed the world almost forgot....May every heart-stopping dive, every retrieved oar, every flawless performance in the obedience or conformation ring, may everything that benefits the breed keep the memory of this sporting gentlewoman ever green."

chapter 3

The Portuguese Water Dog Club of America

While listing the names of Portuguese Water Dog Club of America presidents does not reflect the incredible advances the breed has made, they deserve recognition. Their hard work greatly promoted the breed's renaissance. There have been troubled times in the short period the breed has been in America, and the wisdom of the PWDCA presidents helped spearhead advances made in the dogs' quality and health. Without their leadership, the vicissitudes the breed suffered could have contributed to its extinction.

1972–1974	Herbert H. Miller, Jr.
1975	Melvin M. Dichter
1976	Mrs. Marjorie Ulcickas
1977	Mrs. Hermine H. Munro
1978	Mr. Thomas B. Barrows
1980	Mrs. Deyanne Farrell Miller
1981–1982	Mrs. Pamela A. Schneller
1983–1984	Linwood A. Kulp, Jr.
1985	Mrs. Deyanne Farrell Miller
1986–1987	Karen A. Miller
1988–1989	Carolyn Meisel

1990–1993	Maryanne Murray
1994	David Green
1995–1996	Virginia Santoli
1997	Cheryl Smith

Dog and Litter Registration (AKC) for Portuguese Water Dogs

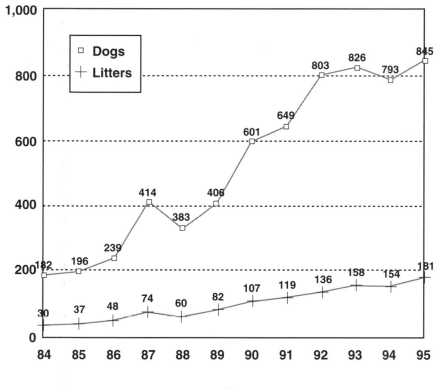

American Kennel Club dog and litter registrations for Portuguese Water Dogs, 1984 through 1995. Courtesy Elsa Sells

GENERAL COMMENTS

The initial nucleus of sixteen members in 1972 swelled to over 1,000 in 1997, with more than 250 nonmembers subscribing to the club's national bimonthly magazine.

The current interest in the breed must be traced to the remarkable dedication of its modern founder, Vasco Bensaude; the continued efforts of Conchita Cintron; the determination of Deyanne and Herbert Miller; and the de Alvalade imports of Dr. Antonio Cabral and Carla Molinari of Portugal, coupled with the tremendous vitality and commitment of Portuguese Water Dog fanciers everywhere.

PWDCA CLUB NEWSLETTER AND MAGAZINE

Communication is the lifeline of a national breed club. From the first meeting onward, the club has published a newsletter. *The Courier* began as a one-pager, graduating to slick magazine format in 1988. From its inception, it has continuously published outstanding material and vital information on the breed's health problems. *The Courier* has been awarded medals three times by the Dog Writers Association of America for being the best national dog club publication in the United States.

AKC RECOGNITION

On June 1, 1981, the American Kennel Club announced the breed's Portuguese Water Dog's acceptance into the Miscellaneous Class (a showcase for rare breeds prior to full registration). On January 1, 1984, the breed became eligible for full AKC registration privileges.

The accompanying chart gives AKC registration statistics from 1983 through 1995. To follow through on all PWD litters and registrations starting with the #1 United States foundation dog (Chenze), please check the Appendix, "Resources for Information."

Available to the public is the PWDCA's *Directory of Dogs*, a valuable resource for those contemplating owning or breeding Portuguese Water Dogs. The PWDCA is the second national dog breed club to publish a yearly health registry, also available to the public, with most members voluntarily disclosing health problems as they arise. The club has been lauded worldwide for its outstanding efforts in protecting and furthering this centuries-old breed, not only for the present but also for future canine enthusiasts all over the world.

The PWDCA has maintained yearly statistics on dogs that have placed in the top ten standings in both the breed and Working Group competitions from 1985 on, with the exception of 1986 and 1987. The statistics for these two years were supplied by The Navigator Book of Records and researched for the author by PWDCA member Karen Arends. This important tabulation runs through 1995.

The memorable Best in Show winner Ch. Charlie de Alvalade (Taro ex Truta de Alvalade) was imported by Deyanne and Herbert Miller, Jr., of New Canaan, Connecticut. Charlie, a brown curly whelped May 16, 1978, was a large force in the breed and the first Portuguese Water Dog to become an American champion.

TOP TEN PORTUGUESE WATER DOGS IN BREED AND WORKING GROUP COMPETITION

1985

Name of Dog	Name of Owner(s)	Breed	Group
Ch. Charlie de Alvalade	D. & H. Miller, Jr.	1	1
Ch. Bandido Do Mar	Dr. R. & D. Woods	2	3
Ch. Sumpwams Neptuno	D. & C. McManus	3	5
Ch. Alfama Uberrimo of Regala	E. Pierce	4	—
Ch. Keel Beleza	J. & P. Schneller	5	6
Ch. Farmion Geo	C. & K. Braund	6	4
Ch. Capricho Do Condinho	A. Summers/A. Vicha	7	—
Ch. Farmion Zimbreira	C. Doyle	8	2
Ch. Brinmar's Nehi to LeHi	J. & F. Ward	9	9
Ch. Rebento Dea of Ilara	C. Elliott/C. Doyle	10	10

Farmion Zimbreira (Ch. Charlie de Alvalade ex Farmion Nazare), owned by Clara Doyle, became the first bitch of the breed to achieve American championship. Courtesy Earl Graham

Ch. Farmion Geo, UD (Farmion Vasco de Gama ex Farmion Nazare), whelped July 8, 1982, was the breed's top producer of champions until mid-1994. Diver is owned by Cyril and Kathryn Brand. Courtesy Missy Yuhl

Ch. Timbermist Lancar Flor de Mar (Baluarte de Alvalade ex Farmion Nascenca), a multiple Best in Show dog owned by Joyce Vanek-Nielsen, became in mid-1994 the breed's top producer of champions. Courtesy Joyce Vanek-Nielsen

1986

Name of Dog	Name of Owner	Breed	Group
Ch. Sumpwam's Neptuno	C. & D. McManus	1	1
Ch. Rebento Don Carlos	H. H. Miller, Jr.	2	2
Ch. Raio	P Preston	3	4

Name of Dog	Name of Owner	Breed	Group
Ch. Timbermist's Lancar Flor de Mar CD	J. Vanek-Nielsen & S. Nielsen	4	3
Ch. Trezena Benquisto CD	B. & K. Arends	5	7
Ch. Regala Brioso Nobreza	A. Nichols	6	5
Ch. Oliverio Agua	Linda D. & J. Mekeel	7	8
Ch. Capricho do Condinho	A. Summers	8	—
Ch. Bandido do Mar	Dr. R. & D. Woods	9	—
Ch. Magia Flor de Mar	H. Kunze	10	—
Ch. Charlie de Alvalade	D. F. Miller	—	6
Ch. White Cap Capitão do Monab C.D.	S. A. Pietros/P. Schnelle	—	9
Ch. Farmion Fairwind	C. Young/T. Johnson	—	10
1987			
Ch. Rebento Don Carlos	H. H. Miller, Jr.	1	2
Ch. Regala Brioso Nobreza	A. Nichols	2	6
Ch. Oliverio Agua	Linda D. & J. Mekeel	3	3
Ch. Zephyr of Dell Mountain	H. & T. Jensen	4	7
Ch. Magia Flor de Mar	H. Kunze	5	4
Ch. Trezena Benquisto C.D.	B. & K. Arends	6	10
Ch. White Cap Capitão do Monab C.D.	S. A. Pietros/P. Schneller	7	—
Ch. Timbermist Lancar Flor De Mar C.D.	J. Vanek-Nielsen & S. Nielsen	8	
Ch. Farmion Geo	K. & C. Braund	9	—
Ch. Capricho Blaze do Rimski	C. & D. Shafer	10	—
Ch. Gozo do Mar	R. & C. Sippel	—	5

Name of Dog	Name of Owner	Breed	Group
Ch. Ilara Sardio	R. Reiherzer	—	8
Ch. Bittersweet Maximilian	P. & M. Edelson	—	9
1988			
Ch. Rebento Don Carlos	D. & H. Miller, Jr.	1	2
Ch. Timbermist Lancar Flor De Mar	J. Vanek-Nielsen	2	1
Ch. Neocles Acabado	H. Conroy/L. Afong	3	4
Ch. Bittersweet Maximillian	P. Chestnutt	4	—
Ch. Zephyr of Dell Mountain	M. Miller/J. Watts	5	—
Ch. Sunrider's Diver of Sete Mares	H. Greschel/L. Carver	6	5
Ch. White Cap First Mate	P. & J. Schneller	7	—
Ch. Magia Flor De Mar	J. & H. Kunze	8	—
Ch. Marmais Double Delight	M. Tassey	9	8
Ch. Gozo Do Mar	R. & C. Sippel	—	3
Ch. Hunter's Vasco De Gama	J. Osran	—	6
Ch. Chandulars Brinmar Blitz	C. Mattingley/A. Bowley	—	7
Ch. Norvic's El Capitan	C. Livingston	9	—
Ch. Oliverio Agua	Linda J. Mekeel	10	—
1989			
Ch. Sunrider's Diver of Sete Mares	H. Greschel/L. Carver	1	1
Ch. Rebento Don Carlos	H. & D. Miller, Jr.	2	2
Ch. Timbermist Lancar Flor De Mar	J. Vanek-Nielsen	3	3
Ch. Bittersweet Maximillian	P. Chestnutt	4	5

Name of Dog	Name of Owner	Breed	Group
Ch. Cutwater's Beroe	M. Volz/J. Harding	5	9
Ch. Neocles Acabado	K. Conroy/L. Afong	6	7
Ch. Anacove's La Primera Samba	C. Cates/C. White, Jr.	7	6
Ch. Hunter's Carbon Copy	E. & M. Lyons	8	—
Ch. Roughrider's Sereia	Anelada Dr. D. & C. Smith	9	—
Ch. White Cap Gemala	T. Brunks/V. Murray	10	—
Ch. Ilara Sardio	R. Reiherzer	—	4
Ch. Gozo Do Mar	C. & R. Sippel	—	8
Ch. Scrimshaw's Opbi Wan Kenobi	S. & J. McMahon	—	10
1990			
Ch. Sunrider's Diver of Sete Mares	H. Greschel/L. Carver	1	1
Ch. Doce Maximillian	P. Chestnutt	2	9
Ch. Timbermist Sea Kaper Hi-Noon	P. & S. Riek	3	2
Ch Neocles Acabado	K. Conroy/L. Afong	4	8
Ch. LeHi's Madeira Lancer	J. & F. Ward	5	—
Ch. Starview Noah	B. Kurtz	6	3
Ch. Bittersweet Maximillian	P. Chestnutt	7	9
Ch. Neocles Brando Nadador	J. Meiloch	8	7
Ch. Hunter's Carbon Copy	E. & M. Lyons	9	4
Ch. Timbermist Lancar Flor De Mar	J. Vanek-Nielsen	10	—
Ch. Jewell De Aguas Windward Lad	R. Zaremba	—	5
Ch. Jewell De Agua Starbaer	L. Philbrick	—	6

Name of Dog	Name of Owner	Breed	Group
1991			
Ch. Sunrider's Diver of Sete Mares	H. Greschel/L. Carver	1	1
Ch. Doce Maximillian	P. Chestnutt	2	4
Ch. Captree's Pirate of Downcast	G. Hawkins	3	5
Ch. Timbermist Sea Kaper Hi-Noon	P. & S. Riek	4	2
Ch. Neocles Duke O' Sunjoy White Cap	B. Jorgensen/P. Schneller	5	—
Ch. Le-Hi's Madeira Lancer	J. & F. Ward	6	—
Ch. Jewell De Aguas Windward Lad	R Zaremba	7	3
Ch. Sea God's Zephyr	R. Benevides/R. Burr	8	—
Ch. Helms A'Lee Jetty Newton Ark	J. Levine/J. Forsythe	9	8
Ch. White Cap Dama of Neocles	B. & K. Arends	10	—
Ch. Neocles Destiny of Mariner	J. Madderra/ C. McCullough	—	6
Ch. Roughrider's Wave Breaker	C. Oakes	—	7
Ch. Jewell De Agua Starbaer	B. Kurtz/L. Philbrick	—	9
Ch. Timbermist's Blackjack Scuba	G. Clark/J. Vanek-Nielsen	—	10
1992			
Ch. Timbermist Sea Kaper Hi-Noon	P. & S. Riek	1	2
Ch. Sunrider's Diver of Sete Mares	H. Greschel/L. Carver	2	3
Ch. Farmion the Bismarck	S. & J. Hawkins	3	5
Ch. Rough Seas' First buoy	L. Guthrie/S. Bean	4	1

Am., Bda. Ch. Roughrider's Wave Breaker (Ch. Farmion Geo, UD ex Ch. Camerell's Roughrider Seeley, CDX), a successful sire, was whelped October 25, 1989 and is owned by Carol B. Oakes. Courtesy Carol B. Oakes

Name of Dog	Name of Owner	Breed	Group
Ch. Del Sur's Blakely at Fairwind	C. Young/T. Johnson	5	4
Ch. Pinehaven's on The Town	B. & T. Rafferty	6	—
Ch. Windruff's Pirate O' The Galaxy	J. Warnsdorffer	7	—
Ch. Helms A'Lee Jetty Newton Ark	J Levine/J. Forsythe	8	7
Ch. Pinehaven's Chantilly Lace	J. Girton/B. Rafferty	9	10
Ch. Dacher's Gotta get A Gund	D. & S. Smith	10	—
Ch. Sunjoy Neocles Forma Grande	D. Kellerman/L. Afong	—	6
Ch. Jewell De Aguas Windward Lad Windward Lad	R Zaremba	—	8
Ch. Timbermist Blackmast Scuba	G. Clark/J. Vanek-Nielson	—	9
1993			
Ch. Farmion The Bismarck	J. & S. Hawkins	1	2
Ch. Dacher's Gotta Get A Gund	Dr. D. & C. Smith	2	3

Name of Dog	Name of Owner	Breed	Group
Ch. Rough Seas' First Buoy	L. Guthrie/S. Bean	3	1
Ch. Timbermist Sea Kaper Hi-Noon	P. & S. Riek	4	4
Ch. Sunrider's Diver of Sete Mares	H. Greschel/L. Carver	5	9
Ch. Sunjoy Neocles Forma Grande	D. Kellerman/L. Afong	6	6
Ch. Cutwater's I'm B.J.of Robel	M. Lowman/E. Volz	7	—
Ch. Fantaseas the Navigator	M. Sparks/N. Carter	8	5
Ch. Neocles Duncan	N. Harris/L. Afong	9	—
Ch. Sete Mares Basil Shanna-Dawn Shanna-Dawn	C. & S. Teasley	10	10
Ch. Sunnyhill's Nobre Espirito	D. & J. Percival	—	7
Ch. Tywater's Skipjack Mate	C. T. Watson	—	8
1994			
Ch. Farmion The Bismarck	S. Hawkins	1	1

Am., Can. Ch. Jewell De Aguas Windward Lad, CDX, Can. CD, WWD, TT, CGC, PT (CH Timbermist Lancar Flor de Mar ex Matia Jewell de Agua), a Best in Show winner, is owned and trained by Robin Zaremba. Courtesy Booth

Name of Dog	Name of Owner	Breed	Group
Ch. Sunjoy Neocles Forma Grande	D. Kellerman/L. Afong	2	2
Ch. Dacher's Gotta Get A Gund	Dr. D. & C. Smith	3	4
Ch. Sete Mares Basil Shanna-Dawn	C. & S. Teasley	4	3
Ch. Cutwater's I'm B.J.of Robel	E. Volz/C. Deloasche	5	5
Ch. Lakeshore Don Bento	R. Araujo	6	—
Ch. Timbermist Agua Lama Ebony 'N Ivory	S. & J. Vanek-Nielsen	7	7
Ch. Le-Hi's Recherche of Tywater	J. & J. Ward	8	—
Ch. Alto Mare Gambol N Man	E. Verkozen/L. Hubbart	9	—
Ch. Dacher's L' Attitude	Dr. D. & C. Smith	10	—
Ch. Rough Seas' First Buoy	L. Guthrie/S. Bean	—	6
Ch. Charkit's Hip Hip Hurray	P. Guthrie/K. Hinnant	—	8
Ch. Sete Mares Windward Breeze	R. Zaremba/L. Carver/ V. Murray	—	9
Ch. Baerbach Campero Negra Jewel	L. Philbrick	—	10
1995			
Ch. Farmion The Bismarck	S. Hawkins	1	2
Ch. Dacher's Monsoon	Dr. D. & C. Smith	2	5
Ch. Pickwick Portago Fish N' Ships	K. Bob	3	6
Ch. Seabreeze Tailor Made	B. & K. Arends/ E. & K. Richardson	4	8
Ch. Sete Mares Windward Breeze	L. Carver/R. Zaremba/ V. Murray	5	3
Ch. Nautique's Neta Isabel	K. Esslinger/D. Glen/ Dr. Fowler	6	—

Name of Dog	Name of Owner	Breed	Group
Ch. Sunjoy Neocles Forma Grande	D. Kellerman/L. Afong	7	1
Ch. Lakeshore Don Bento	R. Araujo	8	10
Ch. Benhil's Rogue Wave	J. & J. Knoll	9	4
Ch. Cutwater's High Fidelity	K. Stalnaker-Spaan	10	9
Ch. Robel First Edition of Bobest	C. & K. DeKoning	—	7

National Specialties

Only four short years after the first lady of the breed, Deyanne Farrell Miller, passed away, the PWDCA held its First National Specialty. The prima event took place in Princeton, New Jersey, for three days, September 21 through September 23, 1992. Members of the Fairfield County Portuguese Water Dog Club, the regional PWD club Deyanne Miller had founded, put the event together.

Over 300 owners and dogs thronged to the beautiful site, not only to participate and share in the festivities, but also to honor Deyanne Miller, to whom the Specialty was dedicated. Everyone who knew her felt certain she was watching from heaven. Member Don Grauer commented, "The second day it tried to rain but miraculously the clouds parted and the sun shone. This was due to Deyanne Miller's intervention, a sure sign that she was watching and still in control." How proud Miller would have been of the sportsmanship displayed, the beautiful dogs her work and dedication had inspired and the sharing of comradeship amongst the participants.

What is a PWDCA National Specialty? What is it like? What is it for?

Join the hundreds who travel each September, in the special days of early autumn, to the current site. The annual PWDCA National Specialty site rotates through a four-year cycle; one year it is held in the eastern United States, next in the central area, the third year in a southern state and finally in the west. The hardworking PWDCA volunteers planning and assembling the Spectacular are, as well as being members of the national Club, members of various regional PWD clubs.

When you arrive at the host hotel and host site, be prepared to stroll across lush lawns, exclaiming with awe at the hundreds of dazzling, impeccably groomed and wagging-tailed Portuguese Water Dogs with their happy

Am., C.B. Ch. Pinehaven's On The Town (Ch. Anacove's La Primera Samba ex Ch. White Cap Graca Bra-vata) was Best of Breed at the PWDCA's first National Specialty (1992). Dillon is shown with his owner/breeder, Beverly Rafferty of Colorado, in Portugal in 1994, where he won his Portuguese championship (CB). Augusto Guimaraes

Five of the then six all-breed Best in Show winners at the 1992 PWDCA first National PWDCA Specialty. Left to right: Ch. Charlie de Alvalade; Ch. Timbermist Lancar Flor de Mar, CDX, AWD; Ch. Sunrider's Diver of Sete Mares; Ch. Jewell de Aguas Windward Lad, CDX, WWD; and Ch. Timbermist Sea Kaper Hi-Noon. Absent from this stellar group was Ch. Gozo do Mar. Courtesy Joyce Vanek-Nielsen

owners. Be ready to join with exhibitors and onlookers at the many carefully planned events, with everyone you meet making you feel very, very special in this infectious atmosphere of celebration and camaraderie.

At this most important yearly event in the Portuguese Water Dog world you are not just sharing in a union of colorful celebrations. The apex of this vibrant drama is the display of the Portuguese Water Dog canine performance events, which show off the breed's working capabilities as well as its beauty. The highlight is viewing the dog chosen by the judge as Best of Breed. This dog exemplifies, in the judge's view, the strides made by breeders in their on-going creative quest for the "perfect" Portuguese Water Dog.

The PWDCA National Specialty is also an event displaying thrilling competitions of canine water workers, obedience and agility performers. The icing on this canine cake is meeting kindred people you haven't met before, greeting those with affection you've missed seeing for awhile and joining seminars devoted to issues important to the protection and furtherance of the breed—such as health, temperament, structure, training and grooming—all conducted by top professionals in the pure-bred dog world.

At the National Specialty there is also ample time to commence or continue "homework"—to peruse pedigrees of desired lines, to browse for puppies to purchase now or in the future, and to buy gifts and dog paraphernalia from the many colorful breed-specific boutiques. A National Specialty is a great number of things; one goes not necessarily to win ribbons, although to win is the dream of a lifetime! It's being there to witness excellence in dogs, to participate in competitions with your PWD, to study, to learn and to join with dog fanciers who admire the Portuguese Water Dog as you do or will.

The memories one takes away—the joy of new friendships, new knowledge and the recurring visions of the beautiful dogs you watched and touched—are unforgettable.

Here are the winning results of the first five PWDCA National Specialties, held from 1992 through 1996.

FIRST NATIONAL SPECIALTY—Princeton, New Jersey, September 21–23, 1992.

Total entries, 353. Judge: Senhora Carla Molinari of Portugal.

BOB, *Ch. Pinehaven's On the Town,* owned by Beverly and Thomas Rafferty, bred by Beverly and Thomas Rafferty.

BOS, *Ch. Cutwater's The Divine Miss M,* owned by Melinda Miller, bred by Jane and Peter Harding.

HIT, *Janota's Cabra De Sorte,* owned by Peggy and Ed Wireman, bred by Jeanette and Howard Babbitt. Score 197, Novice B.

High in Trial under Patricia Scully at the PWDCA first National Specialty in 1992 was Ch. Janota's Cabra de Sorte, CDX (Stone Hollow Regala's Act Two ex Janota's Almejavel Princesa). Owned and trained by co-owner Peggy Wireman (center); co-owner/breeder is Jeannette Babbitt (right). John L. Ashbey

VERSATILITY DOG, *Camerell's Buccaneer Beaver TD CWD,* owned by Beverly and Burton P. Franklin, bred by Cathy Kalb.

SECOND NATIONAL SPECIALTY—St. Paul, Minnesota, August 24–27, 1993.

Total entries, 220. Judge: Mrs. Michelle Billings.

BOB, *Ch. Neocles Duncan CD,* owned by Nancy Harris and Letty Larson Afong, bred by Letty Larson Afong.

BOS, *Ch. Pinehaven's Chantilly Lace,* owned by John Girton and Beverly Rafferty, bred by Beverly and Thomas Rafferty.

HIT, *Ch. Lake Breeze Windward Echo,* owned by Robin Zaremba, bred by D. Gawronski. Score 195.5. Novice B.

VERSATILITY DOG, *Ch Timbermist Lancar Flor de Mar CD CGC,* owned by Joyce Vanek Nielsen, bred by Peter di Capua.

THIRD NATIONAL SPECIALTY—San Rafael, California, August 23–26, 1994.

Total entries, 222. Judge: Mrs. James Edward Clark.

BOB, *Ch Alto Mare Gambol N Man UDX,* owned by Emmy Verkozen, bred by Lisa Hubbart.

BOS, *Ch Driftwood's M-N-M Candy Cookie,* owned by Morgin Costello Quirin, bred by Morgin Costello.

HIT, *Cf Alto Mare Gambol N Man UDX,* owned by Emmy Verkozen, bred by Lisa Hubbart. Score 198. Utility.

Best of Opposite Sex at the PWDCA second National Specialty was Ch. Pinehaven's Chantilly Lace (Ch. Anacove's La Primera Samba ex White Cap Graca Bravata), owned by Beverly and Thomas Rafferty. Haga

High in Trial at the PWDCA second National Specialty was Am., Can. Ch. Lake Breeze Windward Echo, Am., Can. CD, AWD, TT, CGC, PT (Neocles Bizarro 'N Tuxedo ex Jewell de Agua Choco). This was the first time owner Robin Zaremba showed Echo in the Obedience ring. Lee Bros. & Haga

Best in Veteran Sweepstakes at the PWDCA third National Specialty was Am., Mex., Int. Ch. White Cap Dama of Neocles (Ch. Alfama Uberrimo of Regala ex Ch. Keel Beleza), owned by Karen and Bob Arends, the oldest PWD entered in the 1994 Specialty, whelped March 30, 1985. Tom Bruni

FOURTH NATIONAL SPECIALTY—Carlisle, Pennsylvania, September 10–14, 1995.

Total entries, 384. Judge: Mrs. Peggy Adamson.

BOB, *Ch. Nautique's neta Isabel,* owned by Kathy Esslinger and David Glen, co-owned by Dr. Linda Fowler, co-bred by Vivien Pace and Dr. Linda Fowler.

BOS, *Ch. Bobest Roederer of Robel,* owned by Mark and Marilyn Hyner; co-bred by Pat Voltz, Estelle Chakrin and Kit Hinnant.

HIT, *Ch. Pennrico KnollKrest Tugger CD,* owned by Verne Foster, bred by Ruth Francisco. Score 197. Novice B.

SUPER DOG, *Ch. Camerell's Delta Clipper UDX CWD Can CDX NAD ROM,* owned by Verne Foster, bred by Cathy Kalb.

FIFTH NATIONAL SPECIALTY—St. Louis, Missouri, September 25–28, 1996.

Total entries, 595. Judge: Sr. Salvador Janeiro.

BOB   *Ch. Pinehaven's On The Town.* This dog won from the Veteran's Class. He had also been Best in Specialty at the 1992 National Specialty. Owned by Beverly Dees Rafferty and Jack Girton, bred by Beverly Dees Rafferty.

BOS, *Ch. Questar's Athena Nike,* owned by and bred by Marilyn Rimmer.

HIT, *Sandcastle's Princessa Sereia CGC,* owned by Meg and Bud De Fore, bred by Caren Murray, Score 183. Novice A.

SUPER DOG, *U-CDX Ch. Neocles Destiny of Mariner UDTX OA CGC TD1 CWD ROM/POM FDX,*co-owned and bred by Cynthia McCullough and Julie Madderra.

Best of Breed and High in Trial at the PWDCA third National Specialty was Ch. Alto Mare Gambol N Man, UDX (Alto Mare Acalorado ex Ch. Alto Mare Candura), owned by Emmy Verkozen and bred by Lisa Hubbart. He is shown here handled by his breeder, being awarded this coveted win by Mrs. James Edward Clark. Tom Bruni

Ch. Driftwood's M-N-M Candy Cookie (Ch. Old River Ripples 'N The Stream ex Ch. Old River A Lil Minnow) was Best of Opposite at the PWDCA Third National Specialty. She was bred and is owned by Morgin Costello-Quirin. The #1 PWD bitch for 1995, she made the same win at Westminster in 1995 and gained an Award of Merit at Westminster the following year. Tom Bruni

Performing the Veteran Obedience group exercises at the 1995 PWDCA National Specialty are (left to right): Ch. Neocles Destiny of Mariner, CDX, TDX, CWD (whelped 12/87); Ch. Farmion Pflash, CD (whelped 9/87); Ch. Camerell's Delta Clipper, UDX, CWD, NAD (whelped 5/88); Ch. Brinmar's First Encore Galaxy, CD (whelped 7/88); Ch. Kings Cross Fudge of Crystal (whelped 9/86); Ch. Baybrite Algazarra, UD (whelped 4/85); Ch. Beacon Hill Bandeira, CD (whelped 11/86), and Ch. Roughrider Agua Linda, CD (whelped 2/88). The brace (far right) is Ch. Jewell De Aguas Windward Lad, CDX, and Ch. Lake-Breeze Windward Echo, CD. Deborah Lee Miller-Riley

chapter 5

The Portuguese Standard for the Portuguese Water Dog

Defined by the Portuguese veterinarians Dr. Frederico M. Pino Soares and Prof. Dr. Manuel Fernandes Marques, 1938.

The author is indebted to Augusto Guimaraes (De Gifford Kennels) of Cascais, Portugal, who kindly sent me a copy of the original Standard.

Thanks also go to Carol B. Oakes of Potomac, Maryland, American Portuguese Water Dog fancier, for having this Standard impeccably transcribed. With the translation came a certification stating, "...the attached English language documents are true and accurate translations of the corresponding (Portugal) Portuguese language documents to the best of our knowledge and belief."

In very old times, the Water Dog had its home in the whole of the Portuguese coast. Today, due to the continued changes in the art of fishing, it is found principally in the Algarve, which region is its current home. The Water Dog's presence along the coasts of Portugal goes back to times long past, it being considered a national breed.

I. GENERAL ASPECT AND ABILITIES

Mesomorphic dog, sub-convexolinear with tendency toward rectilinear; type pointer (bracoide).

Excellent and resilient swimmer and diver, and inseparable companion of the fisherman, to whom it provides innumerable services in the activity of fishing as well as the defense of the boat and property. During fishing activities, it voluntarily dives into the sea to collect and retrieve fish which have escaped, diving, if necessary, and doing the same if any net or part of any cable comes loose. It is also employed as a communications agent between the boat and the shore, and vice versa, even at appreciable distances.

An animal of uncommon intelligence, it easily understands and obeys with joy all its master's orders.

A dog of eager temperament, willful and haughty, sober and resistant to fatigue. It has a firm expression and a penetrating and attentive gaze. It possesses great visual abilities and an appreciable sense of smell.

Medium linear type, harmonic shape, balanced, robust and well muscled. Appreciable muscular development owing to the constant exercise of swimming.

II. HEAD

Well proportioned, strong and wide.

CRANIUM—Seen in profile, its length is slightly predominant over that of the muzzle. Its curvature is more accentuated at the back of the occipital crest and more pronounced. Seen from the front, the parietals are dome-shaped with a slight central depression, the front has a slight basin, and the frontal furrow is elongated up to two thirds of the parietals and the superciliar arches are prominent.

MUZZLE—Longer at the base than at the end. The nasal bevel is well defined and situated slightly behind the internal eye ridge.

NOSTRILS—Wide, open and lightly pigmented. Of a dark color in dark-colored, light and mixed specimens. In those which are chestnut colored, the color should be that of the fur, but should never be blond (light).

LIPS—Strong, especially in the frontal area. The seam should not be apparent. Mouth mucous membrane (at the roof of the mouth, under the tongue and gums) strongly tinted black.

NOTE: In this paragraph there was no inclusion of brown pigment in the original version. In the first revision by Marques/Soares it was stated: "In browns the nose is of the same colour as the coat. Flesh-coloured or discoloured noses are a disqualification." However, no reference was made for browns on lips or on eyelids. The author believes this was an error of unintentional omission.

JAWS—Strong and correct.

TEETH—Good and not apparent. Strong and developed canines.

EYES—Regular, level, round, distant (set well apart) and slightly oblique. The coloration of the iris is black or chestnut and the eyelids, which are thin, should be rimmed with black.

EARS—Insertion above the eye lines, placed against the head, slightly opened to the back and heart-shaped. Light and their extremities never go beyond the throat.

III. TRUNK

NECK—Straight, short, round, muscular, well forward and of a haughty appearance, connected to the trunk in a harmonious manner. Without collar or dewlap.

BREAST—Wide and deep. Its lower border should touch the flat of the knee. The ribs should be long and normally oblique, giving a great breathing capacity.

WITHERS—Wide and not protruding.

BACK—Straight, short, wide and well muscled.

LOINS—Short and well attached to the hindquarters.

ABDOMEN—Reduced volume and elegant.

HINDQUARTERS—Well formed, slightly angled; symmetrical and almost nonapparent flanks.

TAIL—Whole, wide at the stem and narrow at the end. Medium insertion. Its length should never exceed the hock. At attention, it coils in a circle, never going beyond the mid-line of the lower lumbar. It is a valuable aid when swimming and diving.

IV. FRONT EXTREMITIES

Strong and straight.

SHOULDER BLADES—Well angled in profile and transversely. Strong muscle development.

LEG—Strong and of regular length. Parallel to the middle line of the body.

FORELEG—Long and of strong musculature.

CARPUS—Strong bones, wider at the front than on the side.

METACARPUS—Long and strong.

PAW—Round and spread. Toes slightly arched, of medium length. The digital membrane, which is attached to the toe for its full length, is made up of flaccid tissue and furnished with abundant and long hair. Black ungues are preferable, but, according to color, white, striped or chestnut are also acceptable. Ungues (nails) slightly separated from ground. Rigid sole in the foot tubercle (foot pad) and normal thickness in the digital tubercles.

V. REAR EXTREMITIES

Well muscled and straight.

THIGH—Strong and regular length. Well muscled. The patella does not deviate from the mid-plane of the body.

LEG—Long and well muscled. Does not deviate from the mid-plane of the body. Well angled in the front-back direction. The whole structure is fibrous and strong.

BUTTOCKS—Long and well curved.

TARSUS—Strong.

METATARSUS—Long. There are never extra digits.

FEET—In all manners identical to the paws.

VERTICAL POSITION—The vertical position of the front and rear extremities are regular. Front extremities which are slightly short and rear extremities slightly curved are admissible.

VI. COAT

The entire body is abundantly endowed with resilient hair. There are two types of hair: one long and wavy and the other shorter and curly.

The first variety is slightly shiny and puffy, the second packed together, dull and grouped in cylindrical locks. With the exception of the axillas and groin, the hair is distributed evenly on the whole integument. On the head, they take the form of a turban, in the wavy hair and the curly hair of the other variety. The hair on the ears is longer in the wavy-haired variety.

The coloration of the hair is uniform or mixed: the former exists in white, black and chestnut in tone; the latter, mixtures of black or chestnut with white.

The white hair should be without albinism, except that the nostrils, the edge of the eyelid, and the inside of the mouth should be black in blacks, brown in browns. In the original translation, mention of brown was unintentionally omitted. This was corrected in the second version.

In black and white specimens, the hair (skin) is slightly bluish.

They have no down (undercoat).

A partial clipping of the hair is characteristic of this breed when it becomes very long. The rear half of the body, the muzzle, and the tail are sheared, with a small tassel being left at the end of the tail.

The typical height of males is 54 cm, with a minimum of 50 cm and a maximum of 57 cm being acceptable for classification.

The height of females should be 46 cm, with a minumum and maximum of 43 and 52 cm, respectively.

MEASUREMENTS AND WEIGHT

HEAD	Males	Females
Length of cranium	12.5	11 cm
Width of cranium	11	09.5 cm
Length of muzzle	9	07 cm

THORAX	Males	Females
Perimeter	61	56 cm
Width	15	13 cm
Height	21	18 cm

UPPER LINE OF TRUNK	Males	Females
Length of trunk	45	40 cm
Width of trunk	11.5	10 cm

LENGTH	Males	Females
Of body	51	45 cm
Of tail	32	27 cm

HEIGHT	Males	Females
Of withers	54	46 cm
Of front extremities	29	25 cm
Of hindquarters	52	46 cm

WEIGHT

In males should oscillate between 19 and 25 kg;
in females between 16 and 22 kg.

VIII. GAIT

Unconstrained movement, short step, light and rhythmical trot, energetic gallop.

IX. DEFECTS

HEAD—Very long, narrow, flat and sharp.

MUZZLE—very funneled or pointed.

JAWS—Prognathism in either jaw.

EYES—glassy, light-colored, unequal in form or size, very protruding or very deep.

EARS—bad insertion, very large, very short or folded.

TAIL—cropped, small or nonexistent, heavy, fallen or perpendicularly erect.

PAWS—existence of dewclaws.

HAIR—albinism, hair around eyes a different color entirely or partially, hair of two different types, described.

BODY—giantism or dwarfism.

DEAFNESS—congenital or acquired.

X. TABLE OF POINTS

	Males	Females
Head: bearing, cranium, ears, eyes, muzzle, mouth, nasal muzzle, nostrils	20	20
Neck, withers, shoulders, rear extremities	10	7
Breast, lower lumbar, upper and lower lines of trunk	15	15
Hindquarters, pelvis, rear extremities	10	13
Feet, toes, ungues	10	10
Tail: bearing, form, insertion	5	5
Hair: texture, color, thickness	5	5
General aspect: harmony of form, gait, body, sexual characteristics	25	25
	100	100

chapter 6

The American Standard for the Portuguese Water Dog

Included with the text of the official American Kennel Club Standard is the author's interpretation. It should be understood that this is purely a personal opinion, not an official document, either of the AKC or the PWDCA.

First, let's think about what Tom Horner, a Canadian writer and breeder, wrote in 1982:

> Be mindful always of six essentials of a good dog—type, substance, balance, correct conformation, correct movement and good temperament, the last probably the most important of all. No one wants a dog, however impressive, if it has a poor and unpleasant temperament.

Details of the Portuguese Water Dog, of course, are different from those of other breeds. These details set it apart in type and structure. Here are important characteristics:

1. Rectangular, off-square
2. Substantial strong head, square jaw
3. Short, muscular neck, held high
4. Straight, firm back
5. Strong, wide, short loin
6. Good muscling
7. Strong driving rear, not exaggerated
8. Single wavy or curly coat

68

9. Retriever attitude
10. Looks directly at a person
11. Strength
12. Stoic, zestful yet sensitive; an extremely intelligent animal.

GENERAL APPEARANCE

Known for centuries along Portugal's coast, this seafaring breed was prized by fishermen for a spirited yet obedient nature and a robust, medium build that allowed for a full day's work in and out of the water. The Portuguese Water Dog is a swimmer and diver of exceptional ability and stamina, who aided its master at sea by retrieving broken nets, herding schools of fish and carrying messages between boats and to shore. It is a loyal companion and alert guard. This highly intelligent utilitarian breed is distinguished by two coat types, either curly or wavy; an impressive head of considerable breadth and well-proportioned mass; a ruggedly built, well-knit body; and a powerful, thickly based tail, carried gallantly or used purposefully as a rudder. The Portuguese Water Dog provides an indelible impression of strength, spirit and soundness.

I. Spirited, yet obedient nature.

The PWD possesses an active, zestful, happy disposition. It is stoic and, like all highly intelligent animals, in tune with its environment. The PWD is a sociable canine. This enables it to get along with people and other animals when it is working. We can surmise the dog developed this cooperative spirit after centuries of living in close quarters on small fishing boats. Certainly, no fisherman would have the time or inclination to train a dog unless it was eager to cooperate. Any other attitude would be faulted. When trained in a positive manner, the dog exhibits a strong willingness to please by responding to direction with intelligence and eagerness. If trained without fairness, it becomes stubborn and unwilling to work.

II. Robust, medium build that allows a full day's work in and out of the water.

The Standard states: ". . . Robust, medium build." This breed has exceptional intensity and attitude, so that when working in its natural habitat the dog can endure a full day's work in the water. The ideal PWD's appearance reflects its purpose, as does its health in its sturdy, strong, muscular physique. The PWD's high metabolic rate and normal excellent physical condition play an important role in the breed's fortitude. All in all, the dog impresses your eye with its beauty, strength and "spirited" attitude.

SIZE, PROPORTION, SUBSTANCE

Size: Height at the withers—Males, 20 to 23 inches; the ideal is 22 inches. Females, 17 to 21 inches; the ideal is 19 inches. Weight for males, 42 to 60 pounds; for females, 35 to 50 pounds.

Those who fished from large vessels accommodated large dogs. Variation in the breed's size is because many fishermen went out to sea in small boats, called caiques, containing one to three men and sensibly requiring a smaller dog. Therefore the PWD, due to environmental necessity, has a considerable size range. Weight should be in balance with the dog's skeletal and muscular structure. If a dog is balanced in both vertical and horizontal dimensions and possesses bone structure in keeping with its size, it is preferred over one that is out of balance but within correct weight limit.

Proportion: Off-square; slightly longer than tall when measured from prosternum to rearmost point of the buttocks, and from withers to ground.

The dog is longer than it is tall; an off-square structure grants a dog efficiency in both agility and endurance. The rectangular PWD is able to twist and turn freely in the water. Many early de Alvalade dogs were long and low. Though the trend today is for the squarer-type dog, the Standard states it is an "off-square" breed. Rectangular balance is what is correct for function.

Substance: Strong substantial bone; well developed, neither refined nor coarse, and a solidly built, muscular body.

Each word defines the PWD. The dog must have a strong, muscular body. Thelma Brown, in her book *The Art and Science of Judging Dogs,* said, "A dog's locomotion results from power developed in muscles."

A PWD's muscles should not bulge. The dog is lithely muscled, as in human swimmers or track runners. Again, Thelma Brown explains muscling:

1. Long muscle fibers produce greater action (the length of a muscle fiber tends to be proportionate to the extent of movement it is able to produce).
2. Thin muscles have quicker reflexes.
3. Heavy muscles produce greater strength but slower reflexes (the thick ness of a muscle tends to be proportionate to its power).
4. Reflexes vary in individuals.
5. Thin muscles in proper condition give greater endurance for running.... This author adds: and for swimming.

HEAD

An essential characteristic; distinctively large, well proportioned and with exceptional breadth of topskull.

The PWD needs an impressive head. Its head is chunky, not refined like a Poodle head. It shows plenty of brain room in the skull and plenty of gripping power in the muzzle. In the original FCI translation, the word *massive* was used to describe the shape of the head. This has been changed. While the PWD's head may appear massive when thick curls, waves or groomer-designed topknots cover it, its skull is not massive, but impressive. (I often wonder if in translation from the Portuguese, *impressive* was turned into one of its more intense definitions, "massive.") Run hands down through shaped curls or waves and you'll find the head to be, just as the old Standard says it is, "well-proportioned, strong and wide." For comparison, it is wide like the head of the Puli, Labrador Retriever, Golden Retriever and the older type of Dalmatian head.

The correct head is in balance with the rest of the dog. When you place your hands on a good head, you will feel the occipital crest, a strong back skull; you'll trace the depression running from occiput to nose. Slide your fingers over the stop. It is defined yet not overly cliffed, as in the Bulldog, or all but missing, as in the Bedlington Terrier. (It's important to note that the PWD is a slow-maturing breed. Some heads with stops don't mature until the dog is close to three years).

Head faults are long, narrow, flat or pointed skulls. Muzzles must never be funnel-shaped, overly pointed or snipy.

Expression—Steady, penetrating, and attentive.

If you have judged the PWD, you will have noticed the dogs have a steady, penetrating, highly attentive look. A PWD is not afraid to look at you. It looks directly at you; the dog that looks away from you is not desirable. The natural attentiveness of an adult PWD makes for easy training.

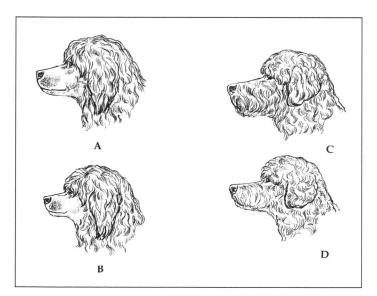

Muzzle, as shown in A, is correct; B is too short, C is too long, and D shows a dog with a snipy muzzle.

Eyes—Medium in size; set well apart, and a bit obliquely. Roundish and neither prominent nor sunken. Black or various tones of brown in color. Darker eyes are preferred. Eye rims fully pigmented with black edges in black, black-and-white or white dogs; brown edges in brown dogs. Haws are dark and not apparent.

The original Portuguese Standard stated it well: Regular, level, roundish, set apart and slightly oblique. Eyes set apart give a dog a wide field of vision, so important underwater, when it is retrieving underwater gear or pursuing a fish that escaped the net.

Dark eyes are preferred in most breeds because in theory, a dark iris protects the dog from bright sunlight. The sun shines on water! However, this has never been proven; many wild animals have light eyes. In black-coated PWDs, eye color ranges from a dark brown to a dilute brown (hazel), with the darker shade preferred. Brown (chestnut)-colored dogs have yellowish-appearing brown eyes. Eye faults are light-colored eyes in black-coated dogs, eyes different from each other in either form or size and eyes sunken or protruding. Eye rims must be fully pigmented—black for black dogs and brown for brown dogs. As the gene pool widens, you will see more lack of pigmentation. Lack of pigmentation in an adult must be penalized.

Ears—Set well above the line of the eye. Leather is heart-shaped and thin. Except for a small opening at the back, ears are held nicely against the head. Tips should not reach below the lower jaw.

Many early dogs had incorrect ears: ears set below the line of the eye, that hung below the lower jaw or that were thick. When the dog is alert, the point of attachment on the head is aligned with the top of the skull. The heart-shaped ear leather should hang close to the head. Note that hair grows on the inside of the ear. Nature may have put heavy hair there to help keep water out. At the present time, hair is gently plucked from ears for cleanliness, but it should never be completely removed. Hair helps keep the inner ear dry.

Skull—In profile, it is slightly longer than the muzzle, its curvature more accentuated at the back than in the front. When viewed head-on, the top of the skull is very broad and appears domed, with a slight depression in the middle. The forehead is prominent and has a central furrow, extending two-thirds of the distance from stop to occiput. The occiput is well-defined. Stop—Well-defined.

Muzzle—Substantial; wider at the base than at the nose.

Jaws—Strong and neither over- nor undershot.

BITES

The words *very broad* (under skull) and *well-defined* (under both occiput and stop) are open to interpretation. Better stated is that the skull is broad. The occiput is defined. The stop is defined. *Well* is a loose word.

If the muzzle is longer than the skull, many dogs will probably have a longer back plus more angulation in the rear. Jaws must be strong. Deyanne Miller said, "Patience is required with puppies. Mouths may not settle down until the pup is ten months to a year in age."

Some PWDs have a narrower lower jaw. The jaw affects the bite, with incisors squeezed together and slightly crooked. There are undershot jaws in the breed, oftentimes caused when breeding a dog with a short muzzle to one with a longer muzzle. Bad jaws and bad bites are difficult to breed out of a line. Ideal is an even, strong jaw.

Nose—Broad, well-flared nostrils. Fully pigmented; black in dogs with black, black-and-white or white coats; various tones of brown in dogs with brown coats.

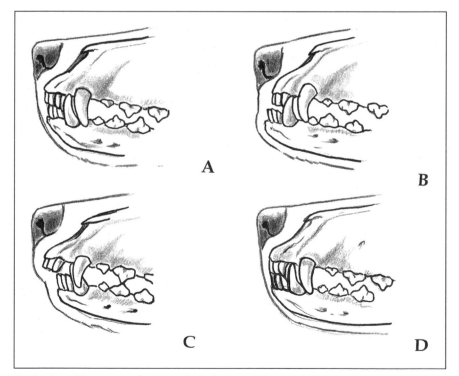

A—Preferred is a scissors bite, in which the upper incisors slightly overlap the lower incisors; B—Underbite; C—Overbite; D—Level bite, which in the Portuguese Water Dog is acceptable. Dogs having underbites or overbites must be faulted.

Lips—Thick, especially in front; no flew. Lips and mucous membranes of the roof of the mouth, under tongue and gums are quite black, or well ticked with black in dogs with black, black-and-white or white coats; various tones of brown in dogs with brown coats.

Dogs that work in the water and carry things in their mouths don't require excess skin around the mouth. This would prevent their grasping wriggling fish. Skin should be thick, tough and tight. The PWD should not have pink on its lips.

Bite—Scissors or level.

Teeth—Not visible when the mouth is closed. Canines strongly developed. A level bite is allowed, but scissors is better.

NECK, TOPLINE, BODY

Neck—Straight, short, round and held high. Strongly muscled. No dewlap.
The PWD's head is carried high on a short, strong and muscular neck, blending smoothly into both head and topline. If the dog is straight in shoulder, or if it has a short upper arm, its neck will look like it is stuck on its body. A correct neck allows the dog to drag boat gear. Even small dogs and bitches have strong necks. Miller said, "The PWD's neck has to be straight and short and round so he can hold his head high to carry fish, messages and nets along with ample muscle for the work he does."

Topline—Level and firm.

Body—Chest is broad and deep, reaching down to the elbow. Ribs are long and well-sprung to provide optimum lung capacity. Abdomen is well-held up in a graceful line. Back is broad and well-muscled.

Loin is short and meets the croup smoothly.

The PWD has to have a firm, level topline. A soft back hinders it in its work. The topline is straight, without any dip where its withers meet its back. Sometimes, muscling causes a dip. It has been found that most females are slightly longer in back. The added length gives them ample room to carry puppies.
Some small pups have deep chests, although most drop as they near maturity. The chest is moderately wide, giving the dog endurance. Excessive width hinders forearm movement, necessary to a strong swimmer. There are pups born with extremely wide chests, which, unfortunately, develop over the years into Bulldog-like chests. The correct chest is well filled, showing

depth down to the elbows, giving the dog ample lung room. Some dogs are narrower in chest; this is acceptable if ribs are long and well sprung. The latter is preferred over too wide a chest, which would hinder progress through the water.

Good tuckup doesn't mean extreme development, as with a Greyhound. The correct PWD's deep, broad chest with strong, muscular loin endows it with a firm, graceful tuckup.

The dog's loin is short, strong and firm. Textbooks say a short loin is synonymous with "strong and muscular." It has to be that way in order to tense and flatten easily, transmitting power and agility as the dog swims. A strong loin enables the dog to turn quickly underwater, to twist and turn to dive, if necessary to herd schools of fish. In my opinion, the Standard should state "a strong, wide loin."

Croup is well formed and only slightly inclined, with hip bones hardly apparent.

Tail—Not docked; thick at the base and tapering; set on slightly below the line of the back; should not reach below the hock. When the dog is attentive the tail is held in a ring, the front of which should not reach forward of the loin. The tail is of great help when swimming and diving.

The croup, in connection with the loin, performs a major function in a dog's movement. It is the source of "rearing" muscles and propulsive effort. The croup should be rounded, with well-developed muscles. A narrow croup indicates weakness; too wide a croup throws off the dog's center of gravity.

The more powerful its croup, the more a dog will carry its tail upward or curved over its back. Not enough attention is being paid to tail sets or length of tail. The dog's tail is a continuation of its croup—at a medium setting—and is of utility in swimming. Although the tail is shaped like those of most dogs, thick at the base and tapering to the end, the way it is set and the way the dog uses it is an important breed characteristic. It carries its tail over its back when it is strutting, "full of [it]self." The dog also flings the tail straight out behind it, or up, waving it like a flag in a stiff breeze. When it is looking at something intently, the dog flips it up and over its back in a ring. But it must never lie there; if it does, the dog has too high a tail set. When diving, its tail is the last part of its body to disappear. Fishermen left the tuft on the end of the tail to help the dog utilize it as a flag and a rudder. The tuft should be left natural in its growth, never trimmed.

Tail faults include a docked, rudimentary or nonexistent tail, or one that is heavy, droopy, held perpendicularly or so short it has to be carried continuously in a ring over the dog's back. Uncharacteristic tail set and action not only detracts from the style of the dog, it destroys the lateral stability so important to this breed.

FOREQUARTERS

Shoulders are well inclined and very strongly muscled. Upper arms are strong. Forelegs are strong and straight with long, well-muscled forearms. Carpus is heavy-boned, wider in front than at the side. Pasterns are long and strong. Dewclaws may be removed. Feet are round and rather flat. Toes are neither knuckled up nor too long. Webbing between the toes is of soft skin, well covered with hair, and reaches the toe tips. Central pad is very thick, others normal. Nails are held up slightly off the ground. Black, brown, white and striped nails are allowed.

People tend to misinterpret "well-inclined." Again, the word *well* can be misconstrued. Angulation of forequarters must balance that of the rear quarters. The PWD's forequarters give power combined with reach and freedom of leg movement. Shoulder blades are set farther apart than those of racing dogs. (With wide-set blades, one has to be careful of faulty fronts.) Rolls of fat along the withers show faulty shoulder construction. Shoulders are firmly placed, sloping onto the back smoothly. The best-formed PWD will have a long shoulder blade and deep chest. The upper arm (humerus) should come down with elbows held close to the chest. Pasterns, while long and strong, are slightly sloping to allow for endurance.

The PWD is web-footed. The webbing is thick and comes out to the end of the toes. The paws are round and spreading, like paddles. Although toes

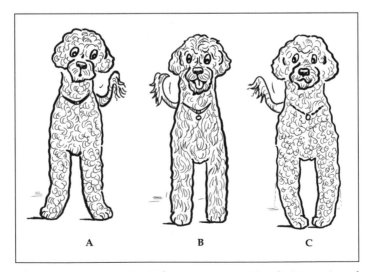

The Portuguese Water Dog's forequarters must give the impression of power combined with excellent reach and freedom of leg movement. A—Toeing out—faulty; B—Correct; C—toeing in—faulty.

are slightly arched, the dog is rather flat-footed, with pads thick and fleshy, never thin. A heavy growth of hair protects the webbing on the bottom of the feet between the toes. (Unfortunately, this growth may become matted on certain terrains, so pads must be checked periodically for mats.) Tops of toes are covered with wavy, rather than curly, hair even in dogs with curly coats. Dewclaws on the hind feet are a fault.

HINDQUARTERS

Powerful; well balanced with the front assembly. Legs, viewed from the rear, are parallel to each other, straight and very strongly muscled in upper and lower thighs. Buttocks are well developed. Tendons and hocks are strong. Metatarsus is long; no dewclaws. Feet are similar in all respects to forefeet.

The PWD has breadth across its pelvis because its strong, lithe muscular hindquarters are there to manufacture power. The dog flies through the water. It literally bounces off the diving board when entering a pool, and it swims with its legs straight out in back of it. Too much rear leg angulation will weaken drive. Notice underwater human swimmers with all forward propulsion coming from the legs—working straight out in back through the water.

Thighs are long and stifles well bent. Look carefully at the angles of the bones. The PWD's moderate angulation is synonymous with agility, power and endurance.

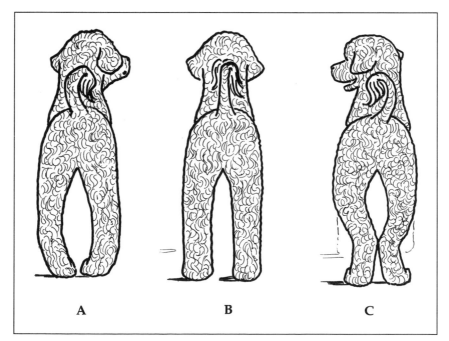

A   B   C

When viewed from behind, as shown in B, hock joints do not lean in or out. Bone is of good substance. A shows a spraddle-hocked dog, and C shows a cow-hocked dog.

Hocks are well developed. High hocks give initial speed; medium hocks equal endurance. The ideal hock starts two-thirds down from the hip.

COAT

A profuse, thickly planted coat of strong, healthy hair, covering the whole body evenly except where the forearm meets the brisket and in the groin area, where it is thinner. No undercoat, mane or ruff. There are two varieties of coat:

Curly—Compact, cylindrical curls, somewhat lusterless. The hair on the ears is sometimes wavy.

Wavy—Falling gently in waves, not curls, and with a slight sheen.

No preference will be given to coat type, either curly or wavy.

It is a single nonshedding coat with body and strong texture. (Dead hairs are removed by regular grooming with comb and brush.) The curly coat has a lusterless, matte finish, while the wavy coat is glossy. Both coat types grow equally long and need to be scissored or clipped. What is important is that hair quality be of strong texture. It needs to be understood that neither coat type sheds water well, so long coats hamper the dog's work; they also gather sand, dirt, mud, twigs and leaves, and in the wintertime snowballs cling to them. On the other hand, while the coat needs to be short enough to dry quickly, it needs to have enough body to repel mosquitoes and other insects that infest beaches and banks where the PWD guarded the catch.

In Portugal, 95 percent of the dogs are wavy-coated. The curly-coated dog was seldom seen in litters there until recently (so said Carla Molinari, president of the CPC). In America, we have many variations of coat in the breed. In wavies we have flat, semi-flat, round and tight, often called a soft curl. Curly types are loose, wide, tight and wiry. Undesirable are too flat a wave and too wiry a curl. Dogs with wiry coats may carry a hair loss factor. (Most coats tend to become wavier or curlier as the dog ages. Fast growth usually occurs over the rump and above the withers, with legs and head hair slower in rate of growth.)

Most litters contain both curlies and wavies, with wavies in most litters dominant. Some breeders claim it is best at this point in time to breed a curly to a wavy, because wiry coats and hair loss seem to be tied together. When breeding curly to curly, wiry coats appear. This is said not to happen when breeding curly to wavy. However, this practice may disperse the gene for hair loss widely!

There are improper coats in the breed. Outcrossing with dogs of questionable pedigrees gave the PWD a wider gene pool, but it also brought in a variety of ancestors. Improperly coated dogs may show resemblance to a Labrador, a Cão da Serra De Aires (a Portuguese sheep dog), a Flat Coated Retriever, a Curly Coated Retriever, and even an Afghan Hound or a

Newfoundland. Improper coats may be short, dense and close lying, or curly or wavy with short hair on muzzles, feet and feathering only on legs. Wavy-coated dogs usually have lots of white, and the Newfoundland-type coat in the improper PWD is long but not fully textured. Different degrees of curls and waves can be found on different parts of the body. The outward appearance of an improperly coated dog may not represent a PWD—inside, the dog's temperament is identical.

The gene for improper coats is present in many PWDs. It takes two to tango, of course: both sire and dam have to carry the gene for improper coats for it to show up in their pups.

CLIP

Two clips are acceptable:

Lion Clip—As soon as the coat grows long, the middle part and hind-quarters, as well as the muzzle, are clipped. The hair at the end of the tail is left at full length.

Retriever Clip—In order to give a natural appearance and a smooth, unbroken line, the entire coat is scissored or clipped to follow the outline of the dog, leaving a short blanket of coat no longer than one inch in length. The hair at the end of the tail is left at full length.

No discrimination will be made against the correct presentation of a dog in either Lion Clip or Retriever Clip.

The Standard states that in the retriever clip, scissoring or clipping should leave hair of one inch. This statement can be interpreted to read, "to a depth of one inch." *Depth* means the blanket of coat should appear no longer than one inch. A grooming guide once sent out to judges by the PWDCA insisting on a one-inch retriever clip was immediately rescinded by the membership.

Grooming should not be exaggerated. The breed has a functional conformation, and even though the breed ring is a beauty pageant, no PWD should look like a cookie-cutter dog whatever clip is used. In the Retriever Clip, the muzzle should be longer than it is in the Lion Clip. And on ears, the length of the hair should be trimmed close to the ear leather. See Chapter 10, "Grooming the Portuguese Water Dog."

COLOR

Black, white, and various tones of brown; also combinations of black or brown with white. A white coat does not imply albinism provided nose, mouth and eyelids are black. In animals with black, white or black-and-white coats, the skin is decidedly bluish.

The Standard states that in animals with black coats, "the skin is decidedly bluish." Where there are white markings that will remain white for the life of the dog, the skin is pink and will remain pink for life. Portugal considers mismarked dogs those with "white collar, four white legs and over 30 percent white on black." United States breeders do not have to follow the restrictions of the Portuguese and FCI Standards and many breed for parti and piebald dogs as well as for the classic black and brown, following the AKC Standard.

Black is dominant, with brown (chestnut) recessive. The distribution of white markings (unpigmented areas) is expressed in the following pattern in all dogs:

1. Self (solid/one color)
2. White on chest, feet, muzzle, end of tail
3. White on whole chest, legs and stomach
4. White extending to shoulders and withers
5. White covering flanks and back
6. White with a variety of spots and splotches

C.C. Little, in his book *The Inheritance of Coat Color in Dogs,* designates spotting as follows: "Self; Irish spotting, chest, feet, muzzle tail, narrow collar on neck or withers; Piebald, whole chest, legs, stomach, shoulders and withers, flanks and back; Extreme, A variety of spots and splotches."

Breeds differ in the amount of unpigmented areas due to modifiers that were genetically honed into the breed. PWDs are black, black with white markings, brown, and brown with white markings. In black dogs, the skin should be bluish. Some black PWDs "rust" during summer from sun or chemicals used in food and shampoos; brown coats fade. Many dogs go "off-black" as they get older; most browns turn dark cream.

The breed also carries the graying factor, which is what makes some dogs appear silver or gray as they mature. If a dog carries the graying factor, gray hairs may begin to appear as early as three months. These first crop up on top of the back, then slowly spread. Usually, the earlier it appears, the grayer the dog becomes. Gray, as a color, is not allowed in the Standard , yet some dogs who express the graying factor are gray by one year. The Standard has no disqualification for gray. Robert Fries, in the book *Origin of the Weimaraner,* calls "silver gray a dulled brown through a process of color degeneration." He also says that continued brown breeding results in silver-brown and gray dogs. In the PWD, black dogs can produce gray ones. Gray and brown hairs often show up on the legs of black dogs, particularly below the hocks. These are not considered faults.

Solid (single/self)-colored black dogs may have a small amount of white hairs on their chest and paws. A few of their nails may be white also. A few additional white hairs, very strong in texture, will appear as they age on skull, chest and tail. These dogs do not have the graying factor. Some dogs both with and without the graying factor grow a ring of white around the upper third of their tail.

GAIT

Short, lively steps when walking. The trot is a forward-striding, well-balanced movement.

The correct PWD moves in a free, energetic, lively ground-covering glide. The word *lively* in the Standard denotes motion, not attitude. The original Portuguese Standard described movement well: "Gay, short steps when walking, a light trot and an energetic gallop."

Unfortunately, the Standard does not say anything about closeness or width in the rear. As a water dog, the PWD is a single-tracking breed. And, although no one has conducted a study to check underwater movement, good land movement makes for good water movement.

The well-constructed, well-balanced PWD combines beauty and efficiency in its movement. The dog moves with its head held high and its tail swinging or flagging high over its back. When moving at a moderate stride or trot, its backline remains level as it floats smoothly over the ground. At the trot and the gallop, action is long and free. Viewed from the front, the legs of the running dog move straight forward, with good reach. There is no interference or twisting in or out at the elbows. From the side, leg action flows rhythmically. Legs do not overreach or strike together. When viewed from the rear, the hocks

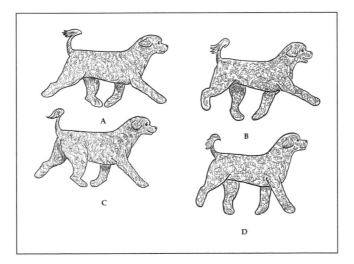

The well-constructed Portuguese Water Dog combines beauty and efficiency in its movement, as shown in A. B has too much front extension and is lacking rear extension; C is pacing, and D shows inadequate front extension.

of the standing dog are parallel, yet when driving forward, its legs merge without rear feet touching or crossing over. Stand behind the dog. Look for strong tendons. Look for drive. Deep-chested (and wide-chested) dogs with medium height on leg usually move closer in the rear than do taller, rangier dogs. This is still proper movement, as Rachael Page Elliott, author of *Dog Steps*, explains: "The criteria of judgment is not whether a dog single tracks or whether he has a wider footfall, it is how and why he moves as he does that must be understood and evaluated against his overall conformation and the purpose for which the breed was developed. The principle of seeking balanced support remains the same for all, as this is Nature's method of off-setting wasteful action that reduces efficiency."

She adds: "Natural convergence should never be confused with the fault of moving close—variations in the dog's height, his width and length of leg make the difference. Misunderstanding of this principle has brought the unjust criticism of moving too close in many a dog that is actually moving well."

Just remember that although this is a water dog, not a land dog, it is necessary that the PWD's movement on land should adhere to the Standard. Ideally, when the dog moves forward, its weight should be centered on the two center toes. Only on turns should the dog put weight on the outside toes. If the heaviest wear is on the thickest part of the pads, the dog lands far back on his heels.

TEMPERAMENT

An animal of spirited disposition, self-willed, brave, and very resistant to fatigue. A dog of exceptional intelligence and a loyal companion, it obeys its master with facility and apparent pleasure. It is obedient with those who look after it or with those for whom it works.

Temperament must be given topmost consideration in breeding and in keeping dogs. The Portuguese Water Dog was a fisherman's helpmate. Along with a sound structure for its job, it had to have spirit and be of willing disposition. The late philosopher Edmond Bordeaux Szekely said, "Intelligence is the ability to adapt oneself adequately to unexpected changes in the environment." This is certainly true of the Portuguese Water Dog. It is highly adaptable. Responsible breeders work hard at keeping the willingness to please in the temperament of their stock, as well as the necessary stoicism and independence this thinking dog must have.

SUMMARY STATEMENT

The PWD is spirited yet obedient, robust and of unexaggerated, functional conformation; it is sure, substantially boned and muscled, and able to do a full day's work in and out of the water.

FAULTS

Any deviation from the described ideal is a fault. However, those inherent characteristics that are imperative for the maintenance of proper type, and that therefore cannot be overlooked, are listed as MAJOR FAULTS.

In judging faults, the degree to which a dog is penalized should be contingent on the extent to which the particular fault would actually affect the working ability of the dog.

MAJOR FAULTS

1. Temperament: Shy, vicious or unsound behavior.
2. Head: Unimpressive; small in overall size; narrow in topskull; snipy in muzzle.
3. Substance: Light or refined in bone; lacking in muscle.
4. Coat: Sparse, naturally short, close-lying hair, partial or overall; wispy or wiry in texture, brittle; double-coated.
5. Tail: Other than as described. Extremely low set, heavy or droopy in action.
6. Pigment: Any deviation from described pigmentation; other than black or various tones of brown eye color; pink or partial pigmentation in nose, lips, eyes or eye rims.
7. Bite: Overshot or undershot.

Approved January 15, 1991

chapter 7

The Character of the Portuguese Water Dog

The Portuguese Water Dog has many layers to its personality. It's a marvelous creature, this boat worker turned companion dog. It's a family dog! It loves people! It's a shaggy dog with great intelligence and an enchanting disposition. It's a fun dog!

But wait.

Although the puppy is absolutely adorable, the adult strikingly handsome, this is not a mild breed. The Portuguese Water Dog is a robust, sturdy handful. It's high-powered. It's strong-willed because it was developed to do a tough, demanding job. If it didn't have the temperament to do its work, it didn't survive.

Our modern PWD is full of the "Let's do it!" temperament of a happy working dog. Its blithe spirit is a grace for owners who are young at heart. For them, it makes an ideal pet. However, a potential owner must look beyond the adorable puppy face, outgoing disposition and luxurious coat to see the dog underneath before purchasing a PWD.

Recently, I had a telephone call from a gentleman who owned a Portuguese Water Dog. During our conversation, he told me, "I didn't know what to do with him the first six months. He was terrible. Maybe it's because he was such a challenge to control that I fell in love with him. Suddenly he became the most wonderful dog in the world. Now I don't know how we ever lived without him."

We hear often from puppy owners: "We survived the PWD's busy puppyhood!" "That adorable face of his gets him out of lots of trouble." "He's a clown and keeps us laughing with his antics." "After he's naughty, we cuddle together on the couch!" "He's like a big fluffy bear and a good friend."

Ch. Nautique's Windward, CD (Ch. Farmion Helmsman ex Ch. Farmion Pflash) owned by Monica and Lanny Kramer and bred by Linda Fowler, upholds the breeds reputation as a fun dog. Courtesy Linda B. Fowler

While friendly and cheerful to everyone, PWDs are loyal only unto their own. The daily hardships the Portuguese fishermen suffered in their dangerous lives at sea are reflected in the breed's almost stoic acceptance of whatever fate has in store for it. Let children pull its hair, let puppies climb all over it, even let a master abuse it—the dog endures. That's the essence of the breed.

Take home a puppy at eight weeks of age and you make an eye-opening discovery. You now own a mouthy puppy! It bites anything and everything. If you tell it "No," the puppy tests you to see if you mean it. (When it does this, instead of scolding, immediately hand the dog a toy it can chew.) The Portuguese Water Dog puppy constantly craves information about everything it sees, hears or touches. Exploring via touch or taste by mouth is an ideal way for it to gain information. We have hands as well as mouths; these puppies have only mouths. And Portuguese Water Dog puppies utilize this aptitude more than any other breed.

While the Portuguese Water Dog is strongly people-oriented, it is also strongly precocious. Your PWD will not allow you or anything around you to be alone. These dogs have an incredible instinct to remain at an owner's heels. They are busy dogs and want you to be busy with them. If you cannot occupy all your time with your PWD, it will find things of yours to be busy with. These "things" might include rosebushes in need of uprooting (thorns

The PWD can be trained to flush out upland game and water fowl. The owner interested in hunting should be sure to cut its coat short so it doesn't pick up burrs and mud. This is Eileen Jaskowski's hunting PWD, Ch. Highseas Blue Boy, UDTX, WD (Agua Linda Macho Man ex Ch. Costa Azul Sophie's Choice). Courtesy Verne Foster

PWDs want to share every family activity. Rovin's Yankee Doodle Dandy (Ch. Brawny Polliwog ex Ch. Charkit Framboesa), owned by Joan Conlon, joins every camping trip and even carries his own food. Courtesy Joan Conlon

taste great to Portuguese Water Dog puppies), bringing flowers or roots from your garden into the house—"Look what I brought you, Mom!" If the flowers and bushes in the yards of its owners could talk, they would scream in anguish as the PWD denudes the very branches the leaves live on.

Give a Portuguese Water Dog puppy a chunk of tree limb to play with. It will rip the bark off with its teeth, expose the spine and proudly show you the remains. It is also skillful at digging holes in lush lawns to munch on grass roots. The puppy believes that young and tender growing greens were planted for its taste buds. Heritage plays a part here. In the Algarve winter, when the sea was too rough for a small boat to go out, the Portuguese Water Dog often herded sheep. It appears to mirror the sheep's grass- and root-eating habits. Don't ever underestimate the creativity of this super-intelligent puppy destined to become a perfectly marvelous adult. Paradoxically, chewing is not a problem indoors. In the house, the PWD can easily be taught to discriminate quickly. It knows its toys and it knows yours. Yours are untouchable. Okay! Your puppy can deal with that.

The PWD *does* make a miserable kennel dog. This brings up an important point. Without exception, dogs prefer to be in the house with owners, not alone in a fenced yard—unless, of course, it's to perform its ablutions! Left outside, your dog will learn to bark continuously so that you'll bring it back inside. It will also learn to climb or jump fences to return to you. It will paw and mutilate a back door when you're inside and it's left out. Not that the dog dislikes the outdoors—it rushes outside to greet rain, wind and snow, whatever the weather, as long as you are with it. Its life is centered around its owner.

Puppyhood is a good time to teach your dog to be content during those times it must be alone. While no puppy or adult should be confined to a crate for more than two hours at a time, it has to understand silence can be golden, with the crate a temporary resting place. The dog can keep treasures there; it can eat treats there; it can nap there. Certainly, it needs to be kept there for short periods while you're busy, until it becomes trustworthy. This, of course, does not apply to bedtime (10 P.M. to 6 A.M.), until a puppy is fully house trained. Better than a crate, in the daytime, is a large double playpen (with a top if the dog is likely to climb out) placed in the kitchen on a heavy-duty plastic mat or carpet. A water dish, a plastic bucket full of its toys and its own sleeping pad, a radio tuned to soft music playing in the background—these amenities should keep the puppy content to be alone for an hour or two.

Portuguese Water Dogs are known to love to grow up in offices, sleeping under the desk of their master or mistress. As long as they're taken out for frequent romps, they are happy.

Watch out! A puppy's playing can be annoying. It will leap up on everyone it greets, as if saying, "Let me be close to your face!" It paws at your legs to get attention. "Look what I have in my mouth," it's telling you. Teddy bears (the bigger the better) and stuffed toys with squeakers inside are its favorites. Teddy bears usually end up with one or no eyes, and button noses disappear—remove them before presenting the toys so they don't end up in your dog's tummy, where they can cause trouble.

Your puppy knows where the squeaker is in its toy when you're on the telephone; making noise is a ploy for attention. One characteristic of the PWD is that it carries stuffed animals, bumpers and bones constantly. It likes to take its treasures outdoors and will do so unless you tell the dog it cannot. It invariably greets you and guests with one of its treasures. Sometimes the toy acts as a security blanket, at other times it's one the dog wants you to see but not take, only to admire.

As the PWD ages, it settles down. It's a joy to live with (unless, of course, you have allowed it to become your boss). It comes to you in the evenings as you sit in your chair, nudging your leg with its nose, asking to be petted. Even if your dog weighs 55 pounds or more, lap sitting is its favorite evening occupation.

A PWD youngster must be kept busy. It won't like sitting in a corner of the living room while you're otherwise occupied unless it's tired from the demands of a busy day. Activities like water work, obedience, tracking or agility are stimulating for your friend and will keep you busy too!

The PWD has an incredible vocal range—and it loves to stage vocal histrionics to manipulate you to do what it wants. In work or play, the dog never takes no as final if it thinks it is right. You must guide it to think right.

Those who claim the PWD as a family member purchase boats, build swimming pools and delight in watching it play. Many owners who only wanted one end up with two—or more! Not only does a PWD enjoy playing with another dog, it wants another to love.

An excellent example of Portuguese Water Dog temperament comes from Felicia Vanoff, who purchased her first for her son, Nicholas, in 1974. Janrol Fortaleza, informally known as Aija, was whelped in the sixth U.S. litter, sired by Ancora do Al-Gharb and Farmion Alcantarilha. Aija lived to be sixteen years old and was active for most of that time, despite various illnesses. "She was an absolutely wonderful animal," comments Felicia. "She loved to play games, particularly hide and seek with our son.

"Watch dog, you ask? She was the best. No stranger was allowed in our house unless I touched the individual at the doorway and told her it was all right. When Aija awoke from a nap, it was her habit to come to me and bark. I let her out—she would dash away to the pool—dive in and lap swim. When she had her fill of swimming, she got out, shook herself off, and ran merrily into the pool house, grabbed her towel between her teeth and brought it to me so I could dry her.

"Oh, what a staunch and stoic creature was Aija. And oh, so funny! To go out and leave her alone courted disaster. We would return to find she had decorated the kitchen with paper towels. However naughty she was, her grace

Ch. Dacher's Gaia Criansa do Rio, CD, CGC (Ch. Ilara Sardio ex Ch. Roughrider Sereia Anelada), bred by Dacher Kennels and owned by Laurie Hardman, shows the PWD has an innate herding ability. Courtesy Angela Harding

Farmion Charlie's Caviar (Ch. Charlie de Alvalade ex Ch. Isodora do Mar) is renowned for his high-flying leaps into the water. His owner, Nancy Vener, took this exciting photo of Cosby doing what he was bred for.

and charm overcame all. When she passed away, it was a very sad day. Deyanne Miller would have had the Portuguese Water Dog flag fly at half mast. Aija was truly a bright light in the lives of everyone who knew her."

William Trainor (Farmion Kennels), breeder, judge and handler of Deyanne Farrell Miller's dogs, says, "The breed is exceptionally intelligent and will try you on everything you try to teach them. They can also be a tough working dog, and unless you let him know you are the boss by the time the dog is six months old, you will be owned and controlled by the dog before he is two years old."

The intelligence of the breed is phenomenal. Carol and Bill Oakes own three PWDS. Mrs. Oakes describes how their youngest, Cruiser

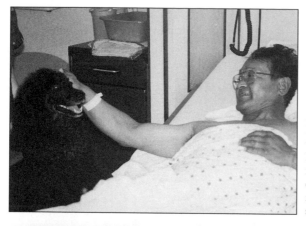

Roughrider's Mandy Lifeboat, CD (Ch. Oliverio Agua Linda ex Ch. Roughrider Diver's Doll), a Therapy Dog, enjoys bringing smiles to hospital patients. Laurie Hardman is Mandy's gratified owner and had the camera ready at exactly the right moment for this sensitive study.

Whatever is required, the PWD is willing to wholeheartedly tackle the job. Sounder, a trained assistance dog, pulls on the strap attached to the wheelchair to move his young charge. Improperly coated, but no less staunch, Sounder demonstrates the closeness to people that has always been an important characteristic of the PWD.

A day in the life of an Arizona PWD and friends. On the raft is Am., Mex., Int. Ch. Pices Hunter Pescador, TT (Paco). In the water is Ha Moreia Do Vale Negro (Mina) and Alto Mares Gentleman's Zack (Zack). Courtesy Arlene Gordon

(Ch. Roughrider's Sea Cruise), prepares for bed: "Cruiser sleeps in his crate at night. Since puppyhood he has always grabbed a stuffed animal from a toy box to spend the night with him. Several months ago, he decided I should tell him which toy could sleep with him. I don't have to go into the family room with him to help him choose. At his bedtime, from wherever I am in the house, all I need to say is 'Get your green monster' or 'Take the gray whale.'

"He'll dash to the family room, sort through the box of twenty to thirty stuffed animals my three dogs own, and carry into his crate the very one I asked him to get. We shake our heads in wonder. His actions bring to mind what people said about Leão back in the 1930s. They said Leão should have been born a human. They said the only problem was that Leão had four legs and couldn't talk. Their intelligence is uncanny—it makes one shiver."

chapter 8

Purchasing a Portuguese Water Dog Puppy

So you want to buy a Portuguese Water Dog puppy?

You want to raise your puppy as a pet, enjoy it as a house dog, a companion animal? Or perhaps you want to rear the puppy as a potential breedable show dog, yet still enjoy it as a house dog and enter it in one or more dog sports.

Whatever your plans, your life style may change in several years. Be prepared to upgrade your goals because you want to do more with your dog than you had planned to in the beginning; be prepared to downgrade if the show potential of your dog did not reach full flower.

The future of this wonderful breed rests in hands like yours. But no one alone can protect it.

Do your homework before purchasing a puppy. Inquire into the history of the breed, and become fully familiar with the breed's temperament and activity level. If a PWD comes to live in your house, is it going to be too active for your family? Too curious? Too busy? Too mouthy? Too difficult to care for on a full-time basis, day in and day out, for the rest of its life? Don't forget, the PWD wants to be underfoot twenty-four hours a day. It's an active, highly sociable dog.

Question whether the dog you are thinking of purchasing is eligible for AKC registration, and if sire and dam are owned by members of the PWDCA. Membership in the national club is not a guarantee of your future puppy's health and temperament; however, PWDCA members are very conscious of health problems, and most share ethical breeding commitments.

"Papas" Allen S. Silver and Herbert H. Miller, Jr., show off three brown puppies from a litter born July 27, 1990 by Ch. Charlie de Alvalade ex Ch. Cocoa Port's Doce Marguerite. Breeders were Sheila B. and Allen S. Silver of the Cocoa Port prefix. Sheila Silver

Have you visited breeders and viewed the living quarters in which their dogs are housed? If a PWD is housed in a kennel full time, stay away. This is a full-time people dog, and a limited-hour (if any) kennel animal.

Think about the things you may not like about a PWD house dog. It is a high-maintenance dog. Though it does not shed, it can leave tiny dead hairs on backs and sides of chairs, on kitchen floors and on your clothes if it isn't combed and brushed often. It requires frequent grooming, clipping or scissoring to keep it looking attractive and mat free.

Not only should the sire and dam be sound and healthy, their temperaments should be spirited (never shy or reticent), zestful and happy, with a willingness to do their masters' bidding. Since the PWD is a thinking animal, it will possess a special touch of independence. It will make for a delightful challenge in training. Still, be on guard—you won't want to live with a pushy PWD who becomes a bully the moment its owners relax.

Consider how you expect the dog to live with you. What kind of housing do you offer? What are your fenced-yard enhancements? If you are looking for a future stud dog or brood bitch, are you aware of the tremendous financial expenditures you have to make for genetic health testing, schooling, showing, grooming, handler fees, advertising, veterinary care, special diets and exercise, plus the extraordinary investment of time?

While it's unlikely that your PWD will be affected with infirmities, tragedies happen. A potential show dog might grow up and develop dysplastic hips, fall victim to progressive retinal atrophy (PRA) or be a genetic disease carrier. Even though your dog's breeder has done all required health checks on his stock, even though the pedigree appears impeccable, some unwanted genes from the past invariably push their way to the present to defeat a potential breeder's dreams. In addition, potential show puppies may develop bad bites (teeth misalignment), roached backs, incorrect fronts, faulty

Do your homework before purchasing a puppy. PWDs grow up to be active dogs. These five are Ch. Charkit Alexander, Ch. Charkit Abril Amar, Whiteposts Queque, Ch. White Cap Craca, CD and Ch. Alfama Ubo. Courtesy Jane Harding

movement or problems with coat or allergies. If you choose a puppy over an adult to answer your breeding dreams, are you prepared to love it for whatever it grows up to be? A potential brood bitch, unencumbered by disease, may not be able to bear puppies. Are you prepared to love her anyway?

After pondering these questions and challenges, recognize that owning a Portuguese Water Dog is accepting the responsibility of caring for an animal for its entire life, despite ups and downs, including possible disquieting moments. To urge you on—yes, the world needs responsible dog owners who love and care for their animals responsibly—let's look for the puppy or adult.

First, the parents. Each sire and each dam must have health checks before breeding. At present there are four required:

1. An Electroretinogram (ERG), a test of retinal function at two years of age to determine whether the dog is free at the time of testing of Progressive Retinal Atrophy (PRA).

2. A yearly Canine Eye Registration Foundation (CERF) examination by a veterinary ophthalmologist to check the health of the dog's eyes. This determines whether the dog is clear of progressive retinal atrophy, cataracts, distichiasis (extra eyelashes) or other eye problems.

3. A Gangliosidosis or Storage Disease GM-1 assay (blood test), giving an approximate Normal, Indeterminate or Carrier genetic status of this disease in a particular animal.

4. A hip X-ray performed by an Orthopedic Foundation of America, Inc. (OFA) veterinarian when the dog reaches two years of age. The dog receives an OFA number when the evaluation by the radiograph shows its hip joint conformation is Fair, Good or Excellent.

When you know these tests have been performed (by papers and/or pedigree nomenclature), examine, if possible, the rest of the pedigree. Pedigree names are just names. You need to inquire into the history of the dogs behind the names. The responsible breeder is the best person to supply the answers. He or she recognizes your need to know about the dogs in the background. Responsible breeders can often become your friends for life when they deem you, too, are responsible. Conversely, do not purchase from a breeder unless you have proof of the health statistics of that person's stock.

Sample questions a prospective buyer should ask:

Please describe what you, the breeder, think are the good and bad characteristics in the breed. How about the dogs you breed? How are they different from dogs of other breeders? If they are, in what way(s)?

What are a family's advantages of owning a Portuguese Water Dog over other breeds?

What are our disadvantages in housing a puppy? an adult?

What are the present genetic health problems of PWDs?

What health checks have you done on your dogs? Are all of these performed by your veterinarian? If not, by what type of specialist?

Do you offer guarantees other than the health guarantee at time of purchase?

Do you stay in touch with your puppy buyers?

What commitments and contract stipulations must a potential buyer make when purchasing a dog from you?

How many years have you been a breeder?

May I visit your kennels to see your dogs?

What books or magazines do you suggest I read for further information on the breed?

There are also a number of questions you must ask yourself. As far as the puppy you wish to own, what are your preferences? Male or female? Wavy or curly? Do you prefer black or brown? Do you want a puppy with white on it, and if so, how much white? Do you like big dogs or small dogs? Do you want a quiet, laid-back dog, or the naughtiest one in the litter?

Males

Males are warm, sweet, sensitive and loving. They are lap sitters. Most respond readily to training. If you purchase a male and neuter him early, he will become a most pliant companion.

The person selecting a puppy from this litter may truly be on the horns of the nicest kind of dilemma. These ten youngsters by Ch. Del Sur's Aguriell, owned by Judi and Dick From and Lana Woodburn, offer a variety of irresistible possibilities. Hmm, decisions, decisions! Courtesy Lana Woodburn

Be aware that the male PWD is no different from males of most breeds. You do not want to house two. When he fully matures (usually at age three), he will seldom tolerate another male living in his house, because it's his territory. He will remain friendly with males away from his home, but at home he will begin to dominate and fight with another male. The time has come to eliminate one male from your household. Don't misunderstand: males make absolutely wonderful pets. While strong-willed at times, they are noble dogs, always proud and full of joy when alongside their owners. Male PWDs become a family's very best friend.

Females

Female PWDs, like males, are sweet, full of fun and happiness, and delight at everything in life. However, if you keep an intact female, be aware she may have mood swings prior to coming into estrus (heat periods). At these intervals, females continually seek your lap for love and take turns at being flighty or exceptionally quiet, sometimes refusing to obey obedience commands. Females are usually smaller than males.

You can house two or more female PWDs in one home; however, if one turns on another, you must then keep them separated. Females who are not compatible are often more vicious when fighting than are males.

Coats and Colors

If you like sheen in a dog's coat, the glossy wavy coat is your choice. Most wavies brush and comb out more easily than do curlies. They look extraordinary in the Lion clip. On the other hand, curly coats are easier to groom for showing in the Retriever clip. Curly coats seem to dry faster when kept short. Long-time fanciers say wavy coats—even when kept short—take longer to dry.

These six Cutwater puppies about to jump out of a Portuguese wine box were reserved long before they were born. Courtesy Animals Only

Black is the classic breed color. Brown is the recessive color. When brown pups appear in litters, they usually do so in a 10-to-20-percent ratio. Most browns carry the graying factor—white hairs may appear on backs as early as three months. As the dog matures, the color change spreads. Entire coats may turn cream-colored, while others turn gray.

Whichever color you prefer, the skin underneath permanent white markings will be pink. White hair is difficult to keep clean. Its texture is also different; many owners say white areas will mat far more easily than black or brown.

Dealing with Unforeseen Consequences

Here are the stories of two PWD owners who have had the uncommon occur when they purchased dogs.

The first owner discovered the unexpected before she adopted her puppy:

After much research, I decided on the PWD because the breed didn't shed, didn't smell, was intelligent, had a herding quality and was a family-type dog. We chose a bitch at three weeks because she had a beautiful white cross on her chest and one white foot with an "onyx" ring on her finger. It was love at first sight. The breeder called when our little girl was almost five weeks old and told me she was suspect of her coat. She had never seen a puppy with an improper coat before, so she wasn't sure. We went out to visit again and again and as the breeder suspected, this puppy's coat was not at all like those of her litter mates. A brother was also "funny haired," although he had more curl—his coat looked like that of a Newfoundland. She looked more like a Labrador Retriever. Both their abdomens were bare of hair compared to the others, who had peach fuzz. Both heads and legs had short hair. We didn't care. And our Nellie has turned out to be an improper wavy, her brother an improper curly.

"It was love at first sight," even though this puppy's coat was not like her littermates' coats. Nellie, an improperly coated PWD, is dearly loved. Nellie, left, is shown here with an unrelated, wavy-coated housemate, Cleo, right.

Now here's the good news. Nellie is 100 percent PWD. She loves the water, retrieves, speaks with the double-octave voice, is everybody's friend. She watches airplanes and helicopters go by. She watches TV. She plays soccer, baseball and street hockey. She ate my sofa and my chair as a puppy. Nellie has a set of teeth that would win Best in Show. She is no different than any other PWD. She sheds lightly. She has no odor. My nephews, who are allergic, can sleep with her without runny noses and itchy eyes. When my Cleo (Wye River Scrimshaw's Cleo) had her puppies last March, Nellie took over the PWD training program, teaching them how to dig a good hole. She was a help to me with puppysitting, as Cleo got acute mastitis after three weeks and couldn't nurse the puppies for several more weeks.

I have been told horror stories about breeders who have put these dogs down at four to six weeks. These "impropers" are incredible companions. This is a cosmetic gene. I know that work is under way to place these dogs in training programs for the disabled and other service-oriented situations. They are so bright they will thrive in these environments.

Cathy Winkler, on the other hand, purchased her PWD with the expectation of breeding it. She then discovered through a health test that her beautiful dog had PRA. She faced her breeder's heartbreak with courage. She wrote in the PWDCA's national magazine, *The Courier:*

I had time to cry and deny and hope that it would all turn out to be a bad dream....I promised myself that I wouldn't cry when I called his breeder, but found myself speechless on the phone.

I guess what I am leading up to is that it is not the end of his life. His new job is to be a much-loved pet. He will remain with us as the perfect house dog, the perfect kid's dog, the perfect companion. PRA is not painful, not expensive, not the end of the world. Even as a small breeder, it is not the end of my breeding program. I have changed plans, reviewed my ethics, revised my dreams.

Not surprisingly, it was my dog, himself, who brought me out of the doldrums. He made me see that it was mostly myself that I was grieving

Breeder Cathy Winkler and Ch. Mariner Bait 'N Switch River Run, TD, were an effective winning team before Cathy discovered through a health check that her handsome campaigner was PRA affected. Kim Booth

for, my broken hopes and dreams, money spent and emotions bruised.... He doesn't care in the least that he has PRA, he doesn't care that he's not going to be a father, or he won't get that elusive Group win or BIS. He *does* care that his family is happy with him. He does care for his human children and his dog friends. Today he is happy, and wants me to be happy and proud of him, which I am.

There is one other little secret I will share with you. My dog will never go completely blind. Never! What he misses with his eyes he will forever see with his heart. Of this I am sure.

Dogs should be sound and healthy, possess excellent temperaments, have all health checks performed and, following the breed Standard, be of correct type and structure. A kennel's objective should be to linebreed and inbreed to establish consistency and produce outstanding examples. Linebreeding and inbreeding help breeders discover and eliminate genes that produce health problems. Periodic outcrosses are also necessary to strengthen lines. It is critical that the breeder community maintain unrelated lines, so that if a health defect is detected in one line, the genetic diversity will protect the breed rather than cause a major problem, such as was the case with progressive retinal atrophy in the early 1990s.

This puppy, owned by breeder Deborah Lee Miller-Riley (Moleiro Kennels), has been taught to sit on command, a good habit it will keep for life. Courtesy Animals Only

Water retrieving at nine months are housemates Moby (left), now Ch. Scrimshaw Seagypsy Moby Dick, and Macy (right), now Ch. Scrimshaw Magellan's Seagypsy. Both are owned and were photographed by Dr. Virginia Brown.

c h a p t e r   9

Rearing the Puppy

TRAINING BASICS

The self-preservation instinct in animals is as strong as the sexual instinct. That is why it is dangerous to be tough on puppies. Many people hit a puppy with a newspaper as a reprimand and wonder why forever after it is fearful of people holding newspapers. Puppies seldom forget an incident from which they have had to protect themselves. Noise and strange sights do not affect them as strongly as the things that may harm them when they are young and highly impressionable.

This response is similar to what can happen when a child goes off to kindergarten for the first time. Something may happen to frighten that child in class, but if no one sees the incident or helps the child overcome it, the child may end up disliking school as a result. However, adults can talk to children and help them understand unpleasant happenings. One cannot do this with dogs. When a young animal is threatened, an indelible mark is placed in its brain. Erasure is difficult. This doesn't mean you can't be firm; it means that you must use common sense to help the puppy get past its problem. Try to visualize how an animal thinks. Don't let your temper get away from you and threaten in a manner a puppy might construe as abusive.

You must, of course—from the moment your puppy first enters your house—teach it your living pattern. That means placing it on your regular household schedule. The puppy should get up when you do, eat its meals at the same, specific time every day on a schedule that is convenient for you, and go to bed at the same time each night. These are the habits that will remain with your dog for life, or until you have to shift your schedule to fit a new pattern.

This doesn't mean when the puppy comes home it isn't taken out every hour until it's house trained (you must do this!) or that you don't get up during the night to let it out of its crate when it whimpers—your dog is telling you it's uncomfortable. And no matter what hour of the night it is, realize it has to eliminate. You must get up and take it outside—always to the same place. If you don't have a fenced yard, the dog must always be on leash when taken outside. Never let it out the door and go back inside by yourself. Go outside with your dog regardless of whether it's raining, snowing, blowing, 30 degrees below or 100 degrees above. Have appropriate clothes ready. You not only give your puppy security with your presence, you give it praise *as* (not after) it eliminates: "Good job!" "Good potty!" or "Good chores!" "Wow, what a g-o-o-d pup!" You are teaching.

During the day, take your puppy outside every forty-five minutes to an hour. Stay with it until it eliminates. Pups have to eliminate after they awaken, eat and play—and the once-every-hour trip outside for both of you must be adhered to until the pup really understands that the carpet or linoleum is off limits. This takes time. Any pup would rather eliminate on a carpet where it is standing, or over in a corner by the closet; these are comfortable things to do.

Novice dog owners believe that roughly scolding a puppy is okay. It isn't. Scolding simply makes the puppy think it shouldn't do what it is doing. If it isn't timed correctly, it doesn't work. For scolding to be effective, it must be given *during* (not after) the infraction; otherwise the pup becomes confused. Novice owners also believe praise anytime after something is accomplished is okay. Professional trainers recognize praise *during* an act is what stimulates awareness in a dog's mind that it's the right thing to do—and that this message has to be repeated over and over until the habit becomes as natural as yawning. Taking the pup to the correct place outside helps it learn what is allowed.

A puppy's brain is in its formative period from birth to about fourteen months. Dennis Charney, head of psychiatry at the Veterinary Hospital in West Haven, Connecticut, says, "The rule for vision, and most likely for the other senses as well, is use it right away or lose it."

Implant good habits right away. This applies to all habits you want your puppy to form. Dogs are creatures of habit. So put your puppy on a schedule. Your dog will gain confidence when it knows it eats at a certain time, goes for walks at a certain time and goes to sleep at night at a certain time.

As with children, early learning in the dog is crucial for rich adult mental development. This doesn't mean that you should push the puppy into intensive training before adolescence. Many canine students pushed into early training burn out by the time they are three. What it *does* mean is that you should establish habits you want the pup to keep for life. If you are consistent in teaching good manners to your puppy, positive courses in basic obedience may begin at about six months of age; puppy conformation classes, however, are a must for both pet and show puppies when they are twelve weeks to four months of age.

OUTSIDE THE HOME

Puppies need to be puppies. The more they can explore the outside—trees, grass, dirt, holes, the more they watch insects crawl and birds fly, the more they can play with other dogs, or travel sitting on your lap in the car and visit downtown scenes with people and auto activity all about them—the more imprinting they will have and the better equipped they will be to socialize in our world as they mature.

Puppies should not be confined in a crate on the back seat of the car to ride alone while you're driving. If you're alone, place the crate on the seat beside you. If your puppy cries, he'll be close to you so you can console it and steady it in his place. If you're not alone, let your front-seat passenger quietly carry the pup on his or her lap. A puppy requires your security and love when learning how to ride in a car, but it must also learn to quietly remain on the seat! Dogs who jump about in a car never learned to ride quietly. They probably rode inside a crate in the back of the car during their formative months, then, when left out, didn't know how to act. Adult dogs who are afraid to ride in cars were probably never carried on laps as puppies and thus didn't develop car "confidence." Your pup was taught to lie down (even when on a lap), so he automatically rides well. Habit formed! Even though any dog is safer in a crate in case of an accident, it must learn to ride quietly on a seat, because many cars are not designed to carry a crate.

One of the best ways to crate train a pup is to take it to neighborhood stores in the car. When you leave the dog in the car, roll down the windows a little for air, place the pup in the crate, lock the car and do your shopping. Your dog will cry, but you won't hear it. By the time you get back, it will be quiet. When you have set your purchases inside, reward the puppy with a tasty tidbit.

Never leave a dog in the car when the thermometer reads over 60 degrees outside. Park in the shade or don't park. PWDs have a high "thermostat," and some have died from heat exhaustion in a crate in a car with windows open and the temperature outside a mere 60 degrees. A temperature of 60 degrees outside becomes 90 to 100 inside a crate, even when windows are open to adequately cool the entire car. If you have any doubt about whether it's too hot to take your dog in the car for a quick visit to the grocery store, leave it at home in its crate!

GREETING YOUR NEW FAMILY MEMBER

"Oh, he's so quiet!" you say on the phone, on the day-after-adoption "is everything okay" call from the breeder. "He's just sits and watches everything. He's as good as gold."

Let your dog explore this strange new environment and make advances toward its new family at the first meeting. Be gentle and comforting. Carry the puppy over your shoulder and let it examine its new world. Give it three

Have your child sit and hold the puppy on his or her lap in a spot where the puppy cannot fall and be injured. Courtesy Dr. Virginia Brown

to four days to adjust. Once settled in, the puppy will come alive. It will grab and chew on fingers and shoes, paw water out of its water dish and cry when you leave the room. In case you didn't realize it before, you now know you own a precocious animal baby that looks to you for its every need.

If you have children, don't allow them to tease, jump around or throw things at the new puppy. Establish proper rules of behavior for them, as well. No carrying of the pup by a child, no wrestling, tug of war or mauling should be allowed. Insist on activities like ball playing—with the child sitting quietly on the floor—or walks. Puppies mimic child activities as much as possible. If children are wild, the pup becomes wild. Puppy mouthing (nipping) does deserve a screech! When your dog chews something it shouldn't, rather than scolding, do something positive. Give it a toy of its own it can chew. Have young children carry one of its toys in their pocket to help teach it proper "chewing" manners. And always supervise a young child with a puppy. You don't want a child hurting a pup in retaliation for a puppy nip.

While puppies don't dismantle too easily, there is a right way to pick them up. Put one hand under the dog's chest and the other hand supporting it from underneath. Lift both ends at the same time. Teach your children how to do this. If they are too young to do it correctly, don't allow them to pick up the puppy; instead, have your child sit on the floor and hold the puppy in his or her lap. Never allow a child to run while playing with a puppy. It's very easy to trip over a puppy and fall upon it, injuring the puppy, the child or both!

An important lesson for a puppy to learn is how to act around visitors in the home. Puppies, like children, are often wary of strangers, particularly if strangers fawn all over them. Have a "dog cookie" jar sitting on a table near your front door. Ask your guests to offer your puppy a treat as they come into your house and then to ignore the dog and let it make the advances.

Carry him over your shoulder and let him examine his new world with his eyes.

Teach the young puppy a whistle recall command. This aids in establishing a reliable recall. Purchase a small field training whistle, such as the Acme Thunderer, from a sporting goods store (never a silent whistle—it might not be working when you think it is). Sound the whistle twice each time you feed the dog; blast it twice each time you call it when you're outside, and reward it with a treat as it gallops to you. After a few weeks, reward the dog with food praise once every three times, then reduce the food praise to every five times. Eventually, reward with verbal praise alone.

PHYSICAL DEVELOPMENT

Most lines of Portuguese Water Dogs are slow developing. One week bodies are long and legs short; the next, the opposite is true. The dog races in circles around the yard. You think, "Gosh, I can take him jogging." Don't do it.

Your puppy's framework at this age is not yet fully calcified and is composed mainly of cartilage. Solid bone doesn't appear until late in adolescence—around fifteen months on average. Don't ruin the dog's hips, leg bones or foot pads by forcing it to walk long distances, especially on cement. Leave it behind.

"It is known," wrote Dr. Jerold S. Bell, PWDCA geneticist, in the club's bimonthly magazine, *The Courier*, "that genetically pre-dysplastic hips can be protected by restricting environmental stress. Some breeders go to the extreme of not allowing stair walking in their puppy contracts. Certainly excessive leaping behavior can alter the shape of the cartilaginous hip at a young age." It's good for puppies to climb up and down stairs, or up and down hills, but not in excess! Again, puppies must never jog or jump (higher than shoulder height) until they're fifteen months old, when bones are set. Of course, they can gallop during free play, as they should. But don't take your puppy on structured physical activities that it might obviously enjoy, such as jogging—its stoic character wouldn't admit to being tired. On a park or yard excursion where it can gallop during free play, your dog will rest when it tires. Its body needs special handling as it matures, just as does his mind.

A puppy's coat can be trimmed for the first time when it is about fourteen weeks old (see Chapter 10, "Grooming the Portuguese Water Dog"). What about new coat growth? The rate of coat growth on the body is about one-half inch a month; on the skull, about one-quarter inch a month; leg coat grows much more slowly. Your puppy should be groomed daily and given a small treat when it poses, standing or sitting. Bathe it every two weeks, but remember that because you have cleaned it down to his skin, you have removed oil. So dry the dog well and keep it inside for the better part of its bath day.

If you've made its grooming episodes happy, your puppy's first visit to a grooming shop should be pleasant. Check out the grooming shops near your home before making a specific appointment. If you were taking a toddler to a barber for a first haircut, you would want the barber to be gentle, soft-spoken and an expert at the work to be done. By the same token you need to use a gentle, soft-spoken, knowledgeable groomer who bathes, blow dries and grooms your puppy while you wait. And if you feel the dog has to be left at a boarding kennel while you're out of town on a weekend, investigate kennels in your area. When you think you've found the right one, take your puppy there for a visit. You need to feel secure about both the environment in which it will be housed and its potential caretakers.

SUPERVISION

Your dog will begin to lord over the house as it grows, if allowed to do so. Even if you teach it not to jump up on the furniture, it will test that no-no when you leave the room. You'll return to find the imprint of its warm body on your favorite cushion.

All young animals need 24-hour supervision. If you're not home, supply artificial supervision—such as crates, playpens and confinement to a safe room—or you may come back to a scene like this.

Your dog is not a wanderer. It stays in its yard—unless, of course, you don't have a fenced yard and let it outside without supervision. Beware: many Portuguese Water Dogs die or become seriously injured as a result of auto accidents. PWDs are not street smart and, as a consequence, many breeders refuse to sell puppies to homes without fenced yards.

All young animals need round-the-clock supervision. If you're not there, supply artificial supervision, in the form of crates, playpens or a safe room. Never leave your PWD in a yard when you're gone, for it might be stolen. They're safer inside—as long, of course, as they have artificial supervision. If you know where your puppy is and how it is protected at all times, it will be all right. As soon as possible after bringing the dog home, check with your veterinarian about having a tiny computer chip implanted behind its shoulders for identification in case it becomes lost. The AKC has initiated a fine electronic tagging program. (See the Appendix chapter for AKC information.)

BEATING THE HEAT

Your PWD should have a plastic tub in which it can wade, unearth toys or recline on a steamy summer day. Neither cold nor rain will bother it. Work the garden on a blustery spring day, dressed in layers; your dog will seek out the nearest patch of snow to lie upon and supervise you. It will lie on the grass as the rain comes pouring down and chew his sterile bone contentedly. (Sterile bones make the best toys. They last for several years and don't compact in a dog's stomach or cause diarrhea, as do many chew bones.)

If you go fishing and your small fishing boat has no shade, pour a thin layer of water along the deck. Your dog will thank you by sopping up the water with its coat as it stretches out in comfort.

At home, it may seek your bathtub to lie in, even when you need to turn up the heat or light a fire. One of its favorite resting places inside the house is a tile floor—if it is only found in the bathroom, that's where you'll probably find your dog.

It's a fascinating baby animal, the Portuguese Water Dog puppy. Enjoy every minute of the fleeting period of its puppyhood.

chapter 10

Grooming the Portuguese Water Dog

A Word to the Newcomer

The "dress code" of the PWD is unique. There are two show clips and several easy pet clips. Prospective owners should observe one of the grooming patterns designed to show off this distinctive breed. Otherwise, why purchase a Portuguese Water Dog!

BASIC GROOMING INSTRUCTIONS FOR EARS, SKULL AND MUZZLE

Portuguese Water Dogs groomed in the Retriever Clip must have a flag on the end of the tail; the hair falling below the ears trimmed close to the ear leather, heart-shaped; and the hair on the top of the skull trimmed to enhance the unique Portuguese Water Dog head look. It's vital that ears, skull and tail conform to the description given in the breed Standard.

If owners have their dogs attended by a groomer every four to six weeks, they should instruct the groomer not to give the dog "spaniel" ears by allowing long hair growth to fall below the lower jaw. Ears are to be trimmed to the edge of the leather! The Standard says: "Ears—set well above the line of the eye. Leather is heart shaped and thin. Tips should not reach below the lower jaw."

The tail should be trimmed to within approximately three to five inches of the end, with hair then left full-length to the tip. This full-length tuft, or Portuguese "flag," is never cut.

The topknot, while scissored to blend with the body coat, enhances the breed's "essential characteristic: head distinctively large, well-proportioned and with exceptional breadth of topskull." To follow the Standard's requirements, keep the topknot full—approximately two inches—as shown in the illustrations accompanying this chapter.

Dogs trimmed in the Lion Clip need longer hair on the ears and skull than do dogs trimmed in the Retriever Clip.

With the popularity of this fascinating breed rising, no matter which of the two show clips or the several pet styles you use, these grooming patterns of skull, ears and tail must be followed.

THE PORTUGUESE WATER DOG LOOK

If you own or anticipate purchasing a Portuguese Water Dog, you know you do not want it groomed as any other breed. A striking PWD, wavy coat glistening or curly coat sculptured, is a product of proper and constant coat care—however brief that daily or triweekly grooming session might be.

Your Choice—Learn to Groom or Hire a Groomer

You need to decide whether you desire to take the necessary time out of your busy daily schedule to groom this long-haired breed. Grooming a dog is relaxing, even though you are wielding a brush, comb, scissors and clippers much of the time. Like animals, who find joy and contentment grooming others, it is therapeutic for owners. After a bustling and stressful day at the office, you may find healing for a troubled mind in this peaceful, creative grooming time.

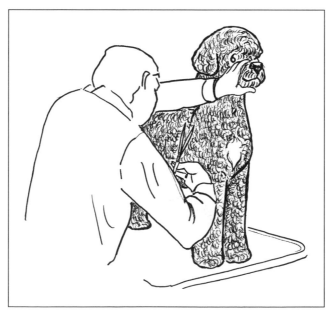

Scissor the legs upward from the feet, blending into the body coat.

Many Portuguese Water Dog owners, however, choose to have a groomer bathe, scissor or clip their dogs. If you intend to use a groomer because you lack the confidence, scissoring skills and time to make your dog look as beautiful as you think it should look, you'll still find pleasure in bathing, drying and trying your hand at clipping and scissoring. Even though not all the clipping or scissoring you do will be perfectly even, there is the consolation that hair grows back, your mistakes will be covered and if you keep at it, your skills will surely increase!

The breed's two historical show clips are the Lion Clip and the Working Retriever Clip. In 1621, Gervase Markham described the cutting and shaving of dogs, particularly the Water Dog:

> ...for the cutting and shaving him from the navill downward, or backward, it is two wayes well to be allowed of that is, for summer hunting or for the water; because these Water Dogges naturally are ever most laden with haires on the hinder parts, nature as it were labouring to defend that part most, which is continually to be employed in the most extremity, and because the hinder parts are ever deeper in the water than the fore parts, therefore nature hath given them the greatest armour of haire to defent the wette and coldnesse; yet this defence in the Sommer time by the violence of the heate of the Sunne, and the greatnesse of the Dogges labour is very noysome and troublesome, and not onely maketh him sooner to faint and give over his sport, but also makes him by his overheating, more subject to take the Maungie.
>
> And so likewise in matter of water, it is a very heavy burthen to the Dogge and makes him to swimme lesse nimbly and slower, besides the former offences before received; But for the cutting or shaving of a Dogge all quite over, even from the Foote to the Nostrill that I utterly dislike, for it not only takes from him the general benefits which Nature hath lent him, but also brings such a tendernesse and chilnesse over all his body, that the

Rey do Al-Gharb, the first all-breed BIS-winning Portuguese Water Dog, shown here in the century-old traditional show clip fashion before the breed appeared in America. Note that some of the hair on the skull is clipped, allowing the breed's beautiful eyes to be seen. This traditional clip also shows to advantage the strong jaws called for in the Standard. Courtesy Conchita Cintron

water in the end will grow yrksome unto him; for howsoever men may argue that keeping any creature cold, will make it the better indure colde, yet we finde by true experience both in these and divers other such like things, that when Nature is thus continually kept at her uttermost ability of indurance, when any little drope more is added to that extreamity, presently she faints and grows distempered, whereas keepe Nature in her full strength and she will very hardly be conquered, and hence it doth come that you shall see an ordinary land Spaniell being lustily and well kept, will tyre 20 of these over shaven Curres in the could water.

Let's observe some pictures of several dogs in the modern version of these show clips and in the breed's unofficial yet comfortable pet clips. We'll then clip and scissor!

Ch. Seabreeze Tailor Made (Ch. Aabest Mr. T Dedemon ex Ch. Seabreeze Nauti-Marietta), owned by Karen Arends, shows his winning form in the Lion Clip.

THE LION CLIP

The Lion Clip, long the traditional clip for the Portuguese Water Dog, is the only trim allowed in the FCI show rings in Europe. In various styles, it appears in early pictures of many breeds. PWD fanciers claim it as their own, with specific differences. The handsome Lion Clip accents the important driving rear structure of the PWD. Unfortunately, breeders claim many would-be pet owners (in countries such as England and Portugal, where the Lion Clip is a must in the show ring) turn away from the breed because of the clip's unusual look. There is very little market for PWD pets in Lion Clips.

The first Canadian parti-color champion, a wavy, Am., Can Ch. Aguarelle's Trek to DownEast, TT, CGC, is owned by Steven Dostie and Claire Dignard. John Ashbey

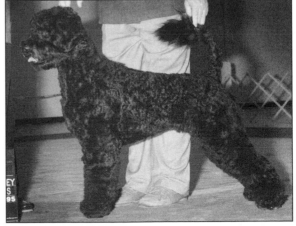

Groomed in the Retriever Clip by Kristi Travellino, the coat one inch on the body with longer hair on the legs, is Ch. Roughrider's Saugus River (Ch. Roughrider's Cisco Pete ex Roughrider's Salt Water Taffy). Steven Ross/Elaine

THE WORKING RETRIEVER CLIP

The Working Retriever Clip, a trim with an approximately one-inch body depth with longer coat on the legs, was designed in the early 1980s by PWDCA members. It was created because Portuguese fishermen stressed utilitarian function rather than the cosmetic considerations that careful, detailed shearing demands. This style was closest to the natural dress of water dog type depicted in century-old treatises on canines. The PWD in Working Retriever Clip even appears on a Portuguese stamp, introduced in 1985. Nevertheless, the American-designed Working Retriever Clip is not allowed in FCI European shows. In America, it, like the Lion Clip, appears in the show ring in various styles—some coats highly structured with no hair out of place, others more relaxed and natural. It is the clip most American owners prefer for their dogs.

Garbonzo, Ch. Dacher's Gotta Get A Gund (Ch. Ilara Sardio ex Ch. Roughrider Sereia Anelada), a top show dog owned by Dr. David, Cheryl and Leigh Smith, is shown in his summer clip. Kathryn Braund

On the show trail Garbonzo compiled an admirable record of top wins. He is shown here winning a Group 1st at the Cyprus Creek (Texas) KC under Judge Lawrence Stanbridge, with handler Bill McFadden. Missy Yuhl

Pet Clips That Make Sense

An unofficial summertime or utility clip is used by many dog owners to keep their animals cool and comfortable during the hot summer months. Ch. Dacher's Gotta Get a Gund (Garbonzo) is pictured here in an unofficial pet clip—short body, longer hair on legs. He is also shown in his show-ring Retriever Clip.

How Seabee grew. The first photo, taken at twelve weeks, shows the puppy brushed and combed. In the second photo, her curly hair has been cut down with a #4 clipper blade at four months; note that her tail hair has not started to grow. The hair on her head and legs is slightly longer than that on her body. The third photo shows her on the day she became a champion. Seabee's registered name is Ch. TimberOaks Seabee Roughrider (Ch. Roughrider's Adventure, CD ex Ch. Sete Mares Storm Diver). Seabee's owner is Kathryn Braund.

A second unofficial pet clip—short body, longer hair on legs—is modeled by Ch. Timber Oaks Seabee Roughrider (Seabee), at four months. Puppies are normally clipped down at three to four months for two reasons: (a) to remove the overgrown birth fuzz with hair that has grown in since (usually well chewed by littermates), and (b) because clipping off old hair is believed to bring in a fuller coat. While the latter may be an old wives' tale, puppy coats respond well to early clipping. Clipping a pup gets rid of fuzz and helps teach the pup what its manners must be during grooming sessions throughout its life.

In the accompanying photo, Seabee has yet to grow the "flag" on the end of her tail, which, in most pups, does not become full until the puppy is almost a year old.

Specifics on Growth and Matting

The Portuguese Water Dog's hair becomes shaggy—whether the dog is wavy or curly—at about four to six weeks. Body hair grows approximately one-quarter to one-half inch a month, with leg hair growing more slowly. During spring, summer and fall, hair becomes abundant; in winter, growth is minimal. Without proper coat care, the PWD's coat will mat—in some cases, readily.

Here's what happens. As new hair grows, old hairs die. In humans, as in other animals, particularly dogs that shed prodigiously, hair falls out as it dies. In the so-called nonshedding breeds, which include the Portuguese Water Dog, dead hairs cling to the new growth instead of dropping off the body. If these dead hairs are not combed and brushed out frequently, they cause intense itching, which then induces scratching. These tiny, irritating dead hairs become snarled with the live hairs and mats develop, forming first beneath the elbows, ears, belly and back legs and between the foot pads. Some dogs also mat along their sides or along the top of their backs. Owners who have light-colored linoleum in kitchens and bathrooms discover the fine hairs when mopping. The little dead hairs stick to the floor as tightly as they stick to the nonshedding dog's coat. I sometimes call my near-white kitchen and laundry room tiled floors, nonshedding!

THE EASY-AT-HOME MAINTENANCE
SHORT GROOMING SESSION

Even a nonshedding breed needs to be groomed regularly. The best schedule is a daily five-minute combing and brushing. If you comb and brush on a daily basis, you'll most likely find dead hairs only in the brush—and very few of them. If a daily regimen doesn't work for you, try five- to ten-minute sessions three times a week.

In these short sessions, first comb the dog down to the skin. Some groomers discourage clients from combing their dogs, saying it can split ends. It is better, however, to have a few split ends than never to encounter mats brushing may skim over. The object of grooming is not only to make the dog look distinctive, but to make it comfortable.

Second, brush (again a reminder that brushing does not always get down to the skin).

Third, scrupulously check paws for mats between the webbing. Also check under ears and elbows. If there's long hair straggling across the top of the ear canals, cut that away, too. Clean ears when necessary.

Fourth, cut away any hair below the eyes that appears to hinder your dog's sight.

Fifth, comb and brush muzzle to remove food and dirt.

Because of a busy schedule, I prefer the three-times-a-week regimen. However, one of my dogs requires fifteen, not five, minutes of grooming using this routine. He mats easily, which neither of us likes. Consequently, it takes time and the proper tools to untangle the hairs that are pulling together into a ball.

If you have decided to take your dog to a groomer every four to six weeks, be observant, at the first session, for signs of separation anxiety. Portuguese Water Dogs, even when socialized to a variety of environments and people, do not like to be apart from their owners for any length of time. If possible, select a groomer who will allow you to remain in your dog's sight at least part of the time during the first session it is being groomed. This shared grooming experience helps your dog stand confidently on its own four paws when you're not beside it. And it will certainly enjoy the final outcome. My dogs are always proud when returning home looking and feeling quite comfortable (and beautiful). Even though you hire a groomer, you must at least three times weekly check over, comb, brush and care for your dog's coat and body so that it is comfortable during the interval between the grooming shop visits.

Ready to Groom?

Ready to tackle the necessary grooming chores? Remember, you are caring for your dog, which is fun. The chores are interesting, relaxing (for both you and the dog) and rewarding. The time required is modest.

Not so with tools. You need more than a modest assortment. (Check with your dog's breeder for sources; also check prices and items at pet stores, in dog magazine ads, in pet supply catalogs and with dog show vendors.)

Tools You Require

GROOMING TABLE

Don't use the top of a box, an old, shaky end table or the top of a washing machine or dryer—you need a standard grooming table (along with a chair). It is the soundest dog equipment investment you will make. Quickly, your dog will learn it is its very own table. It soon realizes it gets attention on its table, thus making the time you spend there together joyful. When your dog becomes an adult, it will probably jump up on the table to take a nap. (Most dogs enjoy observing their surroundings from a high station.)

You may not plan to exhibit your dog in dog sports and decide your neutered or spayed PWD doesn't require constant care and grooming because you keep it in a very short pet trim. However, the grooming experience is still essential. It's wise to teach your dog to accept grooming as a puppy. Even though you don't plan to do much grooming, this is one of the responsibilities you accept in owning a dog of a long-haired breed. If it doesn't enjoy grooming, it's your fault, not the dog's.

GROOMING ARM WITH ATTACHED COLLAR

The grooming arm helps introduce the dog to the ministrations that will be performed on it. The arm works beautifully in helping to teach puppies to stand still.

SEVERAL COMBS

There are numerous kinds of combs available that can be used on a PWD coat. For normal grooming operations, you need: (a) a "Greyhound"™ comb with half fine, half medium metal teeth and measuring $7^1/_2$ inches long, coarse/medium, with $1^1/_4$-inch teeth; (b) a wooden-handled comb with $1^1/_8$-inch teeth; (c) a rake comb, for breaking up and removing mats; (d) an untangling comb, with $1^1/_8$-inch teeth; and (e) a dematting rake.

BRUSHES

While combing is necessary to reach the dog's skin, brushing brings up the coat's natural oil and gloss and keeps hairs in good health. Buy a pin brush and a slicker brush. These are available in a variety of sizes, so find the size with which you are most comfortable. Some PWD owners keep both a regular-size and large brush on hand, but you must decide what works best for you. Be certain to purchase a quality slicker; to do otherwise is a false economy. Lower-priced counterparts are made with cheap wire teeth, which often pull out and damage the coat.

ELECTRIC CLIPPER

Buy a quality clipper with a heavy-duty motor; you'll be using it for many years. If you buy an Oster™ A5, it will probably be fitted with a #10 blade, which will cut the dog's hair to $1/_{16}$ of an inch. If you buy another brand, check the blade for the length of the cut. A #10 blade is fine for use on a pregnant bitch's underbelly or the skin around a male dog's genitals and for fashioning the Lion Clip. Experienced groomers use the #4, #4F, #5 or #5F for the Retriever Clip and the #10, #8½ and #7½ for the Lion Clip. Desirable are snap-on combs (which can be attached to a #10 or #40 surgical-length blade). Accompanying these are mechanical maintenance items such as a blade wash, "kool" lube, clipper oil and clipper grease.

SCISSORS

Professional-quality shears are available in all sizes, shapes and prices. Buy the best you can afford and you will be glad you did. 7½-inch ice-tempered shears are popular with groomers, as are the 8¼- and 8½-inch models. Thinning shears, bent shank shears and nose/ear shears are also very popular. Multiple scissor purchases are dependent on the intensity of your grooming. Start with quality scissors, adding to your collection gradually.

NAIL CLIPPERS

These are a must. All dogs require toenails to be cut at least twice a month. There are two types of clippers: the guillotine and the nail scissor. The guillotine is the best for use by novices. Be sure you purchase the clipper intended for use on large dogs. You'll also need a coagulant on hand in case you unfortunately cut one or more of your dog's nails too short. Every nail has a vein growing down into it. Called the "quick," it carries the blood supply to the nail. Don't worry, though—even experienced groomers cut quicks more often than they may care to admit. While a severed quick causes some pain, it is not a serious matter. A popular coagulant powder called Kwik Stop‰ is available from catalogs and dog show suppliers. Some owners prefer filing their dog's nails with electric nail grinders or canine nail files. You must decide what is best for you.

TOOTHBRUSHES AND TOOTH CLEANING PRODUCTS

Dental care has become an important part of canine maintenance grooming. Dogs taught to accept tooth brushing and gum care are less likely to develop tartar problems with resulting tooth loss. Many canine dental care products are available. In lieu of commercial canine tooth-cleaning products, baking soda mixed with water and rubbed on the dog's teeth with a soft, clean cloth works fine. Do not use toothpaste made for humans.

SHAMPOOS

Dog owners need to be aware that the canine's pH balance is different from that of humans—almost 100 percent of canines fall within the alkaline range of 6.2 and 8.6, as opposed to the average human acidic pH of 4.5 to 5.5. Look at pH balance this way: a pH shift of less than half a point can almost destroy an aquarium within forty-eight hours. The higher the pH balance, the more alkaline the shampoo is and the more cleansing action it has, but it's also more drying to the skin and coat. It can strip the natural oils from hair and can affect color molecules.

If your dog has dry, limp hair, you are probably using a high-pH-balanced shampoo (7 or higher), which is usually tearless. Baby shampoos are 7 pH. On the low end of the pH scale, using a shampoo that is too acidic may deplete the animal's slightly alkaline mantle, which protects its skin, and in time trigger skin problems, which begin with itching. Usually, a shampoo with a balance of 5.5 pH up to about 6.2 pH removes dirt and debris, but not to the point that it removes natural oils. How long you leave a shampoo on a dog's skin determines the cleansing and stripping action of the shampoo and whether or not conditioners are required.

Because the Portuguese Water Dog's skin condition is important to its hair condition, each owner should check the pH balance of a shampoo. Drug stores carry pH test kits that include specially treated paper and a scale with a color code. Touch the shampoo with this paper, then check the color it turns against the color code on the pH paper. This gives the pH balance.

There is a dizzying array of dog shampoos on the market—some tearless (high pH balance), others not; some with and some without conditioners; some medicated; some with flea killers; some with color enhancers. Because most shampoos dilute—3–1, 15–1, etc.—it's economical to invest in the gallon sizes. When you dilute shampoos, concentrate on accuracy to maintain correct balance.

Conditioners are sold separately from shampoos; they, along with sprays and colognes, are numerous. There are also oils and coat enhancers that one can spray, massage or wipe onto the dog between baths to clean the dog and beautify its coat. Be sure to buy small quantities first to ascertain the results. Dogs, like humans, do better on a particular type of pH. Confer with other PWD owners; they'll offer good shampoo choices.

EAR AND EYE CLEANER

These are also necessary. Both should be purchased from your veterinarian. Neither should be used unless the professional directs you to them and explains how to use them. Ear powder and cotton balls are other musts.

HAIR DRYERS

Canine dryers are much better for dogs than human dryers. Most human dryers have high, shrill, powerful dryer sounds that can hurt your dog's ears. The sound may frighten your dog temporarily. There is also a tendency to use human dryers at high heat, which is also harmful to the dog's hair.

There are two basic dog dryers: one emits heat, the other air (with minimal heat coming from the motor). It's practical to have both types if you intend to do your own grooming. The dryer that emits heat is particularly practical in the wintertime, when dogs must be dried fully before venturing outside after a bath. Although dogs can go in and out of lake, river or ocean water with no ill effect, washing a dog cleans it down to the skin, temporarily erasing its natural water-resistant skin oils. When soaked to the skin, dogs become chilled. While the hot-air dryer reduces drying time in half, since its function is to blow moisture out of the dog's coat quickly and efficiently, it can also chill the dog in cold weather. Bathe dogs after they have been swimming in salt or pool water to rinse out the salt or chemicals their coats attract.

SPRAY BOTTLE

Use a spray bottle for applying water or water mixed with conditioner before commencing grooming operations.

TOWELS

A good rule of thumb is to allow three bath towels per dog per bath, plus several hand towels.

Introduce Your Dog to the Grooming Table

Treat any Portuguese Water Dog, even an older rescue dog, as if it were a puppy. You will quickly learn whether the older dog is familiar with a grooming table. If so, do not advance any faster than if it were a puppy. You are bonding and learning about the dog's temperament while grooming it.

You need more than a modest assortment of tools to groom the Portuguese Water Dog.

FIRST WEEK

Whether puppy or adult, acquaint your new PWD with the table the second day it is in your house. Make the introduction short, sweet and fun! Simply place or lift the dog on the table. Slip its head through the grooming noose (be sure to set the grooming arm at the right height for your dog first), making certain the dog is secure. Holding the dog in a stand, commanding "stand" happily, as if it knew what it was supposed to do—no dog does at this early stage of training. Even if the dog squirms, hold it in this position, saying "Good stand" all the while.

How to hold? Here's a rule to remember: control of any animal's head means control of the animal. With your right hand, circle your fingers high on the dog's neck, right under the chin and close to the grooming noose. Your grip holds the dog steady. Keep the dog standing with your free (left) hand under the abdomen, directly in front of the back legs.

Praise "Good stand" and massage with your left hand while smiling and comforting with your voice. Dogs have no idea what is going to happen to them in strange situations; some become intensely frightened, so your calm and soothing voice and actions must make allowances for this. Massage the dog's back, front chest, under chest, head, ears and legs, all the while having the left hand (yes, the one that is doing the massaging) available to steady the dog, if necessary. Although it is trying to sit or flail about most of the time and you continue attempting vainly to stand it, say happily, "Good stand," and keep the dog there.

Then sit the dog, maintaining your grip on it. Your left hand can push down on its rear. As you push down, say, "Sit." Praise the dog to the skies once it sits (yes, you pushed it there—why are you praising? Because it's there!). Elapsed time? Not quite a minute. Give your dog a treat, associating the treat with its being on top of the table. Immediately lift the dog off the table while praising it, then go on about your daily business.

Perform this grooming session twice daily for the next week: place the dog on the table, stand it, keep it standing while you massage it, talk to it, give it a treat and lift it down. Before the week is complete, your dog will have learned to enjoy being on the grooming table. It will also begin to understand the two commands you are attempting to teach it and perhaps begin to automatically respond to them.

If the dog continues to squirm when you lift it up, be calmly dominant while keeping it in place. Dogs that continue to squirm or yell must be made to remain in place. How? Controlling the neck, scold verbally, insisting, with a calmly dominant voice, on appropriate behavior. If you become angry, the dog realizes it has won the battle and will continue to misbehave. If you persist in a calm, authoritative manner, it will respect your leadership and begin to behave.

One important caution: Never allow a dog to stay on a table by itself. If the telephone or doorbell rings, take the dog off the table before answering the ring. Many young dogs are injured jumping off grooming tables when their owners leave them "for just an instant!" Dogs left on the table and held by the grooming noose can choke to death when they try to jump off.

SECOND WEEK

Grooming begins! Show your PWD the comb, let it examine the comb with its eyes and mouth, then comb the top of its ears gently. Yes, while the dog is sitting! Some puppies and older dogs fidget and become frightened again, wanting to know what you are doing. Let your dog examine the comb again. Maybe it wants to smell or mouth it. Okay! Continue combing with a happy, positive attitude that says, "We're grooming. So don't fidget." If you don't assume leadership, if you comb with an unsure demeanor and unsteady hand while the dog fidgets, the dog recognizes it, not you, is in control. And a PWD will test you in every way imaginable!

When the dog stands well on the grooming table, begin teaching it to lie down while you groom. It's easy and makes grooming sessions so much easier for you both. Leaning against the dog's body, take hold of the two legs on the side farthest from you. With your arm around them, lift them off the table as you gather the dog's body against your chest and push forward and down, laying the dog on the table. The dog ends up on its side on the table. Without hesitation, talk sweetly as you begin massaging its tummy. Order "Stay." Massage for thirty seconds. Let the dog up into a stand. "Stand." Praise. Offer a treat. Massage. Command "Sit," as you sit the dog. Groom with a comb. Praise. Praise as you offer the treat. Now end the session.

Your dog becomes confident now. While being on the grooming table is not as exciting as playing with toys or crashing into your legs while following you, it is a positive experience. Add brushing. Let your dog examine the brush before you start.

In a few days, begin brushing the dog as it lies down. Again, allow the dog to examine the brush before you begin. Place it into a sitting position while commanding, "Sit." Praise with "Good dog" or whatever words you prefer. Brush head, neck, forechest and front legs. Place the dog on a stand. Command "Stand." Then praise with "Good job." Brush back, sides, back legs and rear.

Give your dog time to become accustomed to grooming before you use scissors. Not only are you learning how to comb and brush, the dog is learning how to accept these ministrations confidently. It's an enjoyable time together, and while grooming you are also teaching the three important rudiments of obedience: Sit, Stand and Down.

NEXT, THE BATH

If you have rescued a PWD and its coat has been neglected, you must cut the dog down before beginning to groom or bathe. If possible, take the rescued

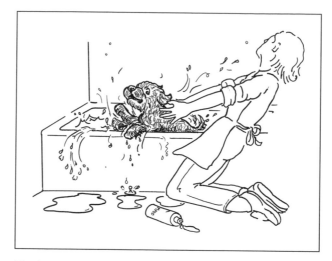

The first time your dog is placed in the tub, it will probably refuse to cooperate.

dog to a groomer who has the expertise to properly trim it. Along with removing mats and imbedded dirt, you (or the groomer) must cut the coat to the skin. If possible, lay the dog down on your table to remove hair, dirt and mats that have developed along the belly, genitals and anus. Grip the scissors securely so they do not slip if the dog moves. These are all highly sensitive areas. Remove hair under and around his ears, which may also be matted and, very possibly, infected. Then bathe the dog in a mild soap several times. If it's necessary to de-flea or de-tick, do so after a mild and thorough cleansing.

Dogs need baths because dogs get dirty! Gone are the days when most lived outdoors and their coats were but minimally maintained. How often should the modern house dog be bathed? Well, some breeds do quite a bit of body cleaning themselves. These may need a bath only monthly, depending on weather, terrain and owners' life style. The Portuguese Water Dog does not do a good job of cleaning; it has too much hair for that. Dogs of both sexes do clean their private parts, but as hair grows quickly there, this too becomes difficult. A good rule of thumb is to bathe your PWD every two weeks.

It's best to thoroughly comb and brush the dog before bathing. If you don't and discover the dog has tangles or mats, water sometimes tightens them, making them almost impossible to unravel. Many busy groomers clip before the bath. But this dulls the blades of any scissors used, and the dog's mats are cut out rather than eased out with fingers or mat combs. Under the circumstances, the final result leaves quite a bit to be desired.

Before you place your dog in the bathtub, be sure the bed of the tub isn't slick. If it is, cover the bottom with a towel or rubber mat. You don't want your dog to slip and panic while in the tub. If it's the dog's first time in the tub, it doesn't need to be soaped and slip too!

Place the dog in the tub gently but firmly, hoping it will understand the bath experience is not to be feared. The first time, however, I can almost guarantee your pup (or adult) will refuse to cooperate. The dog will attempt to break loose of your grip, leap in a frenzy, and perhaps even overpower you and jump out. Use the same tactics you learned when teaching it how to act on the grooming table.

You might fill the tub with water so it reaches the top of the dog's hocks before placing the dog in it, talking sweetly to the dog as it stands in the water wondering what's going to happen next. Also, start out using a cup to fill with water instead of the spray hose, then start soaping. Save the head and neck for last to alleviate fright. If your dog has fleas, however, soap the neck, ears and under ears first. Fleas find havens in these places, along with the top last third of the dog's back, tail and under tail.

Once the dog is thoroughly soaped, massage for a minute while the soap settles into the skin. Leave the lather on the dog for as long as directions on the shampoo bottle indicate. Rinse thoroughly, then soap and massage once more. Too many people soap the dog only once. Common sense tells us that when dirt falls off during rinsing, more dirt must be left behind. The second rinse water draining off the dog will be clean. Nevertheless, rinse and rinse and rinse until the hair slips through your hands with a squeaking sound.

To keep the soap and water out of your dog's eyes, place a hand over the eyes when you soap there as well as when you rinse. After rinsing, towel dry around eyes and inside ears, and then rinse the remainder of the body. If you use a conditioner after the shampoo, the instructions on the bottle will probably tell you it must remain on the coat for several minutes. Utilize this time to massage your dog's back and legs.

Some owners bathe their dogs outside the house with a water hose. Why give the helpless dog a chill? Why pretend to think that cold-water rinsing is thorough rinsing? Any soap left in hair makes it break easily; the skin becomes irritated, causing the dog to scratch. Better to bend down and dirty your bathtub washing the dog, and then scrub the tub clean. A raised bathtub is ideal and a pleasure to use. I have such an arrangement, and it is so easy. My dogs jump into the tub from a grooming table (which they have been trained to jump upon). No back pain for me or spilled water, and it's a comfortable setting for my dogs.

Some owners bathe their dogs in the shower while they shower. Their PWDs like this type of "bath." If your puppy finds its way into the shower after you, pick it up and hold it in your arms until it gets used to the warm spray. Then soap and rinse in your arms rather than placing the pup on the shower floor with the spray hitting it from high above. Of course, I've had owners tell me, "My puppy doesn't need that kind of protection. It loves the shower!" I know a puppy owner whose dog's weekly bath time is playtime. He eagerly watches his mistress while the tub is filled, then jumps into it to play with floating toys and balls before soap and rinse time.

Cleaning the Anal Glands

Before taking the dog out to towel it and blow it dry, clean its anal glands, if necessary. Anal glands of most dogs have to be squeezed periodically to clear them. Never attempt to empty your dog's anal glands until you've been instructed by your veterinarian. Most will be glad to teach you how to do this, since this is not a function they have time to perform regularly. After you've been instructed, it's easy to expel excess fluid from the dog's anal glands during a bath. If your dog licks its anal area often, or if it sits down and scoots along the ground on its rear, check to see if the anal glands need to be expressed. Swollen, impacted anal glands must be treated by your veterinarian. He or she must flush them and place your dog on an antibiotic until the dog heals. This is not desirable, so it's wise to check the condition of the glands before removing your dog from the bath.

Teach your dog to stand in the bathtub with a towel around its body while you squeeze the water from legs, feet and body. Sweet talk it while it stands there, then help lift the dog out (if necessary) onto the grooming table, which you've covered with a clean, dry towel.

Next, slip the noose of the grooming arm over the dog's head. With another clean, dry towel, again squeeze as much water as you can out of the coat. This is when all dogs, yours included, feel they must shake themselves. Say "Good shake" as your PWD does so. Your dog will learn this phrase quickly and will soon shake on command.

Time to Assess the Body

When your dog is on the table, examine it for faults. While the astute dog judge is aware of what a dog looks like under its coat by first feeling for good points and then watching movement, expert grooming presentation can temporarily camouflage faults. It's all an illusion, of course.

The Standard says the skull "is slightly longer than the muzzle." In the Lion Clip, the muzzle is clipped smooth. Be sure the dog's muzzle is shorter than the skull if you utilize this clip. Good grooming suggests a shorter muzzle, with jaws "strong" when it has hair on it. A narrow skull, under expert grooming, appears as the Standard states, "broad."

To achieve the illusion of perfect "Standard" structure, here are other tips:

1. "Strong, substantial bone"—Leave a fuller coat on a light-boned dog to give a "robust" look.

2. "Chest broad and deep"—Leave more coat on the front and side of the chest, and remove enough coat from the inside of the front legs, widening the stance and giving the impression of a wider chest.

3. "Topline—level and firm"—If the dog has a roach back, cut hair shorter in roached area and blend; for a dog with a dip in the topline, leave hair longer inside the dip and blend to the shorter hair on remainder of back. Scissor carefully to make the topline appear level.

4. "Off-square, slightly longer than tall"—On a longer-bodied dog, clip or scissor hair on front of chest and at rear to shorten body. If the dog is cobby (square), add length to the body by leaving more hair at front of chest and at rear. Obviously, this last is only possible if your PWD is in a Working Retriever Clip.

5. "Neck, straight, short, round"—For a long neck to appear shorter, increase length of hair from back of skull to withers, and fill out front of neck with more hair. A dog with too short a neck should have neck clipped short on sides, front and back, with slight clipping down the throat.

6. "Ears, set well above the line of the eye, tips should not reach below the lower jaw"—For large, spaniel-type ears, scissor or clip under ears so they hang close to the head, leave more hair on top of leather below edges and blend the hair on the ears with the topknot to aid in disguising the ear fault.

7. Long-legged dogs: Shorten legs by leaving hair longer above the ribs and under the chest. Keep hair on the legs full.

8. Short-legged dogs: Scissor leg hair short, shorten hair over the ribs and under the chest as well as in front of the chest.

9. Front legs too close together because of narrow chest: Leave more hair on the outside of each leg, and keep hair short on the inside.

10. Front legs turned east to west: Leave more hair on the inside, with shorter hair on the outside.

11. Front feet pigeon-toed: Leave more hair on the outside, with shorter hair on the inside.

12. Rear legs bandy or bowed: Lengthen and shorten the hair to camouflage this fault.

13. Rear legs cow hocked: Cut hair from inside of hock; leave hair full from top of hock to bottom of the rear.

14. Too close in rear: Trim up from hocks halfway. If you trim all the way, you will lose the illusion of width and exaggerate closeness.

All dogs have faults; all dogs are individuals, so you (or your groomer) must evaluate your dog's virtues and faults accurately and clip and scissor the dog to show off its strong points. I don't think anybody can hide faults from truly knowledgeable judges, and they shouldn't; however, good grooming certainly can enhance a dog's beauty. Also, fashions in hair styles change. While responsible breeders breed to improve quality and don't go into the ring just to "win," no breed Standard ever provides exact specifications as how to trim everything; hence "fashions in clipping and scissoring" are created. The current style is usually subtly established by handlers, exhibitors, judges and national club style edicts. Therefore, it is important to remember that while the official grooming guide of the PWDCA should conform to the Standard exactly and not entertain opinions, everybody has his or her version of how to groom a dog, regardless of the breed Standard. The best way to sharpen your grooming skills is to attend dog shows. Whether you own a pet or show-potential Portuguese Water Dog, watch handlers, exhibitors and groomers. Observation teaches!

Remember, coats have to be bred for, fed for and cared for to win in the style in which they are groomed.

Nail Care

Toenails that grow too long force a dog to push its weight back over the pastern and walk in a flat-footed manner, sometimes even producing lameness. Also, when nails grow too long they are no longer nourished by the quick, the live pink flesh inside the nail. The quick gets thinner as the nails get longer. Left to grow unchecked, the nails often fracture.

The quicks in a dog's nails are like the quicks in our own. The quick grows longer as the nail grows and recedes when the nail is cut. Cutting into the quick is very painful to the dog, and results in profuse bleeding. By filing or clipping often, just a little at a time, you won't hurt the dog, the quick will recede and soon your dog will have short nails with nice, tight feet. Clip each nail approximately the same length and you shouldn't be cutting into the quick. If you snip too much, styptic powder will stop bleeding. If your PWD has black nails, be especially careful. The quicks are virtually impossible to see in black nails. Operate with a strong light source and take off only a small amount each time.

It's simple to orient a puppy to the task. With the dog standing, sitting or lying down on the grooming table, get clippers in hand daily and pretend to clip nails. After a few days, begin clipping the edge off several nails, then each nail. If the dog's breeder has been conscientious about nail clipping, the dog will have a general idea of the routine. If not, make certain the dog understands this job is mandatory. Offer a treat when you are finished. If your dog fights nail clipping, lay it down on its side, hold it down with your left arm along the side of its back and talk to it gently, keeping a firm grip on the dog and clip.

Ear Care

Both puppies and adults must become accustomed to having their ears cleaned and checked regularly. Ear care is a weekly chore, although you may wish to look into your dog's ears every few days or whenever it scratches or rubs them continually. Pour a little ear-cleaning solution on a cotton ball, squeeze out the excess, and with the damp cotton covering your finger, gently wipe the dog's ear canal and opening under the ear flap. This procedure avoids injuring the eardrum. Never use cotton swabs, which can be dangerous if the dog moves suddenly or you probe too deeply. Never put anything else into the dog's ears and never clean the inside of the canal further than where the cotton ball on your finger can probe easily.

As soon as the ear is clean, place your hand on the dog's head right against its ear and rub thoroughly. Finally, wrapping a clean, dry cotton ball around your finger, dry the ear canal one more time. If you need to remove a few hairs from the open surface of the ear canal, powder the surface and remove the hair with your fingertips. Then, with cleaner on cotton, clean the ear flap and opening. If your dog's ears have an odor and you extract black material on the cotton ball, take the dog to your veterinarian for further examination. Always dry the dog's ears after it has been swimming. Never pluck the hair from a PWD's ears—it's there for protection.

The Indispensible Hair Dryer

Turn your dryer on to a medium setting. Introduce the dog to the sounds of the dryer and hum of the clipper by turning them on and letting them run as you complete your after-bath ear care. Some people place cotton in the dog's ears before they give the dog a bath; however, they still must dry the ears after the bath. Be sure to dry thoroughly inside ears and ear leather and under the armpits. These areas are hard to dry. Then, with the dryer on the proper setting, eliminate water from the coat as the dryer blows. Run the wide-toothed comb through the dog's hair upward, outward or forward. Lifting the hair in this way helps air circulate through the hairs, and so speeds drying. If you don't want to fluff dry the dog in order to clip and scissor, take the dog off the table and let it finish drying naturally. Give the dog a treat for cooperating so well, and turn off your dryer.

Working Retriever Clip

Fluff or blow drying the dog's hair is absolutely essential if you wish to cut straight with either clippers or scissors. Once your dog's coat is fluffed, you can begin scissoring or clipping.

Holding the slicker brush in your right hand with your left hand grasping the nozzle of the dryer (if that is the type you have), quickly fluff dry each section of the coat. Brush small sections at a time, flicking the brush upwards with quick motions of your wrist. You would be surprised at the number of PWDs with "unforgiving coat." When such coats are cut unevenly, the unevenly cut hairs don't forgive the groomer by blending with other hair. The scissor marks shows until the hair grows out. So be sure to scissor up and down, not sideways; otherwise scissor marks will show.

1. Follow the natural shape of your PWD's body, remembering what the Standard calls for: "Robust, medium build."

2. Top line and sides: Trim with either scissors or clippers to give a level appearance, leaving the coat depth at one inch. Work slowly downwards.

3. Blend the hair on the hips into the coat on the legs.

4. Thoroughly comb out the hair on the hocks and gather the coat on each hock into one hand, cutting the ends off straight from the bottom of the foot to the top of the hock. Carefully scissor hocks straight.

5. Round out the feet.

6. Lift the feet to see if the hair between the pads needs trimming, but do not trim between the toes.

7. Scissor the legs upward from the feet, blending the coat into the hips for a well-muscled look.

8. Now take time out. Look at the dog from the sides and from the rear. You want a smooth line from the hips, right down the long, well-developed second thigh, the stifle, and to the feet, accentuating correct rear angulation if it is present, giving the illusion if it is not.

9. Next, scissor the first two-thirds of the tail slightly shorter than the body coat, leaving the last third its natural length.

10. Lift the hair under the tail and scissor or clip under the tail, around the anus, and make the rump slightly shorter than the body coat, shaping it into a curved contour so the rear appears strong and well developed.

11. Now go to the front of the dog. Straighten the hair again so you can scissor carefully.

12. Scissor, never clip, the skull. Make it slightly rounded and broad. Do not give the dog a "football helmet" look or a "melon-head" look. Follow the contours, yet give the illusion of the "broad, domed" head. Leave more hair on the skull than on the rest of the body to accentuate strength of head. Blend the hair on the back of the skull with the neck hair.

13. In scissoring the face, the hair should be left one-half to three-quarters of an inch long. Length is a matter of personal preference as to what appears to enhance the "wide, square jaw." Scissor the side of the

face, following the natural contours of the muzzle, leaving about one-half inch of hair on the muzzle with cheeks left slightly longer and blended into it.

14. Scissor the ears to about a quarter-inch below the ear leather, following its exact heart-shaped contour. If undecided about what "heart-shaped" is, the underside of the ear will help define the shape, so scissor underneath.

15. Comb the hair on top of the nose and sides of muzzle forward over the nostrils, and trim the extended hair even with the nostrils. Now, using thinning shears, blend face hair on the sides of the face and muzzle, making sure you follow the natural contours of the muzzle. Blend.

16. On the back of the skull, blend the neck hair down to the withers, leaving hair on the withers slightly longer; then blend into the back coat. This enhances the dog's strength of shoulder.

17. Now, using a spray bottle of water (you may add conditioner), spray the dog's coat lightly. Comb it again. Scissor or clip the uneven strands of hair that stick out.

The Lion Clip

The FCI standard for the Portuguese Water Dog says: "As soon as the coat grows long the middle part and hindquarters of these dogs, as well as the muzzle, is clipped. At the end of the tail the hair is left at full length."

Senhora Carla Molinari of Portugal, president of the CPC and a member of the FCI board, in her book on the Portuguese Water Dog says: "It is important to stress that those areas of the body where the hair is kept long should be left as natural as possible, all artificial preparations such as scissoring, fluffing, sculpturing, etc. to be discouraged."

Roughrider's Copper Penny (Ch. Roughrider's Adventure, CD ex Ch. Roughrider's Cinderella, CD) shown at eight weeks. Courtesy Dr. David Smith

Here, Penny is being groomed professionally for the first time. 1. Here the groomer, Laurel, maintains a cheerful mood, putting the puppy at ease while Penny wears a beseeching expression that seems to say, "Please get me out of here."

2. Penny's body coat has now been clipped with a one-inch plastic comb over a #40 clipper blade, with the groomer scissoring in the finer touches.

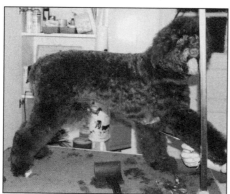

3. Laurel scissors Penny's chest, raising her leg in order to effect the correct coat length.

4. Penny has now settled down and is enjoying the attention.

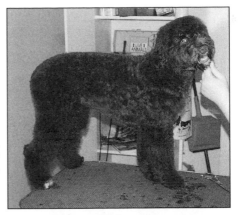

5. Laurel has placed Penny's rear legs on the edge of the table, which helps steady Penny in place while the finishing touches are added.

6. Penny's grooming is now complete.

7. Laurel stacks Penny so the owner can tell if more blending needs to be done. Courtesy Kathryn Brand

At the largest dog show in Portugal (Estoril, June 30, 1996), Augusto Guimaraes demonstrates modern presentation in the Portuguese style to Carol B. Oakes on a dog of his De Gifford breeding. Senhora Carla Molinari, president of the CPC at the time, stresses "...those areas of the body where the hair is kept long should be left as natural as possible, all artificial preparations such as scissoring, fluffing, sculpturing, etc. to be discouraged." Kathryn Braund

The Lion Clip in the United States, as these photos show, is much more involved.

1. The final Lion Clip should follow the contours of the dog's body and enhance the dog's deep, wide brisket or give the illusion of same, as well as following the contours of the body.

2. The starting point of the clip should be approximately halfway down the length of the dog's back—to be accurate, at the second rib. The starting point begins on many dogs just forward of the croup.

3. Some groomers use a #10 blade for all clipping. They clip these areas a week or two before the dog is shown; others alternate blades, using a #8½ or #7F on the body and legs and a #10 on the feet (longer blades may injure the toes or feet).

4. Begin clipping following the lay of the coat, the middle part and hind quarters down to the toes of the hind feet. Clip the first two-thirds of the tail and leave the flag full length on the last third of the tail.

5. Clip the webbing between the toes with a #10 blade only. Be certain no long hair is left between the toes. Trim straggly hairs with the blunt-nosed scissors.

6. Clip the muzzle with one of the three aforementioned blades, clipping sideways across the stop, under the eyes and down the cheeks to below the jaw to the Adam's apple. Remove enough hair from above the eyes so the dog's visibility is not impaired. Clip against the growth of the hair, being careful around the sensitive nostrils and lips. It might help to hold the dog's jaws together firmly so hair can be removed smoothly and the dog does not flick out its tongue to lick its lips and have it nicked. Do not clip the sides of the head, or under the ears or

the throat. Instead, blend this hair into the coat to give the appearance of the broad skull. If you wish to enhance the look of a square muzzle, clip the muzzle several weeks prior to showing in order to allow the hair to grow out. It will show a lovely velvet-like appearance. Scissor the head hair to blend with the sides of the skull, neck and ears. Scissor across the eyes, blending the hair and shading the eyes if the dog has light eyes. Scissor the ear hair heart-shaped to the jawline. You are leaving ears longer in this trim, but not to the length of spaniel ears, which do not flatter the PWD.

6. Scissor the chest coat to two to three inches. You want a workable length. In shaping the hair, follow the natural contour of the body, giving the dog a deep, broad chest.

7. Scissor the front legs. Round the feet off, lifting them to make sure no hair extends beyond the pads, but do not cut hair from between the toes unless matted.

8. Stand back and examine your dog. You want no exaggeration; you want perfect blending.

9. Spray the coat with water, comb it out again and scissor back any uneven hairs that stick out. Karen Arends (Seabreeze Kennels) offers tips on how to groom the curly-coated dog in the Lion trim: "To find the correct place to begin clipping the hindquarters, measure from the middle of the chest to just under the tail and start halfway in the middle and clipper towards the rear. If the body is longer than desired, move the line back toward the rear. The clipper work done on the dog shown in the accompanying photographs is accomplished with a #10 blade (with the grain on the rear and against the grain on the face). Need more substance? Use a #4 or #5 clipper blade or scissors to sculpt rear and face. If the dog needs more width in the rear, leave more of a blanket on the rear and on the outsides of the legs, while scissoring the inside of the rear legs quite close."

SUMMERTIME PET TRIM #1

1. With skull hair approximately two inches long, clip face and muzzle hair to one-half inch; clip entire body with a #10 blade, legs and last two-thirds of the tail and tops of the ears with a #4 blade. Finish scissoring the ears right around the leather.

2. Lift the feet, trim under and round off feet with the #10 blade.

PET TRIM #2

1. Leaving skull hair full and the last one-third of the tail hair full, use a #4 blade on the entire body. Trim ears to the leathers. Scissor leg hair to a length of one inch.

chapter 11

Breeding the Portuguese Water Dog

There's an adage that "Dogs mate when they want to breed and not at any other time."

Nature has gifted the male dog (like the human) with the ability to mate successfully at any time, but there's a catch. Nature, an exact lawmaker, also has an irrepressible sense of humor. She throws in a kicker, allowing the male dog to mate only when the rich aroma of a female in estrus hits his nose. Although he may feel tremendous surges of desire, not always is he afforded the opportunity to indulge in this driving force. In fact, some dogs wait years before that opportunity presents itself.

The female dog, possessed of the same intense primordial sex drive, must also follow nature's inexorable rule of propagation for dogs. She must await the middle part of estrus (heat) after she ovulates (sheds eggs) before she can allow a dog to impregnate her with sperm.

As Cambridge University geneticist Bell Amos said, "Every species has its reproductive strategy—some work better than others."

TERMS

Following are definitions of some of the terms used in this chapter.

AI (Artificial Insemination). The artificial injection of semen into a female's reproductive tract.

Anestrus. The resting stage of the estrus cycle; the period between cycles when hormonally, progesterone levels are at baseline.

Bulb. The portion of the penis that becomes enlarged and rounded during copulation.

Cornification. The process by which ova become fully mature as a prerequisite to a successful mating.

Diestrus. The period immediately following the fertile period. The vulva softens and gets smaller in size; usually the normal discharge is clear, without blood cells. Hormonally, progesterone levels are elevated up to sixty days, whether the bitch is pregnant or not.

Epithelial cells. Normal skin cells lining the walls of the uterus. These become "cornified" during breeding estrus.

Estrus. The fertile period during which the bitch ovulates and accepts penetration of males. The luteinizing begins its surge at approximately six to ten days into estrus.

Erythrocytes. Red blood cells. These appear in large number in proestrus, fade to a few or none during the estrus phase.

Fallopian tubes. Oviducts leading to the uterus.

Flagging. A visual sexual response of a bitch in season at full acceptance, tail held high and to one side.

Infective agent. Any agent potentially harmful to breeding stock, unborn puppies or puppies at any age.

Leukocytes. White blood cells that gradually disappear in proestrus; they reappear late in the estrus cycle, signaling the end of the breeding period.

LH. Luteinizing hormone.

Metestrus. The period immediately following estrus.

Ovum *(sin.),* **ova** *(pl.),* **oocyte.** Egg, eggs.

Ovulation. The act of discharging eggs from the ovary.

Pituitary. The gland that secretes luteinizing hormone.

Proestrus. The period, beginning with vulvar swelling, during which cells in the walls of the vagina become cornified. Males may or may not be attracted. Hormonally, rising estrogen levels.

Progesterone assay. A test that indicates progesterone concentrations.

Prostatic fluid. Fluid from the male's accessory sex gland.

Slide. The vehicle on which vaginal and semen smears (dried and stained) are placed and observed under a microscope.

Smear. A sample of vaginal fluid taken with a cotton swab.

Smell. An odor perceived through chemical stimulation of olfactory nerves.

Testes. The testicles of the male, in which sperm are produced.

Window. A fertile period.

Zygote. The cell formed by the union of the sperm cell and the ovum.

ESTRUS

The healthy, uninhibited Portuguese Water Dog bitch comes into estrus (heat) approximately every four to seven months. Her first heat usually occurs when she has obtained 95 percent of her full growth.

The bitch gives evidence of impending heat several weeks earlier by squatting often to urinate. With her human family she clings to laps and may

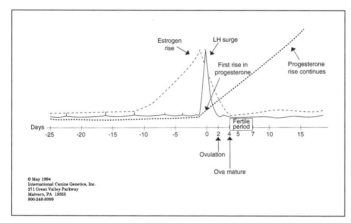

Schematic Representation of the Estrus Cycle of the Bitch. Courtesy ICG International Canine Genetics, Inc., Malvern, Pennsylvania

Portuguese Water Dogs of both sexes are excellent escape artists. The bitch in this series of photos climbed and jumped two fences to mate with a dog. This series of photos, taken from a hiding place, shows how she was able to do it. 1. First the bitch gained momentum by leaping against the barn wall. Note her kennel mate watching intently.

2. She gained enough momentum to reach the top of the fence.

3. Taking hold of the post along the top of the fence, she pulls herself up.

4. She starts over the top with the bitch below watching her, and down she jumps. Her romantic adventure resulted in a litter of seven puppies. Courtesy Kathryn Braund.

continually beg for petting and affection. She may even refuse to work if involved in one of the working dog sports, since hormonal activity is disrupting her normal thinking patterns. She may show awakening sexual excitement even before she comes into estrus by mounting other females or males with whom she lives.

Once in heat, evidenced only by a slight swelling of the vulva and usually (but not always) small spots of blood, which she scrupulously cleans away with her tongue, her sexual urges mount. Some bitches seem consumed by them; others become very quiet. It's as if they are frightened of what is going on inside them. But almost without fail during the time bitches are fertile, they begin flagging (flinging and holding their tails to one side or the other). That's one sign they are in their fertile period, a heady peak lasting approximately five to seven days. This normally begins at about day ten to fourteen of the heat period, although a few bitches will flag at day four and others not until day seventeen. Some breeders say their bitch's fertile period (called the "fertile window") lasts only one or two days, but this has not been proven. What is proven is that bitches with little libido will allow mating only one or two days; others, with stronger sexual urges, allow breeding long before and after the fertile lifespan of the ova. Some invite males to enter them as early as four days into heat (proestrus) and some as late as twenty-eight days in heat or post-estrus (diestrus).

The eggs (ova) are immature when released at the beginning of the breeding period. Studies have zeroed in on the precise amount of time it takes a bitch's eggs to become capable of being fertilized. Phyllis A. Holst, MS, DVM, of Colorado, in her book *Canine Reproduction* (1985), says it is three days, plus or minus a day. She uses the word *day* to denote variation in the time it takes the eggs to become capable of fertilization. "After they have reached this stage," Holst says, "the fertilizable life span seems to be fairly short. This is the reason many matings fail to produce puppies if the bitch is bred too early or too late during her receptive period."

International Canine Genetics (ICG), a Pennsylvania company devoted to animal reproductive problems, gives a longer "breeding window." One of the firm's instruction sheets to veterinarians says, "Ovulation occurs two days after the LH surge. The ovacytes (eggs) then require an additional two to three days to mature, and will live for about forty-eight to seventy-two hours. Thus the fertile period of the bitch falls between days four and seven after the LH peak with the most fertile days being on days five and six post LH peak." Both Holst and ICG state that the word *day* implies variation in the breeding window. (LH will be more thoroughly explained later in this chapter.)

If the bitch lives with and is allowed to mate with a male, her playful, fickle "don't-touch-me" attitude towards him during the first part of her heat disappears as she begins to ovulate (discharges eggs from her ovaries). It becomes obvious that she is experiencing a profound increase in sexual desire. She no longer runs away, tucks her tail or sits when the male comes close.

She'll run around him, dash teasingly away from him, pounce on him, even mount him. She's sexually unrestrained. If no male is available, she searches for one. The accompanying photos show a bitch who located a male two kennels away, tied with him without the knowledge of the stud's owner, and produced offspring. The photos were taken after the fact, after puppies had been whelped, reared and went to homes. They are graphic proof that the bitch in season should always be monitored very carefully.

If you are a breeder, have your veterinarian take a "smear" (a slide containing vaginal cells gently wiped off the walls of the vagina with a cotton swab). Do this without fail on days four through six of the bitch's heat. The veterinarian will place the smear on a slide and examine it under a microscope. He or she may find the epithelial cells fully cornified. Why won't the bitch breed, then, if placed with a male? She has not ovulated!

To follow the pattern of your bitch's heat, have your vet take smears every two days. When she ovulates, the cornified cells seen on a smear are not as round as on smears examined in proestrus (before ovulation); they become irregular in shape, some having several angles. Have another smear taken. If the cornified cells have become thickly packed and angular, the bitch is ovulating. Now keep your eyes on her and the male.

THE STUD DOG IN ACTION

Before the bitch ovaluates, an inexperienced male will attempt to mount her unsuccessfully. An experienced male is interested, but just mildly so. When placed with her, he approaches to read her mating odor in order to determine the state of her sexual readiness. He may or may not attempt to mount her. The experienced stud instinctively knows his role. He cannot mount, penetrate and ejaculate without the presence of the full ovulation aroma. He'll sniff his prospective mate and every foot of the ground around her in desperate search for the odor. He follows her closely as she moves through the area. She teases him, enticingly, squatting often, so he can sample the pools of urine she leaves behind. It's only when her eggs drop that she exudes a smell so utterly intoxicating that he goes temporarily insane.

He, you say, was a paragon of perfection, a perfect house dog, a willing worker, a gentleman animal in every family action? Not now. When the bitch is ovulating, the male stops eating. He sets up a steady wailing and whining. Worse, if he is an escape artist, he flees his yard for hers (up and over or down and under). If allowed to be with her (with supervision, please), he chases the female about when given space to do so. She proves her readiness by halting in front of him, flagging her tail and elevating her rear. He is now absolutely daft. He reaches out with front paws to grab her. If she is still of a mind to tease, she dashes away. He pursues her pell-mell, tongue hanging out, heart beating wildly. Like the virile animal he now is (nature's gift to ensure propagation), he catches up with her, paws her, licks her eyes, her ears, her vulva, and then grabs her tight with his front legs around her waist as she stands for him, flagging, quivering at his attentions. He pulls her rear to him. Thrusting wildly with the rear half of his body in his sexual passion, his penis is now out of its sheath and fully engorged with blood. Somehow, by means of a hit-and-miss process bewildering to the supervising human onlooker, his penis finds its objective—her swollen vulva. With furiously increasing staccato probes, he now enters the bitch. The bulb on the end of his penis swells and the dogs are locked together. Tied!

In the instant of entering, the male, with tail pulsating, initiates a stream of clear, watery prostatic fluid from his sex gland, moistening her reproductive chambers for the next fluid he'll inject—the milky seminal fluid. He then ejaculates intermittent streams of semen carrying millions of sperm. Finally, he discharges a last wave of prostatic fluid. This helps push the wriggling sperm along their way up the bitch's reproductive tract to where precious eggs await them. This third wave not only helps drive the sperm upward, it also aids in neutralizing acidic conditions found inside the vaginal tract. Then, usually within a minute of being tied, the male relaxes his hold on the bitch's waist and turns straight around until the dogs are rear to rear, their bodies and heads facing opposite directions.

RESTRAINTS

The male and female should be supervised during the entire mating sequence. If allowed to mate without leashes, leashes should be attached as soon as the dogs have tied. When the tie has been completed and they are once again separated, the bitch should not be allowed to urinate but should be walked directly to a crate, where she should rest quietly for several hours. The stud dog, after being allowed to clean himself, should also be taken to a quiet place where he may rest without distraction. The stud should be treated with great consideration so no injury to his delicate reproductive organ occurs at this time.

THE TIE

Dog and bitch are now locked (tied) together by nature for from one to five minutes up to an hour or more. Most dogs will tire during a long tie; if left unsupervised a bitch may lie down, pulling the dog down with her. One of the two might become restless. Unrestrained, the two may drag each other about, creating a potential for serious injury. This is why supervision is absolutely necessary. Valuable breeding animals should not be allowed to unintentionally hurt one another, and the potential for damage is so easy to prevent.

All males, during the tie, periodically turn about and kiss the female's ears (thought to ensure a longer tie) and, in turn, the bitch may lean down and around to lick the tied genital area. This further excites both. The dog ejects more sperm and prostatic fluid inside her. The more satisfying the tie is to the animals, the more they shift positions and the greater they pant. When finally they do fall apart, they both sit down and become occupied with cleaning themselves. With the bulb back to normal size, the dog's penis slowly withdraws into its sheath. The bitch, as if nothing unusual has occurred, moves away to seek a quiet place to rest. The stud must rest also; he can repeat the mating act within fifteen minutes.

But nothing the two mated animals can do now will break the chain of coming events—pregnancy and puppies—unless disaster in the form of a vaginal virus or infection contracted at about three to four weeks into pregnancy enters the relaxed vulva. Internal problems may also cause reabsorption of fetuses at about forty-five days. If there are too many fetuses inhabiting the long, narrow corridors of the uterus, several or more of these may be reabsorbed. If there is considerable stress in the life of the bitch, this too may cause reabsorption. Further, if the male is sterile (more common than most people realize), then too there will be no puppies. All males, before being used at stud, should have their sperm count checked by their veterinarian. If you own a male PWD you'd like to use, your practitioner will explain the procedure to you.

ARTIFICIAL INSEMINATION

There are alternatives to breeding from dogs that do not follow the adage "Dogs mate when they want to breed and not at any other time." This phenomenon is not uncommon with Portuguese Water Dog bitches.

Breeding by artificial insemination (AI)—injecting semen into a female's reproductive tract—is becoming increasingly popular in all purebred breeding. Unfortunately, it has already replaced much natural breeding of horses and cattle. An AI is very beneficial when used to aid in fertilizing eggs of a bitch who has some type of psychological or reproductive problem that inhibits normal mating behavior. It is popular with owners who are disinclined to or cannot transport bitches for whatever reason.

An AI is also recommended for matings from a quality male who may live far away from a relatively large number of breedable bitches, in order to spread his desired genes in a different area (another state or even a country on the other side of the world). Semen can be sent to the veterinarian regularly attending the recipient bitch!

While breeding via AI may be slightly less expensive than shipping a dog far away, 1990 American Veterinary Medical Association statistics show that only 60 percent of fresh inseminations are viable. The percentage falls drastically with shipped chilled semen, and it topples again with frozen semen inseminations. To maintain a high percentage of success, veterinarians must be thoroughly skilled with artificial insemination. Many veterinarians and breeders believe healthier puppies come from natural breedings, although this has not been proven.

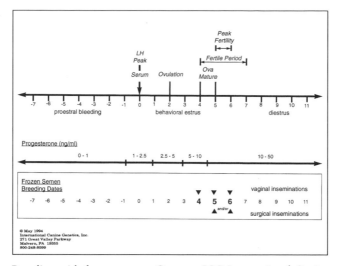

Breeding with frozen semen. Courtesy ICG International Canine Genetics, Inc., of Malvern, Pennsylvania

A FAILED BREEDING

A bitch refuses to mate with a stud she so happily tied with three heats previously. It was the same stud with whom she had produced eight exceptional puppies. Her answers to his present persistent solicitations are growls, snarls and vicious snaps. The breeder takes her to the veterinarian for a thorough health test, even though a complete health exam had been done just prior to her heat. It shows her to be in excellent health. Progesterone assays are performed. Adhering to the results the assays show, she is artificially inseminated three times. Then, a restrained but natural breeding occurs. The outcome? No puppies. Because the bitch is over five years of age, the breeder makes the decision to spay her and not chance another breeding.

What did the veterinarian find when he spayed her? One of her two reproductive tubes was completely filled with serum (fluid). It was not infective (harmful) fluid, at least not at the time of spaying. But the serum during her last ovulation would have drowned any sperm that found its entrance into her reproductive tract. She knew she couldn't breed. So the adage "Dogs mate when they want to breed and not at any other time" holds true here.

DOCUMENTATION OF A BREEDING

The following documents a difficult breeding case. The steps performed throughout this case were done with the knowledge that the recent genetic advances made an LH assay possible. Note that normally, an AI would not be performed on an everyday basis. This documentation was done so experienced breeders could analyze pros and cons.

Fancy, a lovely animal, a dear pet, a valuable breeding animal, a most intelligent PWD, had always been difficult to breed. The first three of her matings—she had to be held while the dogs she was bred to impregnated her—resulted in puppies. She proved to be an exceptional mother. But before her second pregnancy she experienced a split estrus, which was quite frustrating to breeder (me) and stud owner, even though mating was managed at the end of the "true" season. Let's pause here to examine this uncommon occurrence.

"Split estrus periods may be seen occasionally in pubertal (immature) bitches and rarely in mature bitches," states Stephen J. Ettinger in *Textbook of Veterinary Internal Medicine* (W.B. Saunders Co., 1989). This bitch, however, was mature. "Bitches with split estrus periods exhibit signs of target tissue stimulation by estrogens (vulvar swelling, sero-anguineous discharge) for a few days as follicles develop. The bitch may or may not be receptive to mating. This is followed by a regression of vulvar size and cessation of the discharge for a few weeks until the bitch enters a 'true' season and ovulates. If the bitch is mated appropriately during the second part of a 'split' estrus, fertility should be normal."

Her third mating was fruitless, even though AIs were done adhering to the progesterone assays. Two heats later, with smears accompanied by progesterone assays plus one forced breeding, she produced eight puppies.

The puppies were so lovely that the next year she was artificially inseminated three times to the same stud (after several progesterone tests were done). The AIs were performed on the fifteenth, sixteenth and seventeenth days of her heat, supposedly her optimum breeding days.

Unfortunately, three-and-a-half weeks later, I had to go out of town, leaving Fancy in care of the veterinarian where she had been inseminated. She was happy when I left, and plump; she was distressed, ill and thin when I returned five days later. A sonogram revealed she was barren. Statistics told us that if the eggs had been fertilized at the proper time—information from the progesterone assays pointed that way—Fancy should have become pregnant. Despite medical statistics, my gut feeling was that this dog—we were very close—became distraught and unhappy at my absence and aborted (reabsorbed) those fetuses. Medical statistics also bear out the fact that viruses at three to four weeks into pregnancy can make pregnant bitches absorb the fetuses. The truth of the matter is, no one will ever know exactly what happened!

Before her next heat, I decided to mate her with a different stud, since by her past responses it appeared Fancy did not like any male presented to her. I documented every step of her twenty-one-day estrus period:

May 20, 1995. Fancy refuses to work several retrieving exercises I had been training her for in Open Obedience. Heretofore, she had been doing excellent, almost fault-free work. Because of the good work, I had already sent in entries for five Obedience Trials.

June 3. Fancy ran out of ring at an Obedience Trial when commanded to retrieve her dumbbell. This was the first time I (or a dog of mine) was ever excused from a ring! I pull her from the other Trials.

June 10. In fun practice, Fancy still refuses to retrieve or jump with the dumbbell, exercises she had excelled in over the past several weeks. I decide to allow Fancy to have a holiday from training until I can figure out why she refuses to work. Her attitude is puzzling. She has always been such a willing, biddable worker.

June 14. Fancy's vulva is becoming larger and hard to touch (signs of impending estrus); she also wants to sit on my lap every time I sit. Is she coming into estrus? I look back at her heat records. Fancy had last entered estrus February 8, 1995. She was artificially inseminated 2/20, 2/22 and 2/24. She was out of heat February 28. Fancy has heretofore always been on a six-month estrus cycle, so I question the signs that she is coming into heat. She's never been on a four-month cycle before (common in the PWD). But she is getting older, and that will often affect cycle changes. I make arrangements for a stud to visit us should she come into estrus early. Because of her distressed attitude when she is not with me, I will not ship her away to be bred.

June 15. Thursday. Fancy is in heat—four months since the last time! She is a very difficult bitch to monitor for outward signs because she bleeds very little. By inserting a swab gently into her vulva, I am able to detect slight color. It also shows she has a very dry vulvar environment.

June 16. Friday. I take Fancy to one of my local veterinarians. She examines her thoroughly, takes a smear and takes blood for a brucellosis test. Fancy is up to date on all shots and appears in excellent health, and her smear suggests she is in early proestrus (however, I am not able to view the slide). The veterinarian suggests I bring her back in two days (Sunday) for a second smear. She also suggests I make arrangements to fly the stud to my home early. Back home, I segregate Fancy from the other dogs. In my house, a dog in heat is confined to the kitchen and laundry room and to a 30×60-foot yard we call the "funnel yard." My resident male signals interest in her as he sniffs the air on the opposite side of a kitchen gate. I call the stud dog owners and inform them of what is occurring.

June 18. Sunday. I drive Fancy to the veterinarian for a second smear. The veterinarian determines several cells are cornified; there are still leukocytes (white blood cells), along with a growing number of erythrocytes (red blood cells). The veterinarian feels the bitch may be ready to breed as early as the following Tuesday or Wednesday. Later that day I call Dr. Michael Murphy, the veterinarian who helps me when AIs are necessary and who allows me to examine smears. I explain that Fancy is

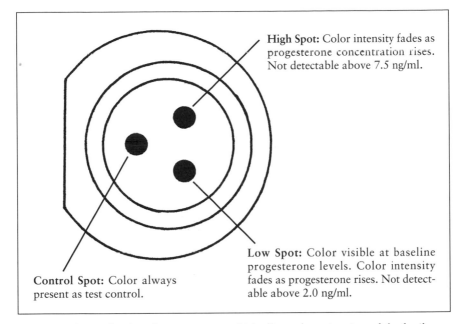

High Spot: Color intensity fades as progesterone concentration rises. Not detectable above 7.5 ng/ml.

Control Spot: Color always present as test control.

Low Spot: Color visible at baseline progesterone levels. Color intensity fades as progesterone rises. Not detectable above 2.0 ng/ml.

Status-Pro detects he rise of progesterone, which allows the estimation of the fertile period. This is important in natural breeding and fresh artificial inseminations. Courtesy ICG International Canine Genetics, Inc., Malvern, Pennsylvania

in proestrus and reviewing the past history of both bitch and stud dog, I wish to breed her via artificial insemination, since this is deemed necessary for a successful pregnancy.

The stud dog's one breeding experience was with a dominant bitch who growled and snapped. Because of her attitude, the impressionable, untried male dared not approach, and an AI became his one mating experience (it produced one puppy). Since I wanted this to be a successful pregnancy with (a) a bitch who doesn't give many outward signs when she is ready to be bred and, (b) a male who doesn't yet know what the breeding experience is about, I ensured that the mating would produce puppies by following through with AIs plus proven artificial tests presently available (progesterone assays and the LH test). The data received from these tests gives extremely valuable information for most breeding situations—although no test is 100% accurate. There are many failed breedings in the PWD, so progesterone assays are of great value.

Progesterone Assay

The progesterone assay reacts with the blood-serum sample of 1ml, with which a drop of pretreatment solution is mixed. The test cup, after a fifteen-minute waiting period during which several drops of different solutions have been added, indicates high or low levels of progesterone through color development. There are three color spots on the test cup: (a) a control spot in which color is always present; (b) a high spot in which color intensity fades as progesterone concentration rises (on the high spot, color is not detectable above 7.5 ng/ml); and (c) a low spot that has color visible at the bitch's baseline progesterone levels. This low spot is the key spot in determining the LH surge, because the color intensity fades as progesterone rises; further, color is not detectable above 2.0 ng/ml.

The first progesterone test should be run sometime during the first five days of proestrus to determine the bitch's "baseline progesterone level, which varies in individual dogs but usually ranges between 0 and 1 ng/ml." At this level the test cup is blue in each of the three spots. Remember, the outward signs of estrus are controlled by changes in the hormone estrogen, which are only approximations of ovulations, and can vary by more than a week, depending on the bitch! The progesterone assay allows fairly true identification of the occurrence of ovulation.

Progesterone assays need to be run every few days; they are often used in conjunction with vaginal smears. When a bitch's smear shows 50 percent cornification, LH tests are conducted every day to find the day of the LH peak. Then, to confirm that ovaluation has occurred after the peak, an additional progesterone assay should be run two to four days later.

LH Test

LH stands for the luteinizing hormone secreted by the pituitary gland, which stimulates ovulation in females. This test is highly accurate. Remarkably, it

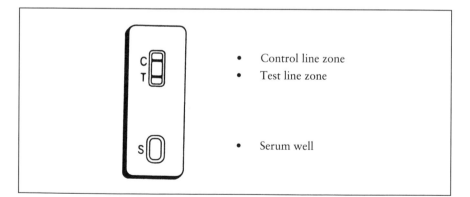

Status-LH provides the ability to identify the luteinizing hormone surge. Used in conjunction with Status-Pro, a high degree of timing precision can be obtained for all breedings. It is especially beneficial for artificial inseminations using chilled or frozen semen, when a more precise identification of the fertile period would be advantageous, or when working with dogs who have a history of infertility. Chart courtesy ICG International Canine Genetics, Inc., Malvern, Pennsylvania

The LH surge is identified by comparing the test line with the control line.

zeros in on the mystery of why some bitches are difficult to breed. Used in conjunction with progesterone testing, blood is drawn daily from the bitch until the LH surges, a rise the LH test identifies. In most bitches, the surge lasts only one day and is detected within six days of testing. The test device has a control zone, a test zone and a blood serum well. At the end of the twenty-minute waiting period for the test to be completed, a pink horizontal line appears in the control zone. This assures the tester that the test is complete. The test zone usually will not show a horizontal line; if it does show one, it will be of a lighter color than the pink line in the control zone. This is because the LH value is less than one nanogram per milliter. On the day of the LH peak, the test zone line will be of a similar or greater color than the color in the control zone. This peak precedes ovulation. No more LH tests need be performed at this point.

The above two tests, used in combination with smears, give almost 99 percent accuracy on when to breed in the following cases: (a) with a bitch who has a history of infertility, (b) with one who has low libido, (c) with one who has limited access to the stud dog or (d) when the stud dog has low semen quality.

Dr. Murphy says, "Okay. See you tomorrow for an examination." I call the stud dog owners and ask them to fly the male, Garbonzo, from his home in San Jose, California, to Portland, Oregon, tomorrow, June 19.

June 19. Monday. Garbonzo arrives in Portland at 11 A.M. He is in a summertime trim. He is a handsome, happy, nicely mannered dog. I am glad I chose him to be Fancy's mate. Certainly, the pedigree indicated an excellent match. Sight confirms it. I drive home seventy miles north, stopping only to pick up Fancy, and continue another 55 miles to Dr. Murphy's clinic. He examines both dogs, does a progesterone assay on Fancy, and takes a smear, which I can view. The cells show her to be still in proestrus. Nevertheless, we artificially inseminate. After the insemination, we check a slide with a drop of Garbonzo's semen. "He has sent out a Chinese army!" exclaims Murphy. I agree. There isn't a space between the seemingly billions of sperm this dog is producing. Back home, I call Garbonzo's owners. "Well," laughs his mistress, after I tell her about the tremendous army of sperm, "he has only been used once so there's a lot to be gotten rid of."

June 20. Tuesday. Back at Dr. Murphy's clinic, the LH kit has arrived. We again take blood from Fancy's front leg (as we did for Monday's progesterone test. Her veins "freeze," possibly from nervousness. It is difficult for the veterinary technician to obtain blood. Finally the tube fills. The LH test shows Fancy is not yet at LH peak. "AI her anyway," I say, still not believing the tests are 100 percent reliable. Fancy is artificially inseminated. Garbonzo's semen evaluation shows us another tremendous army—we compare it to a Roman legion.

June 21. Wednesday. Dr. Murphy suggests I take Fancy and Garbonzo to my local veterinarian (to save travel time) and have a smear taken. If my local veterinarian's evaluation shows that Fancy is close to ovaluating, I am to continue on up to his clinic. I do this. Dr. Mark Giffey speaks with Dr. Murphy by phone and tells him Fancy appears almost fully cornified. I then make the fifty-five-mile drive to Dr. Murphy's hospital. Fancy, although she grimaces when she gets out of the car and sees where we are, without invitation jumps up on the four-foot-high table to have blood drawn. Again her veins "freeze"; it is difficult to draw the blood. We do a second progesterone assay and a second LH test. LH is still low; so is the progesterone assay. She is artificially inseminated, and Garbonzo delivers a third huge army of sperm, as seen in the semen evaluation.

June 22. Thursday. Fancy again jumps onto the high table without bidding. Those standing around are amazed at her agility. Dr.Murphy hugs her. He has to go into the jugular vein for blood. Success in a quick draw! The LH shows she is peaking. She is ovaluating! The superficial cells in the smear show full cornification. The dogs are bred via AI, although Dr. Murphy tries to help Garbonzo mount Fancy. Instead of mounting Fancy, Garbonzo turns to Dr. Murphy! This dog needs to be taught how to mate naturally! We check Garbonzo's semen on a slide. Not one single sperm! Before we viewed the slide, I had taken him back to the car to rest. "Get Garbonzo back in here," Dr. Murphy says, then follows with a second AI. This time the smear does not show an army, but certainly shows a heavy concentration of sperm. Strange that the first AI produced no sperm. Garbonzo waxed very willing! It's wise to check semen each and every time an AI is done. We decide to forgo one day and meet again two days later.

June 24. Saturday. No need of any further LH tests. However, we need to check the progesterone assay. Fancy again jumps onto the high table without invitation or command. "Amazing dog," Dr. Murphy says. "Good girl," as he puts his arms around her. He again goes into the jugular vein for the two ccs of blood necessary for the progesterone test. The assay, like the LH, takes thirty minutes to process—always a long wait for me. It's a high reading, and Fancy's slide again shows full cornification, although now it contains several blood cells. Fancy has ovulated. She is AId. On Garbonzo's slide we note the armies are reduced only slightly. The next scheduled visit is Monday, two days later.

June 26. Monday. Another progesterone assay, another AI, another smear and another semen evaluation. Garbonzo's behavior, as on Saturday, is highly excitable. Fancy is noncommittal except for some "Do I have to" looks at me. Dr. Murphy suggests I attempt to let them breed naturally that evening.

Natural Tie

I do not find anyone to help me effect the tie, so after dinner I take the two into the dogs' bathhouse, hold Fancy by the leash with one hand and attempt to teach Garbonzo how to mount her with the other. It is not easy. After ten minutes of seemingly back-breaking effort on the part of all three of us—Fancy to avoid being bred, Garbonzo to try to mate and me to direct by repeatedly placing him where he should be—we succeed! He mounts, they are tied in seconds, and Fancy smiles! "Are you smiling, Fancy?" I ask, incredulously. "You really like him!" I exclaim. I am elated. They remain tied for twenty-five minutes.

June 27. Tuesday. I call Dr. Murphy. Like me, he is elated. "Well," he says, "you don't need to return here. I am glad they are breeding naturally." So am I. In the evening, the dogs mate again—both eager. It takes only minutes before they are tied. This tie lasts thirty minutes. Fancy appears quite pleased with herself. Whoopee! She's interested in a male during breeding for the first time.

June 28. Wednesday. This evening both dogs are eager to tie again. They tie for thirty-five minutes.

June 29. Thursday. At 6 P.M., Fancy comes to me in the kitchen and touches me on the leg with her nose. She is reminding me it is time to visit Garbonzo. She dashes out of the house and runs through our deck yard into the bathhouse, where she eagerly greets Garbonzo, who enters from his yard through one of the doggy doors. However, after a few minutes together, during which he attempts several times to mount her, she decides their mating period is over. She escapes from his grasp and as he persists, she growls at him. Garbonzo sits back dumbfounded. I keep them together for ten minutes, but it becomes increasingly obvious Fancy will not cooperate. Garbonzo goes back into his big yard. Fancy returns to the house.

June 30. Friday. I place the two dogs in adjacent yards. Then I place them together. When Garbonzo tries to mount Fancy, she resists; they end up playing as good Portuguese Water Dog friends play and when Fancy tires, she lies down on the grass. He stands quietly close by, as if to protect her. Their mating experience is over. (The breeding was successful. Fancy whelped two beautiful puppies. Check the Whelping chapter for the conclusion of the story.)

DOCUMENT OF UNUSUAL BREEDING, CASE III

A veterinary evaluation of the vaginal smear at the bitch's home city shows her to be fully cornified. "She is ready," the veterinarian tells her mistress. "Ship her ASAP."

They fly her that same day to be bred. It is her tenth day of heat. Stud and bitch mate the instant they are placed together. Their mating record is as follows: Breeding No. 1: day 10 of heat; breeding No. 2: day 11 of heat; breeding No. 3: day 13 of heat; and breeding No. 4: day 14 of heat. Day 15 she refuses to accept the male. She remains with the stud's owner five more days until she is out of heat. She is then flown home. No puppies.

What went wrong? Bred too early? Too late? At her next heat she is shipped on the first day her owner notices spotting. Owners, however, often miss the first several days of a bitch's heat, even though they scrupulously examine her vulva daily with white tissues or cotton swabs as her time nears. A smear is taken the day after arrival. It shows her fully cornified!

Returning from the vet's office, she is placed with the stud. They mate within ten minutes. Is she standing early? Has the luteinizing hormone surged this early in her heat?

Stud dog and bitch are allowed to mate daily. On day 10 (the day she arrived during her previous heat), she refuses to stand; she instead tucks her tail and sits whenever the male approaches. She remains with the stud dog owner another five days, then she is shipped back home.

She whelps seven puppies. This PWD bitch's receptive behavior on day two of her heat was because she ovaluates early, but also, her first few days of proestrus may have gone unnoticed. This breeding again tells us that "dogs mate when they want to breed and not at any other time." But this adage does not always mean the dogs mate with proper timing for sperm to impregnate the bitch's eggs.

The last two examples prove the variability of the outward signs of heat and breeding time in the female Portuguese Water Dog. These superficial conditions—flagging, standing, size and softness of vulva and smear examinations—are "primarily controlled by changes in the hormone estrogen," states ICG. "Unfortunately," the company adds, "these changes are only an approximation of ovulation and can vary by more than a week."

While I, as a breeder, and the veterinarians I deal with advocate natural breedings, it is wise for the serious Portuguese Water Dog breeder to take advantage of smears, progesterone and precise luteinizing hormone measurement tests along with the natural breedings to maximize the chances of conception.

chapter 12

Whelping Portuguese Water Dog Puppies

Let me start with some cold, hard facts.

THE DOWN SIDE

Are you ready to get down on your hands and knees and scrub floors twice a day for eight to twelve weeks, or until the last puppy in the litter is sold? Whelping and raising a litter of puppies is hard work. If you're not work-oriented, forget about raising puppies. Yes, there are breeders who whelp litters in basements, in barns and garages, and sell the ones that don't die off as fast as they can to the first potential buyers who call. Don't plan to raise a litter that way. All life put upon this earth must be treated as precious.

Ask yourself:

- Will you object to sleeping in a sleeping bag or on a cot beside the dam and her newborns for the first ten to fourteen days of their lives? You must be beside the dam to help in case there is trouble. As wonderful as you think your bitch is and as healthy as her pups appear, her milk might not come down; she might not have enough nipples for all her pups to suckle (you must feed the ones that don't suckle enough milk from her). Newborn pups may crawl away from the dam and not know how to return. If one is apart, a dam may become anxious watching the puppy crying and struggling to return, push out her paws to pull it back and unwittingly hurt the pup. In the process, she may lie unknowingly on a nursing puppy and smother it, or get up and carry the pup back to the nest in her mouth—a natural, albeit dangerous, thing to do. These incidents, in which healthy newborns perish, are far too common. Be aware that if a pup crawls away and lies alone far away from the litter for any length of time, it can quickly become too cold to maintain life. Newborn pups require a constant source of heat. They are born without temperature controls and cannot shiver to generate heat until they are about five to seven days old.

Some adored pet bitches are notorious for their lack of instinct in caring for their pups—they turn up their noses at keeping their pups clean. In such cases the breeder must take over the dam's chores, cleaning and stimulating the tiny newborns at frequent intervals. You must be there to help those small and weak neonates learn to suckle. Another caution: Pups may get entangled in bedding and smother. Some pups are born with congenital or inherited health problems that show up only in the whelping box. If you are not with the litter on a 24-hour-a-day basis for the first ten to fourteen "newborn" days, you'll invariably lose pups. Last, but not least, while dams need to stimulate the pups vigorously, licking and rubbing (physical stimulation induces growth and warmth), some dams bite and pull and cut umbilical cords too close and a few unintentionally mutilate their puppies—they even may end up cannibalizing them.

- Are you ready to pay an inflated household heating bill? The puppy room should be maintained at 85 degrees for the first week (yes, the dam gets very hot, but she'll survive!), 80 degrees the second, and then down to 75 degrees warm for the next two. When the pups are a little over four weeks of age, you can begin to adjust the puppy room temperature to normal—still remembering that pups under seven weeks of age should not lie on cold floors, even if there is ample puppy bedding around. Why such high temperatures? Although the dam provides heat from her body, as stated earlier, puppies aren't born with temperature controls. Until their shivering mechanisms develop to help them regenerate heat, their body temperatures drop quickly in a chilled environment. A chilled puppy quickly becomes a cold puppy, with pale gums and limp body, unable to sustain life. When the environment is cooler than it should be, the calories the pups receive from their mother's milk must be used to generate heat. Warm puppies use calories to grow; they don't waste them in order to keep warm. However, there is also a risk in being overly warm. Hot puppies rest apart from one another and away from the dam. Yes, heat stress makes limp puppies also.

- Is your automobile fully fueled and packed with puppy paraphernalia? Are you equipped to leave your home at any hour, day or night, in case of a health emergency of dam and/or pups, so you can get to the veterinarian ASAP? You may be lucky, and your dam and every puppy in the litter may thrive blithely through dewclaw removal, worming, vaccination and health check dates at your veterinary hospital without a hitch.

On the other hand, every breeder experiences an "I didn't believe this could happen to my litter and/or their mother" emergency—and not just once. Potential complications include mastitis, eclampsia (low blood calcium), lack of milk during the crucial first 48 hours (caused by temporary hormonal imbalances), infections, diarrhea, lung and heart abnormalities, dehydration—you name it. If a breeder keeps at it long enough, then that breeder experiences it all.

- When emergencies arise, will you have enough money available to pay an emergency all-night animal clinic the high fees for emergency treatment or for a monitored night's stay? Veterinarians seldom make house calls day or night. Instead, all-night and weekend emergency clinics have taken their place, usually operating from 6 P.M. until 7 A.M. For the veterinarians and professional attendants at the emergency clinics to service companion-animal owners, service costs are high, with payment up front before the dam or puppy is treated. Pickup is always by 7:00 the next morning, since the all-night clinics close during the day. If the animal is still in need of professional treatment, it has to be taken to the breeder's regular veterinarian when the hospital opens for the day.

- Will you say yes to spending money for special exams and tests, as well as for the traveling expenses to get you and the puppies to specialists? Puppies' eyes must be examined by a veterinary ophthalmologist to be sure there are no inherited eye problems. Storage Disease (GM-1) tests must also be performed, and there will be veterinarian's fees for drawing the blood necessary for each test and the overnight delivery fees to ship it to the New York State facility where the GM-1 assays are run. A reputable PWD breeder always does required health tests before placing the puppies in a litter.

- Are you committed to be on 24-hour guard to clean up immediately after your puppies, using a quality detergent, and then putting down clean paper or blankets?

- Do you have a washing machine able to alternate between your clothes and the puppies' garments on a daily basis—"garments" like blankets, cushions, pillows, stuffed toys and towels? And do you have ample storage space for what will seem like the tons of paper it takes to cover floors to catch the puppy urine and feces? Where will you dispose of this soiled paper properly and quickly?

- Are you prepared to set one room aside for the puppies for their first four to five weeks? And then to allow them the run of the kitchen and laundry room, or another room with a tiled or easily cleaned floor, where they can be "underfoot"—that means under *your* foot—most of the day? This "underfoot," noisy household socialization is a must if you want to raise well-adjusted puppies.

- Are you willing to remain home—even though a tempting vacation beckons—until all puppies have left for permanent homes?
- Are you committed to spending quality time to socialize each puppy in the litter?
- Are you willing to supply the puppies with quality canned milk, puppy food, puppy vitamins, puppy shampoo and all the other essentials required to raise them right?
- Do you have time and funds to devote to the extensive phone calls you'll have to make to potential buyers? Do you have a computer/typewriter to write up contracts and puppy instruction information?
- Do you have the space and the time to keep a puppy who becomes ill or has not shown optimum development until it is thriving, no matter how long it takes—sixteen weeks, six months, a year?
- Are you a member of the national club, the Portuguese Water Dog Club of America, and do you inform your puppy buyers of the advantages of belonging to it as well as acquaint them with the health guidelines the PWDCA requires owners to follow with their puppy? If you do not belong, do you plan to apply for membership before embarking on a breeding program?
- Are you willing to follow through and accept a dog back that you have sold, no matter what age or the reason for the return?
- Last but not least, are you sure you want your home to become a dog house? Can you learn to live happily with canine-teeth-marked baseboards and cupboards and rugs with chewed edges and/or holes right in their centers?

THE UP SIDE

Birth is a miracle each time it takes place. The moment newborns whoosh out from a dam's womb to a breeder is an absolute wonder. The breeder sees a newborn life as a personal kiss from nature. Each new little life proves the replenishment of the breed the breeder loves. Each little form fits into its own niche in the wonderful spectrum of nature.

So sweet, so tender is the scene—a loving dam and her pups. The joys of being a breeder outweigh the work and the possible agony of potential tragedy.

PREGNANCY

Check the time intervals between your bitch's last two heat periods. About two weeks before you think she is due to come into her next estrus, take her to your veterinarian for a complete blood analysis, a brucellosis test and a worming, plus any other tests the veterinarian deems necessary to ensure both a perfect pregnancy and a textbook whelping.

Set up a record book and record your bitch's first day of heat, the volume and color of vaginal discharge, the day the stud dog becomes interested, days bred, length of ties and end of heat. Keep track of every scrap of information regardless of how trivial it may seem.

FETAL DEVELOPMENT OF PUPPIES

Eggs do not attach to the uterine wall until about seventeen days after conception. At about twenty-four days, the fetuses can be felt by expert palpation on a relaxed bitch. With a tense bitch, the chances for successful palpation are greatly reduced. At this stage of the pregnancy fetuses can also be seen on a sonogram (called ultrasound); their size is about that of an olive. By twenty-eight days the palpation size compares to a walnut. At thirty-five days into pregnancy, small skeletons are recognizable on a sonogram. The veterinarian cannot palpate a bitch for puppies after thirty-five days, because the puppies' amniotic sacs protecting them from injury also protect them from palpation. And neither palpation nor a sonogram can predict the exact number of puppies the bitch carries. Also, until approximately forty-two to forty-five days into pregnancy complete skeletons cannot be seen on X-rays. Avoid having X-rays taken of a bitch in good health, unless an emergency procedure is deemed necessary. X-rays are valuable tools if a health problem is apparent in the bitch or if embryonic lives are threatened. During the last week of pregnancy, pups complete their nail, eyelash and hair growth.

FEEDING DURING PREGNANCY

Keep your bitch on a maintenance diet for approximately four weeks after breeding. The tiny forms do not require additional food. Then reintroduce her to the puppy food she once ate, which, because of its higher protein content, can better nourish her and her growing embryos.

Some bitches are food guzzlers throughout pregnancy. Some, the ones that send their owners into hysterics, look at food askance. "I don't want to eat," they explain in clearly understood body language—they refuse to go near a dish of food. Still others decide that owners will feed them human food right off the table if they pretend they can no longer stomach dry or canned food. I have one bitch who will only eat canned white chicken during the last four weeks of her pregnancy. I also have a matron who wants to be hand fed. She remembered that during her first pregnancy I hand fed her for the last two weeks. I have another who prefers to starve. Nothing tempts her. All of these bitches readily eat dry food, without supplements, when they are not pregnant! (Yes, you could say they are spoiled.)

Fortunately, when bitches are fed quality food throughout their lives, during pregnancy they have ample stored nutrients to give to growing babies; nature makes sure mother and babies are not deprived. A few bitches may develop mild anemia. If your bitch's appetite lags during pregnancy, don't fret; get a daily vitamin down her throat, take her for several good walks every day to stimulate her appetite, run her food through a blender and feed it in small quantities several times a day.

During the last several weeks, the majority of bitches eat minimal quantities of food. No matter where puppies are carried—high, right under the ribs or along the uterine walls—a bitch may experience considerable discomfort as her stomach and intestinal tract become compressed. Feed blender-processed food in small quantities at this time to aid digestion.

MONITORING THE BITCH'S TEMPERATURE

The bitch's normal temperature is between 101.5 and 102 degrees. During the last weeks of pregnancy, it hovers between 100.5 and 101.5, and also can meander up and down.

Begin taking her temperature morning and evening rectally on day fifty-six. This helps keep track of how close she is to whelping her puppies. One evening it may be 100.5 degrees, the next morning 101, that night 100. When the temperature goes down to 100, show her the whelping box. Some bitches will have a temperature of 100 degrees and deliver a puppy several hours later, but most do not deliver until it goes down to 99 degrees. Temperature decline is the most reliable pre-labor sign.

THE WHELPING BOX

Many authorities advise introducing a pregnant bitch to the whelping box several weeks in advance of the whelping date. Nonsense! I have never owned a bitch who wanted any part of this strange bed until her travail was imminent. All bitches prefer to have their puppies on beds, in closets, on the living room's best couch or in a hole she has dug in the garden or under the house!

The reason breeders go with the bitch to the whelping box is obvious. The bitches wouldn't go there otherwise. No spoiled PWD bitch (are there any that aren't?) wants to lie in a room by herself on a bed of newspapers or old blankets with rails poking her in the back and strange wooden sides obscuring her view of normal household goings-on. But with her owner by her side—well, if bitches could speak, they would say, "Okay, I'll stay here if you sit by my side. If you're with me, I'll suffer through however many hours it takes for my puppies to come into the world. Right now, I'm going to sleep. Yes, please watch me closely as I rest."

Along with clean towels, washcloths, alcohol, scissors, thread, a box lined with a blanket, facial tissues and a ready-to-be-warmed heating pad, take with you magazines, books, a telephone, a full coffee carafe, doughnuts, a notebook and pen, several bags in which to place discarded towels and newspapers, pillows, and a sleeping bag or cot if pre-labor hours drags on beyond twenty-four. After fifteen hours, you'll nervously wrap your fingers around the telephone receiver debating whether or not to call your veterinarian. You want reassurance that what your bitch is doing (or not doing) is OK! Your veterinarian, of course, has been prepared in advance that your bitch is due to whelp any minute.

She's restless. Put a leash on her, carry a towel (just in case) and take her for a short walk. Offer her some warm milk. These tactics may help push the puppies down a little faster. Unfortunately, she usually won't want to walk or drink the milk if she's close to second-stage labor. By now she's lying on her side, definitely uncomfortable. Suddenly, she stretches her legs and pushes them against the side of the box. She lets out a soft moan, then relaxes. You've seen a first-stage labor sign. Her uterus is contracting as the puppies move into position to enter life. Here are the other normal whelping signs. She'll display some or all:

1. Restlessness
2. Tearing up newspapers and blankets with her teeth and feet
3. Looking at you, looking at her rear apprehensively, getting up and wanting to leave the whelping box to go to a closet or the living room couch

Ch. Roughrider Diver's Doll, CD (Ch. Farmion Geo, UD ex Birchbrook's Salema) appears to ask, "The last time I whelped puppies they were in this box. Why not now?" The photo was taken one half-hour before D.D. started to deliver her second litter of nine.

4. Shivering

5. Vomiting

6. Panting

As the puppies move down in the uterus, panting increases. The cervix is dilating; the vulva swells, becoming large, soft and pliable so puppies can slip out fairly smoothly. For short periods, she will pant excessively. You feel certain a birth is imminent. No! She settles down again, stretches out and goes back to sleep. You don't dare take your eyes off her. When her body contracts (ah! was that a contraction? It's too slight to be one. Well, she did strain and push against the whelping box. So it was!), write down the time. Watch her closely so you don't miss the next contraction.

At this stage one of my bitches, D.D, jumped up out of the whelping box and sat in the smaller cardboard box lined with a heating pad and several towels—the puppy warmer. This was D.D.'s second litter, and she had remembered that during her first whelping I placed each newborn in this box as she was giving birth to another. I laugh to this day as I recall the scene. After sitting in the box long enough for me to take a picture, she half stood and tried to look down in back of her into the box. Unsuccessful, she got out of the box rather gingerly (after all, she was full of pups) and put her nose down in it, rummaging through the towels. When she again rose, she turned her eyes to me, her expression saying, "They were in the box the last time we were here. Why aren't they in it now? It would be a lot easier for me if they were." With that, she stepped back into the whelping box and a half-hour later began to whelp nine puppies, each of which was put in the cardboard box while she whelped the next and then given back to her when she was at rest.

Examine your bitch's vulva. Has it enlarged?

Write down the time of the first contraction. Watch for her water to break, a bubble to appear at the opening of her vulva. Whether you have to wait ten minutes or three hours for this, it seems like an interminable amount of time.

What is happening inside? One of the two uterine horns in which the puppies were housed has contracted, allowing a puppy to enter the uterus. The uterus contracts; the puppy is being pushed into the cervix. When the cervix dilates, the puppy slides into the vagina. The puppy's water bag (amniotic sac) appears at the opening of the vulva, lubricating the passageway for the puppy. The intervals between contractions diminish as the puppy is pushed toward the vulva. If all goes well, here comes the puppy! If, on the other hand, the wait is long, that first puppy is large or has entered the vulva in a breech presentation (hind feet first) or malpositioned in some other way, its presentation into life can be a bit more difficult. Some bitches work hard to expel the puppy. Others, frightened at the discomforting events occurring inside them, shiver, shake and even get up and come clinging to you. Eventually wanting expulsion of what is giving them pain, they push down as hard

Here the whelping bitch grasps the umbilical cord between her teeth in preparation for severing it.

as they can, contracting three or four times, and out comes a puppy. The rare, frightened bitch who refuses to allow contractions needs help.

As the easily delivered puppy is being born, the bitch will look in back of her and reach out to grab the sac in which the puppy is enclosed. Instinctively, she removes the membranes, starting at its head, then shreds the umbilical cord and after consuming the placenta (afterbirth) quickly, vigorously begins massaging her puppy with her tongue, getting its blood circulating while licking it dry. Leave her alone. Instinctively she knows what she is doing. She's doing fine. There is considerable controversy about allowing bitches to eat the placentas of their puppies. Most pediatric veterinarians agree that the afterbirth contains valuable nutrients and hormones that the bitch needs after a whelping and that eating them also helps bring down milk. This author agrees. I have noted that bitches will only consume as many afterbirths as they instinctively feel they require for nourishment and energy.

Those dams that look askance at the squirming objects and dark, bloody membranes lying in front of them need to be helped—and quickly. Pups that are allowed to lie enclosed in their birth sacs over thirty seconds suffocate or inhale so much fluid into their lungs that they expire. Often, there is little you can do to save them.

If you must, circumvent this dangerous possibility. Tear open the sac at the puppy's head; remove it, working backwards. Rub the puppy briskly with a washcloth (never enter the whelping box without several washcloths in hand). If this newborn is struggling for breath and fluid is leaking from the nostrils, take it securely in both hands, head towards the floor, its belly resting in your palms. Supporting its head well, raise your hands, palms up with the puppy grasped securely, then swing it from high above your head straight down towards the floor. Do this quickly, several times, holding its body and head securely. What you are attempting to do is to harness centrifugal force to expel the liquid from the puppy's lungs.

What if it doesn't work?

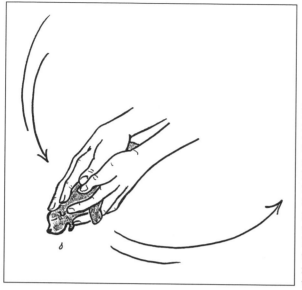

It is common for puppies to have excess fluid in their lungs at birth. To get rid of this fluid, swing the puppy from high above your head straight down toward the floor. Do this quickly, several times, to expel the fluid, but be sure to stabilize the head as shown. Some breeders will use a small towel to hold the slippery newborn while performing this maneuver.

Take a single drop of Duprin (a respiratory aid, which you have obtained from your veterinarian beforehand) and place it on the puppy's tongue. Then place the puppy back with its mother. Immediately, instinctively, she touches her mouth to her pup's nostrils and mouth and with her tongue digs deep into its mouth, wiping up fluid. I have watched a bitch work with her pup for ten minutes, swabbing her tongue deep down into the pup's throat, then bringing it back up, repeating these actions again and again; not getting the response she wanted, she rolled the pup over, wiping it vigorously, particularly around its chest and mouth with her tongue, and then once more began tongue-in-mouth first aid. She saved one of her pups this way. What a stunning expression of canine instinctual intelligence in birthing!

Trouble is brewing when more than three hours have passed before a puppy emerges after the onset of labor. Sometimes, if a puppy can be reached at the vulva, it can be manipulated out, but this should be done only if there is no other option available. Stretch the vulva with two fingers of your left hand and then with a clean washcloth in your right, grasp a foot or head, which should be visible or almost visible. (Obviously, reverse this if you are left-handed.) Be sure your hands are well scrubbed and your nails are well pared. If you can't see the puppy, insert your clean right forefinger up into the vulva to try to feel part of it. Sometimes, the bitch is too frightened or in too much pain to contract hard enough to expel her puppy. Help her. Work the puppy out by pulling—gently—down. Never pull straight out; you'll injure both puppy and mother. And pull down only with contractions. Again, grasp the pup by trying to work your fingers around it, if at all possible (yes, it's difficult to do sometimes, but you can do it). Get that puppy out. When it leaves the uterine horn, it's on its own. If it's squeezed and can't breathe, get it out.

I once had to take a bitch of mine in the car to the veterinarian, five miles away. He carried her to his operating table, laid her down, washed his hands well, then, with an assistant holding her, reached inside her vulva with his right hand—I thought his whole arm would disappear!—and came out with a pup, over one pound. That had been her third pup in a litter of ten. The remaining seven entered the world just fine; the fourth arrived on the front seat of my car as I was driving back home. She never got an infection, and number three pup thrived!

Purchase several whelping books and read them more than once. Carry them with you to the whelping room with the pages open to the words describing problems that arise in whelping. You'll do okay 90 percent of the time—all by yourself.

Sometimes the whelping is too much for a layperson to handle without surgical help. An unborn pup from one of my bitches'second litter almost killed her. Starting at 11 A.M., she whelped nine puppies by 6 P.M., delivering each easily. Then there was trouble. By 8 P.M., Delta began to moan. It being Sunday night (do bitches ever whelp on weekdays or at normal vet's hours?), I was able to reach only one vet.

"Put your finger up her vulva," he commanded, "do you feel a pup there?" I did not.

"Well, she'll last until morning," he said. "See me then." He hung up.

Let me state here that this veterinarian later changed his profession; he had said "She'll last until morning" too many times. I kept trying to reach another veterinarian. The one I did reach was hours away, but he told me about an emergency clinic not too far from where we lived. At midnight, when our bitch was climbing the walls in anguish, we headed south for twenty-five miles in pea-soup fog to this emergency clinic. It was a scary ride, weather-wise as well as for the puppies and Delta.

Thank goodness for credit cards and for good veterinarians. "She would not have lasted until morning," the doctor told me when he showed me the X-ray he had taken to assess the situation. "Look, the pup is sideways across the bony structure above her pelvis. There is no way it can come out. There's no way she could survive this, either."

A Caesarean section was required to remove the pup, whose bones were shattered, and two more pups inside, also dead. It did not matter. Delta was fine. She stayed at the hospital and we returned home to feed the nine puppies already born. Returning for her at 7 A.M., we watched her nurse her first nine the moment she was back home. Wonderful dam, so brave, so stoic! Delta had one more litter for us three heats down the line. She delivered all pups easily, and she enjoyed raising them.

Another heartbreaking event: our bitch Seeley whelped her last litter easily—eight girls and one boy. When I took her back to the vet to have her checked, the X-ray showed her insides to be clean and healthy. The vet even remarked how good her internal organs appeared! But a week later, she came down with acute metritis—an infected uterus. It had spread upward through the birth canal while she whelped or soon thereafter. Oddly enough, Seeley hardly gave an indication of her suffering. I knew something was wrong when she refused food. I took her temperature. It was 105. She was at the veterinarian's office within the hour.

Seeley was spayed and placed on heavy doses of antibiotics. Although she was well within a week, the pups could not nurse from her. My husband and I fed those puppies by bottle every two hours for two weeks straight. No, we didn't have much sleep. It was a very exhausting time. The good news is that our Seeley lived past twelve years of age in the best of health. An admonition: Don't ever have a litter unless there are two of you to whelp and to care for the pups until they go to their homes.

The third heartbreak with a heroic ending happened with my 1995 litters, when Fancy and Cinder were ready to whelp at the same time. Fancy delivered two puppies before dawn on a Monday after beginning hard labor at 2 A.M. At 4:45 A.M. she delivered the first, which weighed eighteen ounces. No wonder she had such an awful time! But Fancy, like her mother, Seeley, has always been a strong, energetic bitch, and she persevered until that huge female pup came out—breech, to make the birthing even more difficult. The second girl arrived, also by breech, this one weighing sixteen ounces. Two overly large pups like this can be tough on their mother in the birthing process. The norm for newborn PWD pups is nine to twelve ounces. (While PWD puppies can also run the gamut from a one-pound birth weight down to four ounces, these puppies are the exceptions.)

We were happy. Even though it was a smaller litter than we or potential puppy owners had wanted her to have, the two girls were beautiful and obviously healthy.

"Well, Cinder, now you can have your puppies," we said to our other expectant mother as she looked over the gate at Fancy, happily feeding and caring for her two babies.

Normally, we take mother and puppies to the veterinarian the day following whelping for checkups. But Cinder was ready to whelp, so we didn't want to leave the house. She began early labor the next morning. At 9 A.M. she did deliver a pup, but it was dead. It was also bloody. Cinder attempted to clean it, then lay down, uttered a loud groan, and looked up at me, anguish in her face. This was her third litter, the twenty-fourth I had assisted; there was something very wrong. I called my veterinarian a half-hour later. Cinder hadn't moved from where she had lay down and her expressive eyes, when I kneeled beside her to soothe her, were full of pain. My veterinarian suggested I bring her to the hospital.

Several hours after she arrived at the vet, Cinder whelped a second puppy. That was with the help of several doses of oxytocin. After this pup was born, repeated oxytocin injections failed to stimulate uterine contractions. We decided on a Caesarean. "She'll be all right, you can go home to wait," I was told, but I wouldn't leave her. I waited three hours. Finally, a veterinary assistant came to the waiting room to tell me they had taken out eight puppies: "Cinder has four boys and five girls! Everyone in back is working real hard, rubbing life into them." "How's Cinder?" She gave me a noncommittal, "All right," then turned and left. I waited another hour. No one brought me the pups; no one brought me Cinder. Assistants entered and left the reception room, but were almost noncommittal at my queries. "Everyone is okay," was the best I got.

Finally, I was informed my veterinarian was able to see me. I went into the examining room shaking. "The puppies are all fine," he told me, "but Cinder has to stay at the hospital until she is stabilized. She is bleeding internally."

Because Cinder was bleeding internally, she had to be monitored constantly, with blood drawn at intervals checking the volume of red cells in her blood. Her blood volume was dangerously close to where a blood transfusion would be needed to save her life.

The veterinarian had taken the pups from the right horn, closed it up, and opened the left horn to remove the pups there. As he did, he saw the right horn fill up with blood. He did not dare give Cinder more anesthesia to go back into the right horn after he removed the remaining puppies from the left one.

I took Cinder's puppies home to see if Fancy would accept them. It was important that the puppies receive the first milk, the colostrum. If they did not receive it, the pups' immune systems would be depressed, and they would have little or no resistance to puppy diseases. If Fancy would not accept Cinder's puppies, I would have to return them to the veterinary hospital to try to have Cinder nurse them. But this would threaten Cinder's life. The third choice was to bottle feed them for the next three weeks until they could be weaned.

If Fancy accepted the puppies, I could leave them with my husband watching over the brood while I returned to the veterinarian's office before he closed his doors for the evening and drive Cinder forty miles north to an all-night emergency clinic. The professionals there would monitor her carefully—draw blood to check blood volume and, if necessary, give her needed blood transfusions. They had a blood donor at hand. I would have to return at 7:00 the next morning and drive her back to my veterinarian for continued monitoring and blood drawing. What a horrible itinerary!

I went home with nine beautiful puppies—eight weighing from nine to twelve ounces, and one that no one thought could make it because he was so small, only four-and-a-half ounces. I also went home with a heavy heart. However, I had no time to ponder anything.

My husband was waiting. Fancy was feeding her two puppies. I gave the box of puppies to my husband, who placed it under a heat lamp, as the puppies were cold. He then took out one puppy, rubbed it all over with his fingers to get his scent on it, then rubbed it again with one of Fancy's soiled towels to put her scent on it, and finally handed it to me. I carried the puppy to Fancy in her whelping box. I held up each for her to clean rears, heads and bodies, and then I placed each at a nipple (Fancy has only eight nipples, and there were now eleven puppies she had to nurse). She cleaned each and allowed each to suckle. We did not rush the process. She accepted every one. She licked and nuzzled the littlest boy as I first held him up to a nipple, then as I milked her. I put my wet finger to his mouth until I was sure he was ingesting the colostrum.

My husband handed me the phone while I was still kneeling in the whelping box beside Fancy and the puppies. I called my veterinarian, Dr. Michael Murphy, who had helped Fancy and Garbonzo in their AI experiences. I told him what had happened and what had to be done. He offered to help. Dr. Murphy sent one of his assistants down to my veterinarian, a distance of forty-five miles, where I met her. She picked up Cinder and took her to the all-night emergency clinic. Dr. Murphy then picked her up in the morning and drove her to his hospital so he could draw blood at intervals and check her hematocrit blood volume the next day. What a wonderful veterinarian!

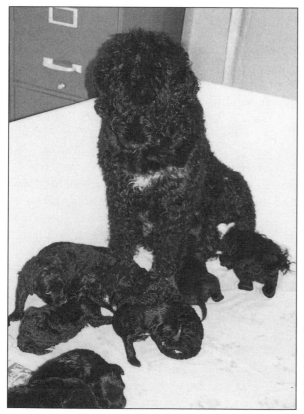

Occasionally Fancy would sit up, stare at her large litter, and then lie down beside them again. She seemed to be thinking, "I don't remember all these!" It is obvious which are wavy and which are curly.

Fancy fed and cleaned "her" eleven pups constantly. She enjoyed the milky food I fed her. Every half-hour I would hold up to one of her nipples the tiny puppy who, thank goodness, was strong and wiry, for he could never have survived if he weren't. My husband and I took turns resting beside the box. There wasn't much chance for sleep. We could laugh, despite the awful events, because occasionally Fancy would get up, leave the eleven pups—her own two four times the size of the other nine—to sit down on the other side of the box, stare at all the puppies, shake her head, and then return to lie down beside them. How clear it was what she was thinking: "I don't remember all these!"

She knew which were hers. While none of the puppies lacked for the bonding and attentions she offered, Fancy always had a special lick and fondling for her two little girls.

Cinder was very ill. Until everyone was certain she had stopped bleeding, she spent her nights at the emergency clinic and her days with Dr. Murphy. I first picked her up when her pups were three days old, but almost immediately had to return her when her temperature soared to 105 degrees with an infection. Thank goodness she was home within a week. Everyone she stayed with enjoyed her—"So sweet, so effervescent, so willing no matter what we did to her." They had to take blood from her veins at least four times daily (the hematocrit test) to measure her blood volume and fortify her with IV fluids.

She never demurred. Upon arriving home, once I allowed her into the living room, she went directly to the room where Fancy and the pups were housed. She sat at the gate first, looking at them, then at me. It was heartbreaking. She knew her puppies. She kissed Fancy when they met in the hall. But we could not allow Cinder to be with the puppies. She was healing, but her stitches could not be touched and her milk had been infected. Also, she was on heavy doses of antibiotics. So we kept her away and after three weeks, Cinder no longer went to sit by the gate looking in at her babies. As the puppies grew and were able to play in the yard, Cinder didn't rush to play with them. We kept a puppy from this litter, who, of course, believed Fancy to be her mom. And Fancy, wonderful dam that she has always been, allowed the puppy to browbeat her constantly. While Cinder plays with her, she feels no motherly bond. What an especial sadness for us, the breeders! The little girl who looks so much like her mother will never know she is.

It's a cold, hard fact. Newborn bonding is essential in animal life.

It's a cold, hard fact. Whelping is hard work.

It can be joyful, it can be emotionally draining, it can be tragic. Whelping a litter is a mixed bag of pain, tears, tragedy, joy and happiness, not only for the dam and puppies but for the humans who decree the birth of these animals.

Are you prepared?

chapter 13

The Portuguese Water Dog Dam and Puppies: The First Eight Weeks

Once the dam has completed birthing and settles into her whelping box, she begins bonding with her offspring. Animal behaviorists call this "imprinting." It's time for the breeder, too, to establish relations. Massage each pup gently but thoroughly: toes, feet, all four legs, tail, body, neck, head, ears and mouth. Do this twice a day. You'll discover, while massaging, that although newborn puppies' ears and eyes are sealed shut, they are able to smell, feel and taste. Our newborns react to both my husband's and my footsteps and the scent of our hands by the second day. Given the opportunity, they will mouth our noses and cheeks.

I suggest bottle feeding each puppy once a day from about five days on, even though most puppies require no supplementation. Do it for bonding. If, at first, they do not like the texture of the "human preemie" baby nipple, they'll change their minds once they taste the milk. My choice is goat's milk. While it is only about 12 percent protein, it is a strengthener and is compatible with a newborn puppy's intestinal tract. They love it! The second time you pick up their little bodies to bottle feed them, they know exactly how you will hold them and will strive to snuggle into place against you. How aware newborn puppies are!

The dam's food the first few days after whelping should be light and milky. Her intestinal tract is sensitive after nine weeks of pregnancy. When you begin feeding her commercial food again, be sure to blend it for the first week. I learned years ago that giving a nursing dam normal-sized meals immediately after whelping increases the chance of her developing caked breasts.

Newborn puppies swallow only small amounts each time they feed. Their dams have consumed placentas, and if not, have been offered and drunk plenty of liquid to maintain and increase their high fluid requirement. If, however, they pant and sweat yet refuse to drink liquid offered by the breeder, the breeder should wet his or her fingers with warm milk and place them inside the bitch's mouth to encourage her to drink. Adequate intake of liquid also helps bring down the milk.

At Roughrider, while our other dogs and human visitors may stand at the doorway and peer over a gate into the room that contains the whelping box and while we lift up a puppy and show it to them, only my husband and I enter the room for the first three weeks. Our bitches are secure in the fact that this is their very special time. Their proud and happy actions prove it. Because they are not threatened in any way and praised often, they are eager to show off their babies from day one. They wag their tails and preen when visitors, human or animal, come to admire. And we encourage all visitors to exclaim to the dam something like, "You're absolutely wonderful! Oh, look at your beautiful babies!" She will positively blossom when her need to be admired is satisfied in this way.

Puppies' ears and eyes are sealed shut at birth. Nature is wise. While immature internal systems are adjusting to the world outside their mother's womb, it would be futile for puppies to be born with the abilities to see or hear. Newborn energies must be devoted to suckling and sleeping. The best growth is obtained, of course, when the newborn is maintained in a warm environment, where it may utilize food calories for growth rather than waste them attempting to keep warm.

Newborn puppies are also active. They move to their mother's nipples, crawl away to nuzzle close to her belly or hug one of her legs. Their sleep is very active. Legs jerk, bodies twitch. After their eyes and ears begin to open, these activated sleep movements will have helped muscles to develop enough so that puppies can get up on their feet to first sit, then stand and begin to wobble about. Ears begin to unglue at about eight to fourteen days, eyes at from ten to sixteen days. Inside corners unlock first. You realize what is happening when a puppy raises its head and moves it about as if it were looking at something. It is beginning to see light—though not much, as its eyes are first tiny slits and slowly open. Even when fully open, eyes are glassy. Objects are blurs. When the eyes are completely open, the puppy may focus on an object, flash its fuzzy image into its brain, and then look at something else. Presenting puppies, at their four to eight weeks' mental development, with bright-colored toys forms an important part of learning. Cloth toys, balls and toys of varying textures and shapes help puppies learn about the world around them.

If the iris in the open eye is light blue, final eye shade will be light to medium brown. If the iris is dark blue, then the pup should develop dark brown, almost black, eyes. Some puppies retain developmental film on their

Two-week-old puppies, by Ch. Captree's Jib of Acton-dale, cdx out of Can. OTCH, Am. Ch. Baybrite Algazarra, Am., Can. UD. Their breeder/owner is Steven Dostie of DownEast Kennels.

These five-week-old puppies, not yet ready to eat blendered puppy food, are enjoying a meal of milk and cereal as they progress toward full weaning.

eyes until as late as eight to twelve weeks. Watch your puppies carefully at these ages; if one shakes its head when approaching you, or perhaps gets too close to a wall or step before realizing an obstacle is in front of it, lift that puppy up, take it to the light and scrutinize its eyes to ascertain whether they still have developmental film streaked across them. If so, supplement the dam with a small amount of vitamin A, and place the puppy on a liquid vitamin-mineral supplement containing vitamin A. The next time the pup goes to the veterinarian, have the practitioner check its eyes; if he or she sees nothing and you are suspect, take the puppy to your veterinary ophthalmologist for an examination. The puppy might have keratitis. (See Chapter 14, "Health.")

Begin weaning when the puppies arc fairly steady on their feet, doing better than just wobbling about. If you begin weaning too early, you won't accomplish much. Portuguese Water Dog puppies should be at least twenty-one days old before being taught to lap. (There are exceptions, of course, such as orphan puppies, but since tummies are still immature, don't hasten weaning.) Most Portuguese Water Dog puppies don't move about much for any length of time before four weeks of age. The supposedly magical time for puppies to come alive is usually this same twenty-one days. Portuguese Water Dog puppies are very slow developers.

Put the dam outside when you begin weaning. As you carry each meal to the puppies—first in communal pans, then in individual dishes—whistle! Some puppies will awaken at the sound of your whistle by the second day of weaning, lift their heads and get up to come towards you. By the end of the first three days of weaning, all puppies will rush towards the food dish as soon as they hear the whistle. We continue this whistle training the entire time puppies remain at our house; in so doing we're teaching a whistle recall!

Allow the dam in to clean the puppies and finish their meal after they've had their fill; they watch and learn quickly by her behavior, becoming experts at lapping within a few days. We start our puppies off with goat's milk, add cereal after several days, then give one meal with meat broth mixed with cereal and finally feed a meat dish. We take our time introducing new foods to puppies. When we do introduce puppy food to them at about five weeks, it's well blended for easier digestion until they are at least six or seven weeks old, since puppies have difficulty digesting chunks. Also, many PWD puppies do not get their baby teeth in until six to seven weeks of age and shouldn't swallow chunks of food. Although we reduce the mother's food by six weeks, dams are allowed to feed their puppies as long as they wish. Puppies love the milk desserts their mothers offer until the day they leave the nest.

At about four to five weeks, depending on their mental development, allow puppies to spend their days in your kitchen. It's best to socialize them under foot. At our home, their mother always precedes them to a new environment. We carry them there; she greets them by feeding them when we place them on the floor in the new space. This maintains a high confidence level. Like introducing new foods, introducing new environments should be gradual. Our puppies find their whelping-box pillows, blankets and toys in our kitchen and extended laundry room; they quickly learn to adapt to appliance noises, rattling of dishes, delicious odors and our big feet. As they gain confidence in these surroundings and the rooms become too confining for their activities, which takes about a week, they find the same familiar items outside in the yard when for the first time they see the sky and breathe the fresh air from an opened laundry-room door.

For their first venture into the outdoors, the puppies are initially carried down the steps to explore the area around the backyard steps and feed off their mother before being carried back inside. Gradually, their explorations take them farther and farther. Young puppies should have as many varied experiences as possible. They need to feel grass, cement, mud and dirt under their feet; they need to take car rides sitting on a lap; they need socialization with adults and children. The more you can provide, the better. Take them to the veterinarian for their first examination and vaccination at six weeks, and be sure their eyes, ears, teeth, jaws, heart, coat and structure are all checked out. If you begin standing the puppies on the grooming table daily when they turn five weeks, continuing their daily massage with a friendly voice and comforting hands, they know what to expect at the veterinarian's.

It's a good idea for breeders to have six-week-old puppies spend nights in an area that is easy to enter and clean up in the early morning. Our six-week-olds spend nights in an insulated, warm puppy room in our barn. It contains a radio tuned to soft music and several open door crates cushioned with soft blankets, stands to jump on or crawl under, pillows, tunnels and other toys. Puppies' toys are learning tools. At 5 A.M. daily thereafter, they troop back into the house, their mother herding them.

An easily built puppy-sized ramp used at Roughrider Kennels. When the author's puppies are about five weeks old, this ramp is placed in the kitchen. The puppies sleep under it, learn to climb up the ramp and then enjoy sliding down it or sitting on its table top and viewing the world below. It is an excellent growth development "toy." This home-built ramp and table is the most popular four- and five-week-old puppy item at Roughrider.

Six-week-old puppies, bred and owned by Maureen Dahms of Bonnydoon Kennels, sizing up visitors walking up the driveway.

Young puppies crave approval when they're bold and need reassurance when something puzzles them. At Roughrider their mom and one of us is always there to offer assistance. Also, their mom, with plenty of space in which to do it, continually teaches. I've watched one dam—with puppies sitting in a semicircle watching her—digging, then looking up at them to see if they are watching, then digging again! I've observed another going in and out of a doggy door while all her puppies watched attentively. As soon as one tried to do the same, she left the scene. Lesson learned! This mother also splashed the water out of her doggy dish, then sat back with that well-known PWD smile, as her puppies followed suit. If a dam doesn't have space where she can remain out of the way when desired, she doesn't teach much. With space, dams sit back and watch, ready to run forward to praise curiosities and bark or scold when puppies fuss too strongly at one another.

We believe shyness is formed in litter play when active puppies keep pouncing upon their slower-developing siblings. The negative input causes the slow developers to hang back. Early mental development in puppies is much more profound than many realize; because of intensive litter interaction, the breeder, as well as the dam, has to be ever handy to make certain each puppy has positive interaction with its littermates. Socialization (exposure to people, other animals and various environments) continues until puppies leave the breeder. Early impressions remain strong; in addition, puppies will reflect the socialization patterns future owners carve. The puppy will mirror, in its attitude, its rearing.

As far as house training, puppies like to keep clean when their environment is kept tidy and when they are able to mimic the actions of their dams. From six weeks on, it is important to take puppies outside often. There will always be house accidents in new surroundings; PWD puppies learn readily but can become temporarily confused—or, as is natural, regress during certain developmental periods.

Raising a litter of puppies is hard, exhausting work, with no time off. Because it is all-encompassing, it also comes replete with high rewards and joys of accomplishment when the breeder sends off an intelligent, well-adjusted canine baby to become a family's treasured four-legged companion.

Do puppies have to go to new homes at the supposedly magical forty-nine days to bond properly? While this may be true for kennel-raised puppies, or for puppies who receive minimal socialization, it is nonsense for well-socialized house-raised offspring. These puppies can go to homes and bond beautifully whether they are seven, eight or eighteen weeks. For guarantees, look at the number of hearing dogs and other assistance dogs that come from pounds and shelters when they are fully mature adults. Dogs are adaptable! If raised correctly, they bond at any age. If you are seeking a puppy for obedience, water work, tracking, dog shows or whatever, the chief thing you need to concern yourself with is the puppy's socialization before you came into the picture.

chapter 14

Health

The Portuguese Water Dog is a characteristically healthy animal. Many of these dogs live to be fifteen years old or more. Noted for strength and stamina, a PWD nevertheless can succumb to diseases common to all dogs. Check the Resources at the back of the book for recommended books on general canine health care and problems common to all dogs.

Competent veterinary care for your dog is essential. Upon purchasing your PWD puppy, take it to a veterinarian for a preliminary health examination. If there are other PWD owners in your area, they may help you find a practitioner who has treated their dogs satisfactorily. Be sure to inquire about the veterinarian's vaccination schedules. You want four, not three, weeks between puppy shots. Find out how emergency calls after normal office hours are handled and what this doctor's specialty is. While all veterinarians are general care practitioners, some specialize in particular canine health areas such as allergies, dentition or orthopedics. Your dog's veterinarian becomes your friend for the life of your dog.

Four health problems, in particular, presently afflict the Portuguese Water Dog: progressive retinal atrophy (PRA), hip dysplasia (HD), Addison's disease and storage disease. Dr. Jerold S. Bell, a clinical veterinary geneticist in Enfield, Connecticut, and the PWDCA's geneticist discusses these four health problems. I will then acquaint you with other health problems, common to all dogs, that you must be aware of when caring for a Portuguese Water Dog.

PROGRESSIVE RETINAL ATROPHY (PRA)

Progressive retinal atrophy is a genetic disease that causes a late-onset, slowly progressive loss of sight in Portuguese Water Dogs. This disease is present in many other breeds, with varying ages of onset and rates of progression. In the Portuguese Water Dog, the disease can present clinically to the owner as

Bonnydoon Obolo and Bonnydoon Poncho (Ch. Raio ex Cherna Albeheira), shown here in 1987, were whelped on October 15, 1982. Poncho passed away in 1994 and Obolo in late 1995, both having lived long and healthy lives. Obolo, better known as Lefty, sired twelve champions. Courtesy Maureen Dahms

Four senior citizens, all over fourteen years. The bitch on the extreme left was seventeen-and-a-half years of age when this photo was taken. Courtesy Cheryl Shaker

Victor's Vibrante (Farmion Azinhal ex Lusitania Joanica), whelped July 10, 1980, died August 14, 1994, after enjoying good health all her life. Petie was whelped in Helen Roosevelt's litter in which two puppies developed symptoms of a disorder later identified as storage disease.

early as fourteen months of age. Affected dogs will first show signs of difficulty seeing at night or in dim light. This can progress to total blindness, although some dogs affected later in life can retain limited vision (light/dark discrimination). There are affected dogs ten years of age who are not experiencing noticeable difficulties in their degree of visual acuity. The age of onset, progression and severity of the visual deficit can vary within litters.

Progressive retinal atrophy in the Portuguese Water Dog is caused by a simple autosomal recessive gene. Affected dogs receive the defective gene from *both* parents, who are carriers. Carriers of the defective gene are normal in all aspects except for their ability to pass the defective gene to approximately half their offspring.

Since 1990, there have been more than seventy-five Portuguese Water Dogs confirmed with PRA. The defective gene is widespread in the PWD gene pool. There are many kindred dogs with PRA that go back to dogs imported into this country in the 1960s. There are also affected dogs who have recently been imported from Portugal.

PRA can be diagnosed by a board-certified veterinary ophthalmologist during a direct ophthalmoscopic examination (which can also be referred to as a CERF exam). CERF is the Canine Eye Registry Foundation, a national database for canine eye diseases. Portuguese Water Dogs from 2 to $8^1/_2$ years of age affected with PRA have been diagnosed by a direct ophthalmoscopic examination. There are affected dogs who had normal CERF examinations at six years of age. An electroretinogram (ERG) can identify affected Portuguese Water Dogs earlier than a CERF examination. This can be performed at a limited number of veterinary facilities in the country, and it requires general anesthesia. At this time, experts feel that 99 percent of affected Portuguese Water Dogs can be identified by two years of age by specific techniques of electroretinography.

A direct ophthalmoscopic or electroretinogram examination can identify only affected dogs. There is presently no clinical test to identify carriers of PRA (those dogs with one defective gene for the disease). The only way to identify a dog as a carrier of PRA is if it (1) produced an offspring with PRA, or (2) is an offspring of an affected dog.

To identify a dog statistically as a carrier or noncarrier of the defective gene, a test mating can be performed by breeding to an affected dog with PRA. If a minimum of seven offspring have normal ERG examinations at a minimum of two years of age, then the tested parent is statistically clear of being a carrier of PRA with greater than 99 percent confidence. (Test matings to carriers of PRA can also be performed with a minimum of sixteen normal-testing offspring produced.) Because of the need to follow offspring for a minimum of two years, the expense of ERG testing and the emotional toll of breeding and placing puppies who may go blind into pet homes, test mating is not an option for many breeders.

Presently, the only way to find a dog's risk of being a carrier or affected with PRA is through a relative risk pedigree analysis. This process considers the known PRA risk inherited from ancestors in the dog's pedigree. It can also be used to predict the carrier and affected risk of a proposed mating.

Dr. Gustavo Aguirre, at the Baker Institute for Diseases of Dogs at Cornell University, is presently conducting research that is aimed at producing a blood test to identify carriers of PRA. The PWDCA is a financial supporter of his research.

As of early 1996, it is estimated that 36 to 38 percent of the breeding population of Portuguese Water Dogs are carriers of the defective gene controlling PRA. Anywhere from 6 percent to 10 percent of all Portuguese Water Dogs are affected. Until a genetic test for the identification of PRA carriers is developed, we cannot expect great progress in decreasing the PRA risk in the breed.

It is currently recommended that all pet and breeding Portuguese Water Dogs have an annual direct ophthalmoscopic examination by a board-certified veterinary ophthalmologist. Remember, a normal CERF or ERG examination shows only that a particular dog is not affected at the time of the examination. It proves nothing about the possible carrier status of the dog. Breeders should attempt to breed only to dogs whose carrier relative risk is lower than the average of the breed. They should attempt to reduce the carrier and affected risk of their own dogs with each generation. Once a genetic test for carriers is available, we can proceed with testing and breeding, and work toward reducing the extremely high level of the defective gene in the population.

STORAGE DISEASE

Storage disease (GM1-gangliosidosis) is a genetic disorder caused by a simple autosomal recessive gene. Only Portuguese Water Dogs who receive a defective gene from *both* parents are affected. They will show neurological deterioration and will die by six to eight months of age. There is no treatment or cure for the disease. A dog with one defective gene is a healthy carrier but will pass the gene to approximately half of its offspring if bred. At this writing there are nineteen Portuguese Water Dogs confirmed affected with storage disease.

The PWDCA administrates a blood test for storage disease status, which is run by the New York University Neurogenetics Laboratory. This test can be performed on dogs as young as five weeks, the limitation being the size of the puppy for the amount of blood needed. This is not an absolute test of a dog's genes, but a statistical assay for blood enzyme levels. It produces results of affected, normal or carrier with 95 to 99 percent confidence, or indeterminate (if the confidence between normal and carrier is less than

95 percent). If a dog tests indeterminate (IND) on multiple blood samples, the ratings of its parents, and its behavior, conformation and functional qualities should be considered in determining its future breeding potential. There is a 2 percent mislabeling error expected with this type of assay, where a dog will test other than its genetic status.

Beginning in 1990, dogs could be assigned "litter-tested normal" (L-rated) status if they produced seven normal-testing offspring and no carriers. Their offspring were assigned "ancestor tested normal" (A-rated) status. This system created more accuracy, because it was based on progeny testing of the offspring instead of single blood tests on individuals. Puppies out of two parents who are either L-rated or A-rated do not need to be blood tested before being sold and are assigned an A-rating (—A) themselves. Portuguese Water Dogs with A-ratings do not have to be blood tested unless they are going to be used for breeding. All dogs not eligible for A-ratings should be tested as puppies before being placed in homes. All Portuguese Water Dogs should be issued an official PWDCA Storage Disease Certificate as puppies, and all puppy buyers should receive a form on the purchase of their puppy stating its blood test result or ancestor tested normal (—A) status.

At the time of the development of the blood test for storage disease in 1987, approximately 14 percent of the breed were carriers of the defective recessive gene. For all dogs born in 1990, the carrier population had been lowered to 6.1 percent (40 carriers), with 77.6 percent L- or A-rated. By 1992, some breeders felt that we did not really need to control the breeding of carriers because of the accuracy of the blood testing system. As a result, the population went back up to 12 percent testing carrier (64 dogs), with only 66.4 percent of the population A- or L-rated. For dogs born in 1995 tested through March of 1996, the breed was back down to 4.3 percent testing carrier, with 80.4 percent of the population being A- or L-rated.

The breeders are now able to eliminate the defective gene for storage disease from the Portuguese Water Dog gene pool. After nine years of the genetic disease program, a goal of not breeding or producing carriers by the year 2000 is realistic. Portuguese Water Dog breeders have done an excellent job of controlling the defective gene. They took strong measures early by calling for a six-month breeding moratorium while the blood test for carriers was being developed in 1987. The Portuguese Water Dog is now on the verge of being one of the few breeds to eliminate a defective gene that was once widespread in the population.

ADDISON'S DISEASE (HYPOADRENOCORTICISM)

Addison's disease results from the autoimmune destruction of the adrenal gland. Its clinical signs usually begin in young to middle-aged dogs (average age four years) with vague symptoms of lethargy, vomiting, inappetence, depression and weakness. Because of the vagueness of these symptoms, and the fact that routine blood tests will not directly identify the disease, a diagnosis of hypoadrenocorticism may be overlooked. A misdiagnosis of kidney disease (due to secondary elevation of kidney enzymes) or Lyme disease (due to the symptoms, although no fever is associated with Addison's) might be made on initial presentation. An affected dog may also present with an acute Addisonian crisis, which if not treated quickly may result in death. The disease can be diagnosed upon postmortem examination.

Addison's disease will respond to generalized treatment such as fluids or prednisone, but will relapse once these treatments are stopped. A blood cortisol level, dexamethasone suppression test and/or ACTH stimulation test is necessary to confirm a diagnosis. The disease is treated with oral drugs or long-acting injectable drugs.

There is a 66 percent to 34 percent ratio of affected females to males. This is also the exact ratio found in the general canine population, as well as that found in humans. It is scientifically established that disorders involving the immune system have a female preponderance in dogs and in humans.

Addison's disease is usually an uncommon disease in the dog. Studies show that in the general population, the disorder is diagnosed in only one out of every 1,500 dogs. There are presently more than fifty Portuguese Water Dogs confirmed with Addison's disease. By conservative estimates, this is a frequency of one out of every 125 Portuguese Water Dogs—ten times the prevalence in the general population.

Scientific references cite hereditary Addison's disease in Portuguese Water Dogs, Standard Poodles, Labrador Retrievers and Leonbergers, a giant breed originating in Germany. McKusick's *Mendelian Inheritance in Man* states that familial aggregation is found in Addison's disease in human beings, most often with an autosomal recessive pattern.

Portuguese Water Dogs affected with Addison's disease have been tracked by the PWDCA Addison's Committee since 1983. Pedigrees of affected PWDs represent the genetic spectrum, including Algarbiorum and Alvalade breeding, original imported stock, and recent imported stock from Portugal. A genetic study of Addison's disease in Portuguese Water Dogs shows that affected dogs are clustered in closely related kindreds. Most of the affected dogs are from two normal-appearing parents, although some have an affected parent. Several affected dogs have littermates who either were affected or are themselves parents of affected dogs. Some parents of affected dogs, when bred to other mates, produced additional affected dogs or dogs who were themselves parents of affected dogs.

Based on the genetic transmission through the pedigrees and the frequency of occurrence, the data suggest that there is a major autosomal recessive gene involved in the transmission of Addison's disease in the Portuguese Water Dog. It appears that only dogs with two defective recessive genes can develop the disease. We cannot say at this time whether this is a simple autosomal recessive gene or if additional genetic factors are involved.

It is possible that the gene(s) for Addison's disease in Portuguese Water Dogs shows incomplete penetrance. This means that some genetically affected dogs (those with two defective recessive genes) may never show signs of the disease. In spite of this, these clinically normal but genetically affected dogs could pass on a defective gene to *all* of their offspring, making them carriers.

It is well documented that stress can cause the onset of clinical signs of Addison's disease in genetically predisposed dogs and people.

In these individuals, environmental or metabolic stress (pregnancy and whelping, debilitating illness, etc.) can overtax a genetically weakened adrenal gland system and bring on the first signs of the disease. This does not mean that *all* Portuguese Water Dogs have a genetic predisposition to Addison's disease. The majority of PWDs who whelp or fall ill do not end up with their adrenal glands destroyed. Whether genetically predisposed dogs can live their entire lives without some environmental or metabolic stress causing the onset of Addison's disease is not known.

There is presently no gene probe or test available for Addison's disease in man or any animal. The PWDCA Addison's Committee, guided by experts in this disease, is investigating whether tests are possible to identify genetically affected dogs or carriers of Addison's disease.

CANINE HIP DYSPLASIA (HD)

Canine hip dysplasia is a disorder of the hip joints that affects many dog breeds of all sizes. The hip joint is made of cartilage at birth and slowly changes to bone by the age of sexual maturity. Due to the cartilaginous nature of the hips in young dogs, they are pliable, and their anatomy is receptive to change.

To control hip dysplasia, its cause must be understood. As a polygenic disorder, many genes and environmental factors affect the occurrence of hip dysplasia. A critical threshold of these factors must add up to cause the disease. As the genetic factors are the sum of what is passed on from the parents, both parents of affected dogs must be viewed as carrying some "dose" of genes predisposing to hip dysplasia.

Breeders have attempted to control hip dysplasia by breeding only from dogs whose hips have been X-rayed and certified by the Orthopedic Foundation for Animals (OFA). The lack of a significant response to such selection suggests that there is not a gene for OFA-certifiable hips, and that all dogs do not have hip dysplasia due to the same genetic factors.

When evaluating dogs for hip dysplasia, breeders must gather all clinical data that might relate to the genetic factors involved. This data includes (1) palpable joint laxity under anesthesia, (2) clinical signs of hip lameness and (3) radiographic signs of hip subluxation (laxity or distraction index) and/or bone malformation (depth of socket, femoral head).

Laxity and subluxation in a dog with normal anatomy probably have different genetic causes for hip dysplasia than in a dog with no subluxation but malformed sockets. These components of the pelvic X-ray must be reviewed, as well as the OFA grade. Genetically controlled rapid growth in a young dog can cause an incongruity between the bone and soft tissue components of the hip joint. As the head of the femur and the hip socket require congruity to form normally, this can lead to both joint laxity and malformed hips. By selecting against such traits (as opposed to hip joint status as a whole), breeders may find a better genetic response in the offspring.

It is best to do hip evaluations after the recognized age of onset of hip dysplasia (95 percent by two years) but before the genetic potential can be altered (due to osteoarthritis, remodeling and long-term environmental influence). The pelvic radiograph is an objective tool that is part of the total picture of hip dysplasia control.

It is known that "genetically pre-dysplastic hips" can be protected by restricting environmental stress. Such precaution is wise for pet dogs. Current recommendations to get off rapid-growth-promoting puppy foods early and encourage a slower, more uniform growth rate are helpful. Some breeders go to the extreme of not "allowing" stair walking in their puppy contracts. Certainly excessive leaping behavior can alter the shape of the cartilaginous hip at a young age. An area of debate rests with breeding dogs. Do you want to restrict environmental stress, and thus mask the genetic potential of dysplastic development? Most breeders take a middle-of-the-road approach and do not overly restrict or stress young dogs, allowing for a "natural" development of the hip joints.

The most important lesson we learn from studying hip dysplasia is that the breadth of pedigree is as important as the depth. This means that besides determining the hip status of the breeding dog and its parents, breeders must determine the hip status of both the full-siblings of the dog and the full-siblings of the parents. Mating the only two dogs to receive OFA certification from their respective litters does not necessarily increase the chance of producing offspring with good hips. With polygenic disorders, the littermates mirror the genetic potential of the individual breeding dog. In addition, the offspring of breeding dogs should be monitored to see which are passing normal hips with higher frequency, and especially when bred to different mates.

In summary, selection against polygenically controlled disorders such as hip dysplasia involve (1) identifying traits that more closely represent genes being selected against (not OFA grade, but laxity, malformation, clinical signs, etc.), (2) the elimination of nuisance factors that can limit selective pressure against the genes (such as standardizing environmental stress and radiographing at two years of age) and (3) selecting for both breadth and depth of pedigree.

OTHER DISORDERS AND HEALTH CONCERNS

Canine Allergies

Allergies are inappropriate responses from the body's normal defense mechanism (the immune system) that contain bacteria. There is a strong inherited predisposition for allergic reactions. *Contact* allergies occur when the dog rubs repeatedly against an allergen or gets it on its skin. These include, for example, shampoos, grass, or chemicals in carpets and plastics. Antibiotics can also trigger this allergy. *Inhalant* allergies include skin reactions to inhaled substances such as pollens, dust, molds or feathers. *Flea allergy* or *flea bite dermatitis* is yet another vexing problem. Summer eczema is usually caused by fleas and other external parasites. Vegetation, and fungus that lives on vegetation, may also cause allergies. Most allergies are seasonal, lying dormant during the cold months of the year. Symptoms for most allergies are irritations of the eyes, throat or skin, while dogs with frequent ear infections and swollen ears are reacting to food allergies.

Treatment for allergies consists of finding the cause and trying to eliminate it. Antihistamines, such as Benadryl, give temporary rather than long-term relief, but antibiotics do not do much good. In severe cases, veterinarians prescribe cortisone, food additives or changes in diet to relieve intense itching, but bear in mind that allergies are treated, not cured.

Pruritis is a skin disease that begins as an allergic reaction to flea bites and causes intense itching, prompting biting and chewing of hair.

One of the most perplexing allergies to treat in Portuguese Water Dogs is pruritis, a skin disease that begins as an allergic reaction to flea bites. Pruritis causes intense itching, leading to biting and chewing of hair, and sufferers often pull their leg hair out. Treatment with fatty acid supplements provides some help, while switching the dog to a product that contains ingredients the dog has never eaten before, such as fish and potato commercial dog food, helps others. Another treatment is combining the above with antihistamines. Again, an evaluation by your veterinarian is important.

Some PWD puppies whose immune systems are slow to mature may develop an intense, life-threatening allergic reaction to a chemical binder in vaccinations. Scheduled immunizations are usually given at six, ten, fourteen and eighteen weeks. The second and third shots in the vaccination schedules seem the most dangerous. Treatment for the reaction is a powerful antihistamine given by the veterinarian. Only one in several hundred puppies is adversely affected.

Anorexia

Anorexia (loss of appetite), while not frequently seen, may be inherited in Portuguese Water Dogs and is more common in certain lines. Puppies who exhibit an aversion to food may also have developed this behavioral trait as a psychological problem in the whelping box. It is difficult to cure. Rather than lavish too much attention on the puppy when it refuses to eat, dose it with a liquid vitamin daily and add peanut butter or spaghetti to meals at random. Most anorexic dogs outgrow the habit by two years. But some never like dry commercial foods due to its texture. Suggested treatment for these dogs is to feed half dry and half canned commercial dog foods, always picking up the dish after fifteen minutes whether or not the dog has eaten. Any remaining food should be immediately discarded. Another suggestion is to mix a half-cup cooked pasta, flavored with tomato sauce, in with the dog's meal. Spaghetti is a sure-fire canine appetite builder! Because anorexia may be a response to illness, any dog showing the symptoms should have a thorough health check by a veterinarian.

Brucellosis

A small, gram-negative bacterium, *Brucella canis*, causes brucellosis. The disease triggers infertility, resulting in late-term abortions (45 to 55 days gestation), abnormalities in and early death of newborns. It is easily transmitted between breeding dogs at mating, from a dog who either has the disease or is a carrier. Brucellosis spreads quickly through a household (or kennel) by contact with infected tissue or discharges from diseased animals. Some animals with an active infection may show enlargement of the lymph nodes; in others, joints may become swollen temporarily. However, the only sign many dogs exhibit is reproductive failure. While brucellosis is not a common disease among dogs, there is presently no vaccine or treatment either for prevention or cure. All breeding animals should be given a basic serologic (blood) test for *Brucella* by a veterinarian before being bred or exposed to another breeding animal. Many owners of dogs at public stud insist on proof of such testing in bitches presented for breeding.

Calluses

A frequent question from Portuguese Water Dog owners concerns calluses, which are not health risks but often cause discomfort in dogs. Calluses are thickened skin areas that exhibit loss of hair. They form in areas of pressure, usually on elbows and hocks. Some owners rub skin ointments on the affected area. Despite treatment, calluses usually remain for life.

Cancer

The most common tumors of intact females, and the leading form of malignancy, are mammary gland tumors. Because they grow with considerable variety, they may be difficult to detect. Usually these tumors appear at ten or eleven years, although they can occur earlier. A high risk of cancerous tumors exists in Poodles, a near relative of the Portuguese Water Dog.

Other cancers occur in the PWD, including lymphatic cancer, which affects lymph nodes. One of the first signs is swelling of the nodes on the throat, around the testicles or in back of the thigh. Because lymph nodes are interconnected, they can become cancerous before the life-threatening disease is observed. At present there is no cure, but professional treatment can prolong the dog's life. Not all swelling of lymph nodes is cancerous; but when it is noted, make an immediate appointment with your veterinarian for an evaluation.

Cataracts

A cataract is a mark on the lens of the eye, usually developing as a small white area and hardly discernible to the naked eye. Cataracts may involve one or both eyes, completely or partially. Sometimes a cataract is the result of trauma, inflammation or nutritional deficiencies, but frequently it is inherited. Many old dogs develop cataracts, and since the cataracts do not grow rapidly, vision usually is not totally impaired. Cataract surgery is not recommended for dogs. At present, there is no treatment, and a dog so afflicted compensates well with its senses of smell and touch. If in doubt about your dog's vision, a yearly Canine Eye Registry Foundation (CERF) examination by a veterinary ophthalmologist will disclose its formation and growth.

Coprophagy

Coprophagy is the technical name for stool eating. It is neither a disease nor a symptom of one, but rather a habit—an unseemly habit to people but quite natural to dogs, especially those who live in packs. Dogs who practice this unsightly habit develop it genetically or by observing other dogs (usually within their family). It must be remembered the canine is primarily a scavenger; even today, in villages throughout the world dogs are kept to clean away droppings as well as garbage. Treatment consists of keeping premises "squeaky" clean and punishing the older puppy and/or dog at the first sign of indulgence (usually futile, since the habit is self-rewarding). There have been many recommendations to effect elimination of this habit, including (1) placing various ill-tasting products on stools left in yards and (2) mixing products directly in the dog's food that do not hinder it from eating, but that render its waste distasteful to it.

Nursing mothers, of course, clean up their puppies' waste from the moment of birth until puppies are approximately six weeks old. Some puppies practice coprophagy as soon as they are up on their feet. Despite the many advised treatments, there is no cure. Most dogs that manifest the habit prefer fresh stools, which may contain undigested food. In winter months, frozen stools, if not picked up during normal cleaning operations, may be carried around and played with. Dogs that practice coprophagy avoid stools in summer months when swarms of insects feed on the nutrients, leaving only bulk. They usually avoid old stools that have lain on the ground for a period of time, because what they seek from stools are nutrients and old stools no longer contain these. Dogs also seek nutrients from the fresh droppings of other animals, particularly rabbits, horses and cattle. In a similar vein, dirty puddles, which can contain parasites that infect dogs, also can contain minerals dogs crave. To avoid health problems, keep your dogs away from puddles and strange waters.

Diarrhea

Diarrhea is a symptom of a disease or other problem. There are many causes. Simple diarrhea in dogs can be caused by bad food, parasite infection, overfeeding, changes in diet or allergic reactions to inoculations. If your dog is also lethargic, vomits or passes blood in its stool, it needs to be seen by your veterinarian as soon as possible. For short-term home treatment of diarrhea: (1) withhold food for twenty-four hours; (2) if the dogs weighs from forty to fifty-five pounds, give a full tablespoonful of Pepto-Bismol, Kaopectate or Immodium AD every four hours (for smaller dogs, give half a tablespoonful); (3) offer ice cubes, instead of water; (4) after twenty-four hours, offer small amounts of bland food such as boiled white rice and yogurt. Never dose a dog who has diarrhea with antibiotics unless your veterinarian has prescribed them.

Distichiasis

This is a term for extra eyelashes in the upper eyelid out of the neibomian glands. The condition is inherited and is seen in the Portuguese Water Dog.

In most instances, it goes unnoticed by the dog. If severe, it can cause tearing, keratitis and corneal ulcers. Treatment consists of surgical removal of extra lashes.

Epilepsy

Epilepsy is a nervous system disorder that attacks the muscles and can be seen in most breeds. During an epileptic seizure, neurons (nerves) within the brain work independently of each other. Without coordinated effort of the neurons, dogs may lose consciousness or simply become temporarily unaware of their surroundings and have rapid, uncoordinated body movements.

There are two types. In *symptomatic* epilepsy, seizures occur because other physical problems exist (liver disease, impaired circulation, renal disease, brain tumor, etc.). *Idiopathic* epilepsy is characterized by seizures for which no diagnostic cause can be found. This latter type may be inherited and has been seen in the PWD. It probably has a higher incidence in certain lines, but no statistics are yet available. Idiopathic seizures may include a brief loss of consciousness with the dog paddling its feet, urinating or defecating. The seizure ends as suddenly as it appeared. It may also exhibit itself in bizarre behavior patterns, characterized by alterations of thought, perception or emotion. Watching invisible things (called "fly chasing"), aggression, cowering, barking incessantly and hiding are manifestations in otherwise normal animals. Reactions to toxic chemicals may also cause seizures and persist until the toxic material is removed from the environment. Normal age of occurrence in dogs is upon maturity, but epilepsy can appear earlier or later.

If your dog has a seizure, there is nothing much you can do at the moment it occurs. It's better to leave the dog alone while making sure there's nothing it can hurt itself on. Never insert anything into the dog's mouth to try stopping a seizure. Veterinarian-prescribed medicine that is given to help prevent future seizures is available.

Follicular Dysplasia

Dr. William Miller of Cornell University has researched follicular dysplasia for the PWDCA. This rare form of hair loss is an inheritable condition in the Portuguese Water Dog. Loss of hair occurs on flanks, chest, back, abdomen and around the anus. Hair may regrow only to be lost again as the dysplasia progresses. Sometimes loss is so widespread the only hair that remains is on the face and skull. At present, there is no treatment. It has occurred in PWDs with wiry, curly coats with no sex predisposition. Affected dogs often have dull, dry, brittle and thin coats prior to massive hair loss, leaving considerable hair in combs and brushes during grooming. It can begin around the eyes in puppyhood. To eliminate this dysplasia, breeders recommend dogs be bred wavy to curly, not curly to curly. (This author believes the intense inbreeding required to resurrect the breed helped disperse this dysplasia. Breeding wavy

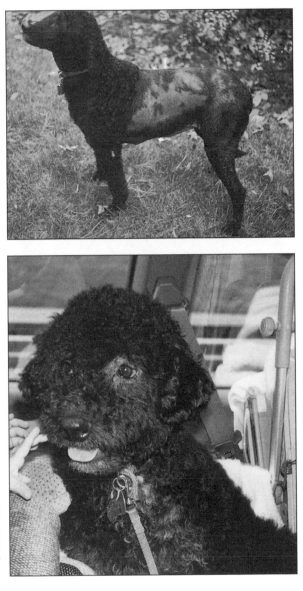

Follicular dysplasia is a disease of the hair follicles. The dogs remain healthy but suffer cosmetic disfiguration most of their lives.

Carriers of the genes for hair loss, as well as those afflicted by follicular dysplasia, often show slight hair loss around one or both eyes whenever stressed.

to curly will only disperse it further.) While dogs with follicular dysplasia are healthy, the cosmetic disfigurement is disturbing.

Foxtails and/or Grass Awns

Foxtails are dangerous barbed grass awns that are easily inhaled. They seek animal passersby and lodge inside ears and noses. While foxtails and grass awns are not a disease, they can cause symptoms that appear to be disease-caused. They not only stick to the coat but can penetrate the skin and, as noted, work their way through tissue to joints.

Dangerous barbed grass awns seek passing dogs and lodge inside their ears and noses.

We had a dog returned to us with a chronic ear and eye problem. Initial examination by our veterinarian uncovered at least ten foxtails embedded deep inside one of his ears. The dog was treated for infections caused by these imbedded foxtails. Investigation into the dog's one weepy eye and prolonged treatment by our veterinary ophthalmologist dissolved one foxtail that had evidently traveled from inside his ear to the optic region of his eye, almost causing blindness. It's been documented that foxtails have traveled through dogs' bodies into their hearts and lungs.

Prevent this environmental hazard from causing harm by keeping your PWD away from fields and roadsides that are overrun with wheatfield weeds. Foxtails are most prevalent from late spring through late fall. If your PWD has traveled in these areas, examine it closely, especially its ears, belly, anus, vagina or penile sheath. If you find a foxtail lodged in one of these areas, take the dog to the veterinarian to remove others, because foxtails seldom travel alone.

Hypothyroidism

This metabolic disease results from a deficiency of hormones secreted by the thyroid gland. It is prevalent in many breeds, including the PWD. Symptoms are hair dryness, hair thinning and weight change. PWDs, with their thick coats, don't usually sit in front of a fire on a cold night or seek the sun on a warm day. However, those with thyroid problems do, because one symptom is for the dog to seek warmth.

Thyroid deficiency can be determined by the veterinarian from a skin biopsy. Dr. Bell suggests the test be done "via a thyroid panel that checks not only T3 and T4, but also T3 and T4 autoantibodies and TSH levels." Treatment consists of veterinarian-prescribed medication given for life.

Temporary Inner Ear Balance Problems

The slower-developing Portuguese Water Dog puppy may experience inner ear balance problems. PWD puppies who suffer from this imbalance often become nauseous during car trips. When at one year these puppies reach full development, balance malfunction, which causes the nausea, disappears. Treatment consists of giving canine anti-nausea pills when traveling. However, this is not a serious problem, and the dog should outgrow it.

Keratitis

Keratitis is inflammation of the cornea, which may be caused by bacteria, viruses, fungi and sometimes by the chemical reaction from puppy vaccinations. The developmental eye film of puppies, which normally dissipates by six weeks, may not leave some puppies until ten to twelve weeks of age; this may be a mild form of keratitis. There are risks of permanent damage to the eye if either of these related conditions is left untreated. A mild keratitis often heals by itself, but a veterinary ophthalmologist examining a puppy at eight weeks of age can determine the exact cause and treat the inflammation successfully with drops and ointments. PWD breeders are wise to have all puppies examined by a veterinary ophthalmologist at eight weeks of age so any eye abnormalities can be identified and treated.

Lameness, a common condition among active breeds, must never be dismissed lightly.

Temporary Lameness

Lameness is a common ailment in active breeds, particularly Portuguese Water Dog puppies. Because they play hard, unmindful of slipping on ice or other unstable ground, and because some actively seek escape from exercise pens, crates and fenced yards by clawing, circling wildly, climbing and jumping out, they pull or tear ligaments. An injured foot, stones under the toes or a broken nail can also cause lameness. Lameness must never be dismissed lightly, so let your veterinarian observe it for a complete diagnosis and the most appropriate treatment.

Lyme Disease

The *Borrelia burgdorferi* bacterium that causes Lyme disease is transmitted by ticks, namely the lone star tick, American dog tick, Pacific coast tick, deer tick, black-legged tick and western legged tick. Difficult to diagnose, the disease begins with fever, lethargy, lymph node enlargement and joint pain with lameness. It is essential to have the dog treated with antibiotics immediately by your veterinarian. In dogs there is a low incidence of chronic complications, as compared to humans, in whom arthritis is likely to set in. Lyme disease is usually, but *not always*, self-limiting in dogs. A vaccine is available. Research is ongoing.

Microphthalmia

When a puppy's eye develops with an abnormally small globe, it is caused by a congenital, recessively inherited defect affecting both eyes, microphthalmia. This disorder is present at birth, but not discernible until the puppy opens its eyes. Accompanying this condition in Portuguese Water Dogs may be cataracts, glaucoma and lack of lenses. Some eyes appear abnormally white when opening, others normal. Affected puppies are often small, require hand feeding, do not thrive, are clumsy, and compensate for loss of sight by use of scent or hearing. There is no treatment available. All PWD puppies, before placement, should be examined by a board-certified ophthalmologist no earlier than eight weeks. Should microphthalmia be diagnosed, culling is, unfortunately, the best course of action. Rarely do dogs afflicted with microphthalmia grow to adulthood; if they do, they are sterile.

Persistent Pupillary Membranes (PPM)

These are remnants of blood vessels in the eyes that do not dissolve normally. Most PPMs disappear by the time the dog is a year of age. If not, vision is impaired and blindness may result.

Pesticide Poisoning

Allergic reactions to herbicides, pesticides and fungicides are common among dogs. There are no data that clearly define the effect of long-term exposure;

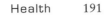

Chemicals used in treating your lawn could harm your dog.

however, it's suspected that these chemicals affect the immune system as well as fertility in animals. Many lawn chemicals are categorized as probable or possible carcinogens. After treatment of your property or that of a neighbor, keep dogs away from the treated area for several days, although there's no proof these chemicals are safe once they are dry. They can remain active for months, during which time they can release toxic vapors.

Symptoms of poisoning from garden products can be deceptive. If a dog develops skin rashes, drools excessively, wheezes, coughs, has muscle pain, cramps or diarrhea, or has a seizure followed by falling into a coma, take it and the product container (if available) immediately to the veterinarian for treatment. Bettina Francis, PhD, a toxicologist, says the symptoms of pesticide poisoning may include breathing difficulties, skin irritations and burns, swelling, loss of weight and appetite, headaches, muscle aches and fever.

Problems with Teeth

In prognathism, the lower jaw is longer than the upper. In lay terms this is often called "undershot jaw." This is evidenced in approximately 20 percent of Portuguese Water Dog puppies. (Prognathism was a prevalent fault in Vasco Bensaude's kennel.) A level bite, where incisors meet tip to tip, is a mild form of prognathism. Another jaw condition seen in the breed is a lower jaw narrower than the upper jaw. This is frequently caused by a faulty bite (malocclusion).

Dr. Gene Rivers, Fellow, Academy of Veterinary Dentistry, says:

Perhaps the most ignored teeth in dogs are the deciduous (baby) teeth. The dog's deciduous teeth normally erupt between three and six weeks and are usually lost before the puppy is six months old. Since the deciduous teeth are present for such a short time, it is easy to ignore them. The deciduous teeth have their own set of problems, however. Ignoring these problems can cause significant damage, while treating them in a timely and accurate manner can have significant benefits for the animal.

Many veterinarians who are not veterinary dentists will recommend watching and waiting when the deciduous tooth remains in the mouth and a permanent tooth is coming in right next to it. Dr. Rivers warns that this is not in the dog's best interest:

Retained deciduous teeth usually cause deviation of the permanent counterpart and result in many malocclusions. These deciduous teeth should be removed as soon as the diagnosis is made. They force the permanent tooth to alter its eruptive plan and may result in a permanent source of pain or infection for the dog. This inevitably leads to periodontal disease, malocclusion or both. If a base narrow condition or dental interlock (*deciduous tooth and permanent tooth*) exists, it should be relieved immediately by a qualified veterinary dentist (Fellow of the Academy of Veterinary Dentistry or Diplomate of the American Veterinary Dental College), who has specialized facilities in his/her office. Two teeth should never be competing for the same socket at the same time.

If you think your PWD may have dental problems, contact the American Veterinary Dental Association, at 1-800-332-AVDA. Its secretary, Carol Barnett, will forward to you names and addresses of the veterinary dentists in your area.

Worms

Worms do great damage to animals. The damage is as varied as the worms themselves. Worms cause gastrointestinal problems, compete for and interfere with nutrient absorption, damage intestinal linings, cause chronic bowel problems (irritation and blood-tinged diarrhea) and on migrations through the body disrupt normal functioning and cause severe skin irritations, often on the feet and legs. Heavy infestations of worms are particularly devastating to puppies and can kill their hosts.

Types of worms are roundworms, hookworms, whipworms, tapeworms and heartworms. Heartworms, of course, are presently the most feared, because they live in the heart and the main arteries to the lungs, causing congestive heart failure. Coccidia and giardia are intestinal parasites, but they are not worms. (Check resource materials.)

A dog owner should use only worm medicines acquired from a veterinarian and follow the veterinarian's instructions. Worm medications differ, and great harm can be done to a dog by dosing it with the wrong kind of worm medicine. Collect a stool sample (a thimbleful is more than enough) and take it to your veterinarian, who will identify the parasite, ask you for your dog's exact weight and give you the proper drug in the proper amount to cleanse your dog of the worms present. Some worm eggs (particularly roundworm eggs) are extremely hardy and remain "infective" in soil for months or even years. Amazingly, freshly passed feces is not infectious; thus, if your dog practices coprophagia (stool eating), this will not spread hookworms or roundworms, although it may infect the dog with other parasites or diseases. Some worms, like hookworms, gain entrance to a dog's body through the skin. Worm treatment is given at intervals of one to two weeks by your veterinarian because worm eggs are only produced at intervals. Tapeworms, however, are not found by routine fecal examinations. Owners of dogs find tiny, white rice-like segments shed on stools. If you observe tapeworm segments on your dog's feces or clinging to his anus, take him to your veterinarian for treatment as soon as possible. Prevention includes quick pickup of your dog's stools, not allowing him to sniff other dogs' feces, keeping his water dish full of clean, fresh water and maintaining a clean environment. It is sometimes necessary to treat heavily infested ground with fresh top soil or to cover the ground with gravel or cement. Reputable breeders have their animals checked for worm infestation each spring. An annual inspection ensures your dog's health and safety from invasion by any worm that threatens.

VACCINATIONS

Every puppy needs to be vaccinated at six weeks against infectious diseases such as distemper, infectious hepatitis, parvovirus, leptospirosis and paraninfluenza. Three more puppy vaccinations follow at ten, fourteen and eighteen weeks. These last three will include the vaccine for coronavirus.

At birth the puppy receives immunity from its mother via her first milk, colostrum. If puppies do not receive this milk due to a dam's inability to nurse or due to her death, they are subject to the above diseases, fatal in many instances. Colostrum protection begins to wane at about five weeks, with protective titers decreasing. A vaccination at six weeks returns the titers, keeping them at an optimum level for another four weeks. Some veterinarians still believe that vaccinations should be given three rather than four weeks apart. However, most agree that titers from previous vaccinations protect the puppy adequately for four weeks. I agree with the latter findings. Why overdo a chemical injection if it is not necessary? At eighteen weeks a rabies vaccination is usually included with the final immunization. In some areas, particularly along the East coast of the United States where there are rabies epidemics in the wild animal population, a puppy's first rabies vaccination may be given at twelve weeks. Also, no puppy can be transported to Canada after twelve weeks of age unless it has had a rabies vaccination.

Every puppy needs to be vaccinated against infectious diseases.

These last puppy vaccinations are good until the dog reaches a year; the dog must then be vaccinated yearly with the second and succeeding rabies shots given, good for from two to three years. Don't neglect the important vaccination program for your dog.

FEEDING YOUR PORTUGUESE WATER DOG

Portuguese Water Dogs are enjoyable to watch eating. Most breeds devour their food without giving a thought to what they are eating. PWDs eat heartily, yet slowly, tasting and enjoying each morsel before they swallow it, be it a dry piece of kibble or a tidbit of fish or steak.

Feed only high-quality food. Dogs fed a quality diet are better able to withstand invasions of parasites—external and internal. Dr. Melinda Beck of the University of North Carolina says, "Disease causing viral mutations slip through the immune defenses of people or animals who are weakened by nutritional deficiency." Since the PWD's background has been oceanic for centuries, a tablespoonful of canned tuna fish (processed in water) or other ocean fish mixed into its commercial food ration, at least three times weekly, is recommended. Be certain all fish and meat is thoroughly cooked. Oil from ocean fish imparts that special sheen to the PWD coat.

Always measure the amount of food you feed at each meal. It is the only way to know how much your dog is or should be eating.

You may wish to add supplements to your dog's commercial diet, such as cottage cheese, tuna fish, tofu, yogurt, simmered ground beef, chicken (completely de-boned), lamb, vegetables and eggs. Raw carrots and bananas are savored by most dogs, as are many kinds of fruit and vegetables. My dogs also dine on outdoor flora, such as field grasses and mushrooms. They happily feast on berries and apples that fall from our trees.

Nutritionists emphasize that supplements should never exceed 25 percent of the dog's commercial intake. If you feed a diet that exceeds this amount, these experts explain, you unbalance the commercial food. Remember, premium commercial dog foods are excellently balanced.

Some also believe dogs do not care if they eat the same food day in and day out. Conversely, those of us who supplement feed our dogs discover they certainly enjoy variety. Dogs not fed natural supplements, we feel, have been deprived!

Feeding Plan

- *Puppies, 8 weeks to 5 months*: Three feedings a day of quality commercial puppy meal, approximately 26 to 27 percent protein, from three-quarters to one cupful at each meal. A variety of supplements may also be fed—cottage cheese, tuna fish, canned puppy food, etc. A valuable food for weaning puppies is ground beef wrapped tightly around grated carrots, baked or microwaved until the meat is done.

- *Puppies, 5 months to 15 months*: Two feedings a day of quality commercial puppy meal, approximately 26 to 27 percent protein, with supplements as desired. According to the dog's weight, feed approximately one to one-and-one-half cupfuls of food at each meal.

- *Adolescents, 15 months to 2 years*: Two feedings a day of quality commercial adult meal, with supplements as desired. The dog should consume (according to weight) from one to two cups of food at each meal.

- *Dogs 2 to 8 years of age*: Two feedings a day of quality commercial adult meal, approximately 21 to 22 percent protein, with supplements as desired. Keep weight optimum. PWDs are prone to "middle-age spread" without sufficient exercise. If by sight and feel (ribs should always be felt) the dog appears to be gaining weight, decrease food intake without resorting to generic or cheap diets containing such undesirable byproducts as processed feathers, corn husks, animal toenails, etc. Adding fibrous, low-calorie foods, such as string beans, may satisfy the dog's hunger when its regular ration is decreased. Give a canine balanced vitamins daily if food intake is decreased by more than one half.

- *Dogs over 8 years of age:* Two feedings a day. Use a quality adult *light-salt* commercial meal. If the dog reduces its desire for exercise, you must reduce the quantity of food. An obese older dog will have a shortened life span.

END OF LIFE

We are indebted to Michael C. Murphy, DVM, of Steamboat Animal Hospital, Olympia, Washington, for the following observations:

Animals do not and never have died of 'old age.' There must be an organ failure. Frequently the heart, kidneys or liver are the reason. If your pet's quality of life is starting to decline, find out why. If you assume it's old age and the time has come, you may prematurely end your friend's life. I have seen many animals make a strong recovery and go on to live another year or two. Keep in mind, an additional two years to a ten-year-old dog is an additional 20-percent life span.

If your pet has a confirmed disease that is unresponsive to traditional or alternative therapy, then it is a matter of understanding what quality of life is for the pet. Every pet and pet owner will interpret this a little differently. This is as it should be, because only the person who is closest to the pet has the real ability to understand how the pet is feeling. If your animal is in pain or is unable to eliminate without soiling itself, then these are clear indications that the time has come. Animals have their own version of honor, and we should respect it.

Pets can die naturally, and sometimes the heart will fail completely and the pet will pass away quickly. More often, the animal becomes compromised, and there would be a period of suffering before death that would 'naturally' occur.

There is a problem with expecting a pet to die 'naturally.' The animal has been taken from its natural wolf ancestry and has been domesticated. In the wild, when an animal starts to fail, nature generally takes the animal's life rapidly, thus minimizing the pain and suffering. People have taken animals out of their natural environment; therefore we have the responsibility for their whole life. Death is the final act of living. Don't be afraid; rather, embrace the responsibility and help your pet transition from this world to what will come after. Keep in mind, your dog was only supposed to live ten to fifteen years. If your Portuguese Water Dog has had a good life of fun and love, let's make sure the end is as good.

chapter 15

Genetics

Exploring canine genetics offers insight into the very essence of life. Scientific advances made during the latter part of the twentieth century are so impressive, future decades promise exciting solutions to hitherto genetic mysteries. Learning about canine genetics opens up a new world. Let's look at some basics together.

Each animal carries gametes, or germ cells, inside its reproductive system. In bitches these gametes are called eggs, each containing thirty-nine chromosomes. She sheds some at each estrus, with the number of ripe eggs shed determining the number of puppies she can carry. An important role of a male's gametes or sperm during fertilization—each carrying either a female or male gene (individual units of inheritance)—is to fix the sex of the puppy.

The eggs descend from the bitch's ovaries and float into the Fallopian tubes (oviducts). There each awaits a male's germ cell (sperm), each of which contains thirty-nine chromosomes (the same number as for the egg). During a mating, millions of sperm, carried forward like a riptide, stream into the tubes. Only one sperm can attach itself to an egg; all others are repulsed, to die. The union of the egg and sperm, each containing thirty-nine chromosomes, now produces a new cell called a zygote. The zygote, containing seventy-eight chromosomes—half from each parent—will, upon maturity, become a newborn Portuguese Water Dog puppy.

Housed inside each of these seventy-eight chromosomes are thousands and thousands of genes. They are lined up like decorated soldiers along the length of each rod-like chromosome. Nature, in its grand and varied panorama of life, sets the scene for the next act: birth of a new life. A puppy will be born in about sixty days with half of what its dam has contributed to its life and half of what its sire has given.

Amazingly, genes are passed down from generation to generation on the chromosomes belonging not only to the dam and sire, but to their ancestors as well. It's a fantastic mosaic pattern. Each newly paired gene contributes physical and mental characteristics to the developing puppy. Since there are over 25,000 genes on each pair of chromosomes, each dog is unique, even within the same breed! Each is uniquely designed. This makes breeding fascinating and intensely creative to the breeder.

When breeding dog to dog, when understanding the laws of genetics, when knowing many of the genes the sire and dam possess and some of what their ancestors possess, breeders can be pretty sure certain traits will be passed down to the puppies.

But here's a kicker! Even the most astute breeder does not know all the traits the genes carry. As you will see, that's why inbreeding and line breeding should never be attempted by a novice. For certain, they are done cautiously by experts. Responsible breeders do not want their bitches to whelp defective puppies.

INBREEDING

Incestuous breeding, generally termed inbreeding, is designed to produce identical genes mirroring physical and mental characteristics of one or more ancestors. The breeder selects dogs of superior quality, close relatives of dogs in the pedigree—sister to brother or mother to son are examples of inbreeding. The breeder is "doubling up on genes"—preserving genes present in the animals being mated as well as seen in the ancestors who preceded them.

Unfortunately, inbreeding doesn't always work. Not all of the genes that come forward in a mating will be good. Some are defective, and others simply don't yield the desired results. Inbreeding, therefore, should never be attempted by anyone not familiar with the genetic material of ancestors in a seven- or eight-generation pedigree. This is a plea to beginning breeders never to attempt inbreeding until you have first-hand knowledge of the favorable and unfavorable genes present in the lines with which you are working. You learn this by investigating the health and temperament of the offspring whelped in previous matings, or, if this is the first time the particular dogs are being used for breeding, by making full inquiries via telephone, letters and photographs into as many of the ancestors and their offspring as possible. Puppies born with health problems are not easy to discard, unlike vegetables, trees or plants grafted together for certain characteristics that don't work out. Faults that sneak in from the past make for heartache. Nevertheless, inbreeding, judiciously practiced, "stamps" a strain with a certain look, and most breeders inbreed to create their own strain.

LINE BREEDING

Many reputable kennels practice line breeding, which is a gentler form of inbreeding. It, too, requires excellent dogs, with both sire and dam conforming to the breed's Standard. Common ancestors may be niece, uncle and cousin. Line breeding takes more time than inbreeding to create the strain the breeder seeks, but is not as risky. Naturally, line breeding exposes genetic faults as well as genetic virtues. These, in the hands of a knowledgeable breeder, can be eradicated or perpetuated through a continuous breeding program. This looser type of breeding allows variations in type, soundness, balance and size.

Reputable breeders using inbreeding and line breeding study genetics, investigate pedigrees of sire and dam, chart two to three options they believe may occur in planned breedings, breed, study results, chart what is learned, and replot another breeding. A second mating of the same bitch and stud may produce completely different puppies. Nature, with irrepressible humor, tells us, one and all, that life is change! Each life is new! Life is unique each and every time expressed. Dr. Jerald S. Bell says, "While we expect uniformity in inbred and tightly linebred litters, the appearance (phenotype) of the offspring depends on which one-half of all genes are inherited from each parent, and how they combine with the genes from the opposite parent."

OUTCROSSING

Outcross breeding is used when purebred dog breeders wish to infuse their strain with a quality it needs that another strain possesses. Properly, once the gene is implanted in their line, they then return to line and inbreeding.

Outcrossing is the popular system. The outcross scenario goes like this: dog owner advertises she is looking for a stud (of the same breed) with AKC papers. What the bitch's owner usually wants to do is to produce puppies that are like the dog she presently has.

Unfortunately, unless you have conducted a study of the ancestors of the dogs you are breeding, this type of breeding is like filling a bag with marbles of all colors. Take out a handful, say six or seven. What you see is what you get. Pedigree evaluation in too many outcrossings is not important; no one can predict results when there are few so known hereditary factors. Undesirable inheritable traits may haunt the puppies produced. When a breed becomes popular and a puppy with no known pedigree information is offered for sale, be forewarned. Many carry temperament and physical problems that will send them to pounds to be euthanized once their cute puppyhood is over and defects appear.

TEST BREEDING

If a purebred line has health faults caused by a simple recessive gene, and there are no genetic tests to identify the carriers of the defective gene, then some breeders espouse "test breedings." Tests are conducted with the knowledge the breeder is going to spend great amounts of money clearing the line of a particular health problem.

Let's examine a test breeding of a Portuguese Water Dog whom the breeder wishes to clear of being a carrier for Progressive Retinal Atrophy (PRA):

1. Breeder chooses a top-quality dog—as close to mirroring the Standard as possible—that has been tested and cleared of PRA.
2. The breeder mates this dog to a dog that has the disease.
3. When the puppies are born, the breeder places them with owners willing to accept a puppy who "might go blind within a few years."
4. When the puppies reach two years, the breeder pays for individual ophthalmoscopic (CERF) and electroretinogram (ERG) examinations. If none have the disease or show signs of its development at this point, and if seven or more individuals are tested, the breeder receives notification from the testing institution giving the confidence of normalcy that the dog now has (greater than 99 percent confidence with seven normal offspring and none affected).

But if some of the two-year-olds show signs of the disease, the tested parent is now known to carry the defective gene. It is an *obligate carrier* for PRA and must not be used for further breeding. All puppies in the litter are also obligate carriers, being offspring of the original affected dog. Mathematically close to one-half of the litter will be affected; the other half will be carriers of the defective gene. All of the litter should be neutered or spayed. As Dr. Bell says, "Test breedings to a carrier parent instead of an affected one require sixteen normal offspring and none affected to attain 99 percent confidence of normalcy." (Refer to Chapter 14, "Health.")

If there were not at least seven puppies in a given litter, the money spent and the breeding will have been wasted, unless the breeder repeats the breeding to statistically clear the dog. (Seven puppies are needed for statistical clearance.) The breeder has to repeat the "test breeding."

Scientists rate a dog's PRA status in three ways: dogs who do not test as having the disease are classified *normal*; dogs who carry the defective gene but do not have the disease are *carriers*; and dogs who develop PRA are *affected*.

If a normal dog is bred to another normal dog, all offspring will be normal. If a normal dog is bred to a carrier, while none of the offspring will have the disease, approximately half will be carriers. If a normal dog is bred to an affected, *all* will be carriers. If a carrier is bred to another carrier, approximately one-quarter of the offspring will be affected, one quarter normal, with the other 50 percent carriers. If a carrier is bred to an affected, 50 percent are affected and 50 percent are carriers. An affected parent bred to another affected will produce all affected offspring. This can be a desperate situation.

At present, dogs can be ERG tested at two years of age to determine whether they have the disease. There is presently no test that identifies carriers. Until carriers are identified and removed from breeding programs, PRA has the potential to spread throughout the gene pool.

Simple Recessive Gene (applicable in Portuguese Water Dogs to PRA and GM-1).

Note: A simple recessive gene is a gene complete in itself. It does not require the action of other genes to become active.

N/N—Normal to Normal—all normal offspring

N/C—Normal to Carrier—50% normal, 50% carriers

C/A—Carrier to Affected—50% affected, 50% carriers

C/C—Carrier to Carrier—25% affected, 25% normal, 50% carriers

N/A—Normal to Affected—100% carriers

A/A—Affected to Affected—100% affected.

As one breeder, former PWDCA president Maryanne Murray, said:

If I bred a bitch tomorrow for my own test breeding, I'd have puppies in two months. They'd be ready for CERFs and ERGs in two years. If everything went perfectly (and how often does that happen?), if I had seven healthy pups and they all ERG'd clear I'd be in great shape. I'd have devoted two years to this testing project plus a great deal of money. On the other hand, if all did not go perfectly, I would have invested two years, many dollars and a lot of effort into producing (possibly) PRA affected animals. Now I'm back to square one. Do I start over again? What's the point? It certainly would be a lot easier and less heartbreaking to put the dollars spent on test breeding into donating that money to research so scientists can develop a blood test which could be available in the same two to three years to everybody (not just myself).

What Ms. Murray says makes sense. Why take a chance on producing dogs who will go blind in two to three years? It wasn't so many years ago that test breedings were necessary in order for scientific advances to be made. Today's research by animal geneticists render many of these breedings unnecessary and cruel. Today, the answer is to fund research programs for scientists. Let scientists develop programs designed to find out the cause of a disease and eradicate it efficiently. Cooperative efforts benefit all. Single efforts benefit only a few individuals and do little to remove a defective gene from the breeding pool.

MISALLIANCES

Accidents occur. Dogs who should not mate sometimes do. If one of your prized bitches is bred accidentally, wait out the pregnancy. Few facts are known about short- or long-term side effects of hormonal shots given to abort pregnancies. Place resulting puppies in pet homes after you have them spayed and/or neutered at eight or ten weeks.

"NICK" MATINGS

Some breedings "nick," or prove highly successful. Such a mating produces uniformly excellent puppies. If you are fortunate enough to have conducted such a breeding and can do it again, by all means repeat it!

FLYERS

Flyers are outstanding puppies. These never go through the awkward stage during adolescence that most puppies do. They come into the world with superior structure and temperament and retain their coveted quality throughout life.

MUTATIONS

Mutations are accidents of nature. They are genetic abnormalities. If undetected, they have the potential to damage a strain, a line or a breed. The PRA gene is one example of a genetic mutation.

A SPECIAL GENE?

There are several breeds of dogs who have the ability to "grin" (e.g., Dalmatians and Doberman Pinschers). The gene that controls the grin works with the upper jaw in these breeds. This gene is not expressed in the Portuguese Water Dog. However, the PWD has the ability to smile with the lower jaw. They have the ability to drop their lower lip, exposing their lower teeth. It is the only breed I know of with this ability.

WHAT TO LOOK FOR—THE STANDARD TELLS US

By studying the words in the Portuguese Water Dog Standard, you learn what to look for in choice of bitch or stud. Let's examine, for a moment, some of the words in both the FCI and American standards that tell us about body lines. The FCI Standard states under General Appearance and Aptitude: "Meso-morphal, sub-convexilinial type showing tendencies towards the rectilineal; bracchoid form....Well balanced, robust and well muscled."

What do these words mean to the layperson?

Meso-morphal designates a muscular, physical body type. The American Standard describes it as "strong substantial bone, well developed, neither refined nor coarse and a solidly built, muscular body.

Rectilineal means characterized by straight lines. The Portuguese Water Dog is characterized by straight lines in its firm, straight back and balanced body: "Legs, viewed from the rear, are parallel to each other, straight and very strongly muscled in upper and lower thighs."

The American Standard, unlike the FCI Standard, which calls for a square dog, calls for an off-square body, "slightly longer than tall when measured from prosternum to rearmost point of the buttocks, and from withers to ground."

Even though the two Standards differ slightly, they both call for balanced dogs. The FCI states the requirement as "balanced"; the American Standard implies the same in "unexaggerated, functional conformation."

It is which dogs are chosen from the litter that determines how the breeder's line looks. While the Standard is the architect's drawing plan, the breeder is the builder. The Algarbiorum dogs of Bensaude's had long legs and were off-square in build. The de Alvalade dogs of Cabral were smallish, had shorter legs and were long in back. Sometimes breeders build on flood plains, so to speak, in choosing a puppy. If the breeder chooses a puppy because she wants a lot of white, and that puppy has short legs, her stock stands a good chance of being flooded with pups who have short to medium legs along with the generous white markings. Breeding a short-legged dog to a long-legged dog yields variances in the legs of their puppies, because modifying genes (genes that effect a change in the trait of some dominant and recessive genes) play a part in leg length. At present there are allowances for leg length in the PWD. The accent is on strong, substantial bone and solidly built, muscular bodies. That's why the type of leg presently seen in the show ring varies. As long as the breeders' selections move their legs in a straight line and display the suppleness necessary to this muscular working dog, these variances are allowed. Diversity is permitted in the growth of a breed (the spreading of genes) as long as breed type and soundness are maintained.

Coats, both in texture and type, will remain variable for a long time. Even though the Portuguese Water Dog wears either a wavy or curly coat—both breed characteristics—there are variations within these categories. Wavy coats may be flat or may have loose waves, a cluster of loopy waves or tight waves. Curlies range from loose curls to compact curls, tight curls and wiry curls. The Standard calls for wavies to have coats "falling gently in waves, not curls, and with a slight sheen." Curly coats must be in the form of "compact, cylindrical curls, somewhat lusterless." A wiry coat is not desirable; the loose curl falls apart in grooming. Coats dry better if texture is strong. You can tell which puppies will be curly when they are still wet with birth fluids—their coats form tight little ripples. Puppies with slight coat indentations may develop soft curls. The true wavy newborn coat looks like a seal's, shiny and smooth.

Some wavy coats remain absolutely flat without any wave until puppies are six to eight months old; other coats indent within a few weeks of birth and end up with tight, loopy waves. It is extremely difficult for a breeder to tell which are "improper" coats at birth. Sometimes the improper coat carries a red cast. As these puppies develop, no hair grows between toes, belly hair is scant, leg hair only feathered and hocks and muzzles clean. Improperly coated PWDs cannot be definitely evaluated until pups are up on their feet, at about five weeks old. A responsible breeder who encounters improper coats in a breeding with a particular bitch or stud informs all potential puppy buyers of the fact.

Two photographs showing the same improperly coated dog. The first photo shows the bitch at five weeks; the second photo shows her at one year. The feathering on the legs, hocks and pasterns consists of incorrect, straight hair. Courtesy Kathryn Braund

Which coat is dominant—wavy or curly? Many breeders have bitches who whelp only wavies even if the stud and most of the dogs in the pedigree are curly. In my research, in most litters, wavies outnumber curlies. PWDCA member Ms. Sandy Saybolt has done an in-depth study on coat dominance in the Portuguese Water Dog. Her findings indicate the curly coat dominant, wavy recessive. Dr. Bell says, "In a genetic database, there are 2,474 curlies and 2,189 wavies. Of course this cannot have a great bearing, unless examined with the parent and offspring types." Ms. Saybolt's analysis of coat type, based on information in the PWDCA's *Directory of Dogs*, is convincing evidence for curly being dominant over wavy. Research is ongoing.

COLORS

Black is dominant, brown (red) recessive. Distribution of unpigmented markings (white areas) follows the same pattern in all dogs: (1) white on chest, feet, muzzle and end of tail; (2) white on whole chest, legs and stomach; (3) white extending to shoulders and withers; (4) white covering flanks and back; and (5) white ending with a variety of spots and splotches. Unpigmented areas are due to modifiers which were genetically honed into the breed. (For more information, refer to Chapter 6.)

Bensaude bred for solid colors. His first litter, Leão ex Dina (May 1, 1937), consisting of four males and four bitches, contained one male, Lagos, who was completely white; one male, Olhão, white and light gray; one bitch (name unavailable), white and gray; and one bitch, Fuzeta, brown. The other puppies were black with white markings. His tenth litter, Leão ex Murta (Leão ex Venesa), whelped September 23, 1941, consisted of six males and five bitches. One male, Alvor, was white, and one bitch, Bolina, black with white markings. (The other puppies in that litter were small and weak, and because raising them would have been difficult during wartime, they were culled.) Because Bensaude did not like the lack of pigmentation on noses and around eyes in the dogs with a great deal of white, he did not continue the process of breeding for white. Neither did he like spots or blotches or gray on black, even though in 1950 he registered a black-gray dog (not a black dog with the graying factor, but one born black and gray). Bensaude bred for solid blacks and solid browns by avoiding parti-colored and piebald dogs in breeding. He preferred rust brown or coal black animals, although few were self- (solid) colored; most showed Irish spotting (dominant over solid color). Coats of some of his dogs did change to salt and pepper, which is still common today. Bensaude's Algarbiorums' main problem was a tendency toward undershot jaws.

Many PWDs have a graying factor. A recessive gene, it may show up in 25 percent of the dogs in a litter. Some puppies turn gray during their first year of life; others retain black hairs until three years of age. Most browns clear to a cream or gray out by maturity. Undoubtedly, if brown is bred to brown for several consecutive generations, color will dilute to cream. For depth of color, breeders have to replenish pigment and breed brown back to black periodically. The few white hairs self-colored or Irish spotted dogs get as they age are not due to the graying factor, but are a natural manifestation of the aging process. They come from a separate gene modifier.

Coat Color Genetics of Portuguese Water Dogs

There are two main coat colors in PWDs, black and brown. In genetic language, color genes are given symbols. The capital letter B stands for black, the lowercase letter b stands for brown. A dominant color gene is always expressed with a capital letter; recessive genes are expressed with lowercase letters. All genes occur in pairs—one from the dam, one from the sire. For example:

Sire is black (BB). Dam is black (BB).

They have four puppies. All puppies will be black. In genetic language they are *BB, BB, BB,* and *BB*.

Sire is brown *(bb)*. Dam is brown *(bb)*.

All four puppies will be brown. In genetic language they are *bb, bb, bb,* and *bb*.

Now, suppose the black sire carries the recessive brown (b) gene. He is a color hybrid (Bb). If the black dam is genetically pure for the dominant trait (BB), all the puppies from this mating will be black, but 50 percent will have the mathematical chance of carrying the brown gene: BB, BB, Bb, Bb. For each puppy in the litter to carry the brown (b) gene, one parent must be brown: Bb × bb. The pure recessive (bb) parent can contribute only the recessive brown gene to its offspring. The puppies produced could be Bb, Bb (two black puppies carrying the brown gene) and two brown puppies: bb, bb. If a male Bb is bred to a female Bb, the puppies could be all black, or at least three of the four puppies should be black (because B is dominant), yet all will carry the brown gene. If a hybrid black (Bb) is bred to a pure dominant black, half the offspring will mathematically be BB and half Bb.

BB × BB = BB, BB, BB, BB

bb × bb = bb, bb, bb, bb

Bb × BB = Bb, Bb, BB, BB

Bb × bb = Bb, Bb, bb, bb

Bb × Bb = Bb, Bb, bb, BB

NOTE: The mathematical average of 25 percent is seldom expressed. In PWDs, brown dogs from Bb ×Bb litters (as stated above) usually fall in the 10 to 20 percent ratio.

When an advertisement carries the words "Our Black stud carries the brown gene," you know that either his dam or sire was brown, the other black; you also could know this because the stud produced brown in previous litters. If the owner of a bitch tells a breeder, "We'd like to breed our black bitch to a brown stud to see if she carries the brown gene," you know both parents were black, with one carrying the brown gene. She must be bred to a brown to determine whether she is *BB* or *Bb*.

In Portugal, a Water Dog with more than 30 percent white is disqualified from becoming a champion. However, the American Standard calls for no such disqualification. As a result, departure from expected coat color variations in black or brown PWDs are considerable. Genetic coat color definitions in dogs have not been studied by many geneticists; an exception was Clarence C. Little, Sc/D, who was a director at the famed Jackson Memorial Laboratory in Bar Harbor, Maine, and author of the world classic book *The Inheritance of Coat Color in Dogs.* Much of our knowledge of canine color genetics come from his profound study of the subject.

Some genes listed below have alleles. Alleles are modifiers of a dominant gene.

A controls the *distribution* of dark and light pigment.

As permits distribution of dark color over the entire body.

At produces *tan points,* bi-colors (black and tan), as seen in Doberman Pinschers.

av indicates various areas of *persistent* dark pigment with other areas where pigment varies tremendously (as in the browns not determined in PWDs).

B produces *black* pigment in *any* area.

b produces *liver* (brown) pigment in *any* area.

Series C gives *full* pigmentation, like *dense* black.

c ch causes pigment to *turn light cream or white.*

D controls *density* of pigment.

d indicates blue *dilution* (not determined in PWDs).

Series E allows *formation* of black or brown pigment over the whole body.

e indicates *suggestion of red* in dark-pigmented hairs.

G indicates *graying factor from birth* to old age.

g produces *white hairs* as animal *ages*.

M, the merle gene, also produces *irregular patches of color along with increasing areas of white*.

MM, the double dominant gene, is semi-lethal. In some breeds it causes deformities, sterility, blindness and completely white coat color. It causes microphthalmia in some breeds, including the PWD. Microphthalmia is caused by a congenital, recessively inherited defect. The puppy's eye develops with an abnormally small globe, with affected puppies small and unthrifty. Accompanying this condition in Portuguese Water Dogs may be cataracts, glaucoma and lack of lenses. There is no treatment available, and rarely do puppies afflicted with this disease grow to adulthood; if they do, they are sterile.

pp produces *champagne* and *silver* by *reducing* dark pigment.

Series S involves *solid* or *self* color. Some dogs may have *minute* white markings; toes or chest are the definite locations.

NOTE: Although parti-color is not a technical term, at present the Portuguese Water Dog Fancy defines dogs with more than 30 percent unpigmented areas (white) as parti-colored.

s, indicates *Irish spotting* (definite locations are muzzle, forehead, feet, tail tip, belly, throat and neck.

Parti-colored C. Camerell's Delta Clipper, UD, owned and photographed by Verne Foster.

s$_p$ indicates *piebald spotting*, with only *15 to 20 percent of coat pigmented*.

s$_w$ indicates *extreme* piebald spotting, with *only ear, eye or tail patch colored*.

Series T acts as a *dominant*, producing in white areas *flecks* or *ticks* of color.

tt indicates dogs with *clear white* areas *without* ticking.

Piebald spotted Ch. Down-East Double Take, TT, owned by Steven Dostie.

This parti-colored puppy was one of the first to appear in the United States from American breeding. The puppy is from a litter out of Cherna Abialheira (Ch. Charlie de Alvalade ex Granja Cherna) and was whelped on October 15, 1982. Maureen Dahms was the breeder.

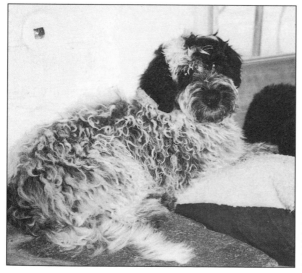

Roseknoll Spencer Crest Sunrider, a double Irish-ticket parti-color owned by Phyllis Zusman and Helen Ruvelas, at fourteen weeks. Courtesy Phyllis Zusman

In December 1981, two piebald PWDs were whelped in the United States. Shortly thereafter, three more breeders told of parti-colored or piebald PWDs being whelped. Donald F. Patterson, DVM, D.Sc, Chief, Section of Medical Genetics at the University of Pennsylvania School of Veterinary Medicine, was asked to evaluate the color of one. He stated, "The S series of alleles is greatly influenced by modifying genes which affect the degree of white spotting." He said it was not easy to discern from looking at the dog its exact genotype.

Genetic study tells us solid color is dominant over Irish spotting and Irish spotting is dominant over piebald. In the PWD, Irish spotting appears dominant over solid color. Only dogs who have been given a "double dose" of the piebald allele would have piebald spotting.

Dr. Patterson did not see any specific health problems with these color patterns in the Portuguese Water Dog except in noting that some breeds with extreme degrees of white spotting, such as the Dalmatians, have a problem with deafness.

The American gene pool of the Portuguese Water Dog carries these color genes, since "anything goes" in the contemporary color pattern of American PWDs.

A	B	C	D	E	G	M	P	S	T
as	b	ch	d	e	g	MM	pp	si	t
at								sp	
av								sw	

For a full understanding of color genes, refer to Clarence S. Little's book, *The Inheritance of Coat Color in Dogs.*

Petra Schaefer, who conducted an intense genetic survey for the PWDCA in the late 1970s and early 1980s, stated, "There will be many different types of patterning, as well as many color patterned combinations introduced in the gene pool to be seen in the future if one perpetuates parti color." Schaefer also stated that to "cull Parti, eliminate parti color dogs and all identified carriers from the breeding pool. To perpetuate parti, selectively breed parti and/or carriers for parti color." Schaefer also stated that the gene for eye color "is not linked to any of the color related genes, thus will segregate independently."

chapter 16

American Breeders of the Portuguese Water Dog

The responsible purebred dog breeder's story is one of love—of dedicated people banded together to develop the best companion animal they can. Not only do they strive to improve the breed they love but also to place dogs with others who wish to share and benefit from the true breeders' level of commitment.

These accounts detail how some of the premier Portuguese Water Dog breeders became involved and made their imprint on this exciting canine's modern history.

ALTO MARE

Lisa Hubbart of Petaluma, California, has been involved in grooming, showing, breeding and raising dogs for most of her life. She handled approximately twenty-five Portuguese Water Dogs in the show ring before beginning her own breeding program. Her favorite canine family member is Int., Am. Ch. Alto Mare Candura, CDX, CGC, JWD. Lisa and Candy made their debut in the Obedience ring at the first PWDCA National Specialty (1992) in New York, winning their class. At the second National Specialty (1993) in Minnesota, Candy won an Award of Merit and at the third National Specialty (1994) in California. Hubbart, with a broken toe and injured knee, entered the ring with one of Candy's sons and won Best in Breed. From 1988 through 1995, Lisa Hubbart has produced thirty-two PWD champions.

Lisa Hubbart with Int., & Am., Ch. Alto Mare Candura, CDX, after winning a first in the obedience trial at the PWDCA 1992 Specialty. John Ashbey

Ch. Brinmar's Back to the Future, a double granddaughter of Ch. Keel Tonel, owned and handled by Maryanne Murray. John Ashbey

BRINMAR

Prior to becoming active with PWDs, Maryanne Murray of Lansdale, Pennsylvania, competed in Obedience with German Shepherd Dogs. Her involvement with PWDs began in 1979 when she purchased Brilha (Trezena

Konstelada) and became a devoted fancier. She has served as PWDCA president, corresponding secretary, member of the board of directors, editor of *The Courier*, chair of the breed Standard committee, chair of the inheritance of color committee and general education coordinator, as well as a participant on other club committees. Murray also is the first owner-handler to put a conformation championship on a PWD in the United States—in February 1984, with Brilha. She continues to handle her own dogs in the conformation ring.

CAMERELL

Breeder Cathy Kalb says, "The one factor that sets Portuguese Water Dogs apart from other Working breeds is their water abilities. Because of the multifactored nature of their tasks, they were required to be a brave, thinking, and at times, independently functioning assistant to the fisherman. We who have chosen to preserve and protect PWDs must always value their working abilities first and foremost."

Kalb's foundation bitch was Meera, Ch. Natale do Mar, a natural around boats and water. Meera whelped four litters totaling thirty-one puppies, twelve of which became champions. Camerell dogs have achieved impressive performance records. Camerell's Call Me Cooper, CDX, AWD, AAD, ROM, was the first dog of any breed to obtain the Agility Dog title, and Ch. Camerell's Buccaneer Beaver, UD, TD, AAD, CWD, obtained the first Courier Water Dog title.

COCOA PORT

Sheila and Allen Silver purchased their first PWD, a brown curly named Mindy, Ch. Firmamento's Zingara do Mar, in the early 1980s for their

Cathy Kalb's Ch. Natale do Mar, dam of twelve champions. Meera is shown here three weeks before the birth of her first litter.

children. They soon became devoted fanciers and dedicated breeders, with Mindy producing in 1985 the first litter from brown American champion parents. In 1989 the Silvers became concerned when they felt a newly proposed revised breed Standard placed undue emphasis on pigment, which they believed would ultimately lead to discrimination against brown dogs, resulting in a narrowing of the already narrow gene pool. Due to their efforts, no change was made. The Silvers continue to breed occasionally.

CUTWATER

Jane Harding of Darien, Connecticut, never intended to become a dog breeder, yet she has been one since 1985. A rambunctious black wavy puppy, White Cap Craca, changed Harding's mind. Craca's second litter contained the top-producing, top-winning and performing Ch. Cutwater's Bonaventure, and life for Harding hasn't been the same since.

   Through December 1995, Cutwater has produced thirty-eight conformation champions, five with water titles, four with Obedience titles and three winning Agility awards. "My goal," says Harding, "has always been to produce Portuguese Water Dogs that are healthy, beautiful, easy to live with and capable of working. I'm very fortunate. I started out with a beautiful bitch who proved herself in both rings, and through effort and luck, I was able to create a breeding program that now has several generations of dogs who have proven themselves in both rings."

A multi-performance dog, Ch. Cutwater's Bonaventure CD CGC AWD USDAA Agility Dog, bred and owned by Jane Harding, Cutwater Kennels. Courtesy Animals Only

DACHER

Dr. David and Cheryl Smith of Los Gatos, California, purchased their first Portuguese Water Dog in 1987 and have been actively breeding and showing since 1990. They have bred and campaigned four dogs in the PWDCA's Top Ten Show Dog standings each year since. Among their most notable winners are Ch. Roughrider's Sereia Analada, Ch. Dacher's Gotta Get A Gund, Ch. Rough Seas Monsoon and Ch. Dacher's L'Attitude. In 1991, Mrs. Smith became founding president of the regional club, the PWDC of Northern California. She has been a co-chairman of two PWDCA National Specialties, in 1994 and again in 1996, and has served on the PWDCA Board and as a club officer. The Smiths train their dogs in both agility and water work.

DE LEÃO

Renee Reiherzer of Newburgh, Indiana, became a member of the PWDCA in 1986. Her foundation stud, Sardio, Ch. Ilara Sardio, Reiherzer says, "is the heart and soul of my kennel." Sardio had Working Group placings in 1987, 1988 and 1989. A popular stud dog, he earned his Apprentice Water Dog (AWD) title in 1995, just ten days before his tenth birthday. Says Reiherzer, "Sardio proves that it's easy to teach an old dog new tricks. It takes patience to work with the owner."

Reiherzer waited two years for her first Portuguese Water Dog. "Sardi came home with me at seven weeks of age and spent the first twenty-four hours on a pillow. I remember looking at him and wondering where the heck

Ch. Ilara Sardio is the foundation stud for Renee Reiherzer's De Leão Kennels. He is shown here, with his owner at left, winning Best of Breed under Muriel Freeman at the 1989 Purina Invitational dog show. Kim Booth

the excitement was! But a day later he got off the pillow and we've never looked back. As a breeder and exhibitor I've made good friends nationwide. I've often been asked if this is my profession. The answer is no, but it's my passion."

DOWNEAST

Steven Dostie of Greene, Maine, grew up with dogs. Involved in showing, training and breeding for many years, Dostie's first PWD was one of his obedience students. "Betsy was a three-month-old ball of brown fluff, hobbling into my obedience class. She had broken her toe the day before and her owner, a veterinarian, put a cast on half-way up her front leg. When her owner found out she could not keep her, I took her in, but with no plans to keep her. I was active working with my three Rottweilers. But Betsy fit in fine, working her power over my dogs. The rest is history. She used her power on me, too, and grew up to be one of the most titled Portuguese Water Dogs."

One of the first PWD Utility Dog titlists, Betsy is the breed's first Canadian Obedience Trial Champion, winning that title at eight years of age after five years of retirement from the ring. The dam of ten champions and numerous Obedience and water-titled offspring, she is the dam of Dostie's stud dog Diego, Am., Can. Ch. DownEast Diego de Armada, Am. CDX, Can. CD, TT, AWD. Diego won a blue ribbon at the PWDCA's first Specialty, going first in the six to nine months puppy dog class. Two years later he won Best of Winners at the third PWDCA Specialty. In 1995, he became the first PWD groomed in the Lion trim to win Best of Breed at the Westminster KC show. He also won an Award of Merit at the 1995 PWDCA Specialty.

Ch. DownEast Diego De Armada, CDX, Can. CD, owned by Steve Dostie, DownEast Kennels. Tom Bruni

FARMION

William J. Trainor, a former Poodle breeder, renowned professional handler and American Kennel Club judge, and his wife, Elizabeth Trainor, DVM, handled Ch. Charlie de Alvalade, Ch. Rebento Don Carlos, and many other PWDs for Deyanne and Herbert Miller, Jr. After Mrs. Miller passed away, Herbert Miller asked the Trainors if they would like to carry on with the dogs, under the Farmion name, as his main interest had been Charlie. The Trainors say, "We never regretted the decision, and shall continue to breed PWDs under the Farmion banner into the distant future."

HELMS ALEE

Joanne Forsythe of Gig Harbor, Washington, started her kennel with Roughrider's Megan of Jaisal, who had begun her show career with this author after being returned from an unhappy owner. Megan became an outstanding producer. One of Megan's daughters, Am., Can. Ch. Helms Alee Summertime, became the first PWD (and the only female through 1995) to win a Best in Show in Canada. The exciting date was January 30, 1993; the show, Ladies Kennel Club of British Columbia.

JEWELL DE AGUA

"An Alaskan fisherwoman at the time I acquired my first PWD," says Katrina Jez, "my primary concern was to own a good boat dog. Matia Jewell de Agua (Ch. Farmion Geo, UD ex Starview's Sarah Emmaline) was all that and more, a diplomat for the breed in every harbor. She became the foundation bitch of my kennel in 1989 with one of her sons, Ch. Jewell de Agua Windward Lad, winning a Best in Show." Jez breeds for the all-around dog, with the desire to keep water work ability foremost. It is her hope, Jez says, "that the perpetuation of water work will nurture a breed whose form indeed follows function."

LA SERENE

Dr. Thomas Strain of Albuquerque, New Mexico, conducted a vast amount of breed homework before purchasing his first PWD. His dogs' successes in both the conformation ring and whelping box prove the value of his thoughtful study in acquiring the best foundation dogs possible. His South American, Int., Puerto Rican, Am. Ch. Regala's Cierra of La Serene, CD, TD, was the first bitch with these titles, winning all before she was twenty-eight months old. At home, Dr. Strain's dogs enjoy roughhousing with his three sons and swimming in the family pool. Dr. Strain breeds occasionally.

Ch. Farmion Geo, UD, and Ch. Roughrider's Megan of Jaisel, handled by the author, shown here winning Best of Breed and Best of Opposite Sex under judge J. Council Parker. Megan became the foundation bitch for Joanne Forsythe's Helms Alee Kennels. Steven Ross

Katrina Jez was a fisherwoman when she obtained Ch. Matia Jewell De Agua, CD, WWD. One of Matia's sons, Ch. Jewell de Agua Windward Lad, was a BIS winner. Courtesy Tom Collins

LEGADO

Ch. Lucia Flor de Mar (Baluarte de Alvalade ex Farmion's Nascenca) arrived at the Phoenix, Arizona, home of Janis Watts and Mart Miller in 1984. Gentileza do Mar (Baluarte de Alvalade ex Morena do Mar), a half-sister of Lucia Flor, later to become a champion, arrived as a puppy in 1985. Gentileza became the foundation bitch for the Legado PWDs, since Lucia became dysplastic. Watts says that Gentileza, a brown wavy, had a head with a design directly from the AKC Standard. Ch. Thor of Dell Mountain (Ch. Charlie de Alvalade ex Isodora do Mar), now retired, was Legado's first stud dog. In 1995, two bitches, Lula, a black curly (Tigre Preto do Mar ex Gentileza do Mar), and Lindy, a brown wavy (Legado's Campion de Ashbe ex Odinha do Vale Negro), joined Legado. Watts has served on the PWDCA Board for several years.

NAUTIQUE

Dr. Linda M. Fowler of New Port Richey, Florida, a PWD breeder-judge since 1992, became involved in showing purebred dogs in 1976. When the AKC recognized the PWD, she contacted Deyanne Miller and after a year-and-a-half wait, received from Miller a black wavy male, Ch. Farmion Helmsman, CD (Noah). Bred fourteen times to eleven bitches, Noah produced multiple champions. Fowler acquired her second PWD, also from Miller, in 1987. This one, Ch. Farmion Phlash, CD, served well as her foundation bitch. Bred only to Noah, Phlash became the top PWDCA brood bitch in 1993. During her productive years, she whelped forty-four puppies in three litters (fourteen, seventeen and thirteen).

NEOCLES

A longtime purebred dog fancier, Letty Larson Afong, formerly of West St. Paul, Minnesota, now of D'Iberville, Mississippi, exhibited several other breeds before discovering Portuguese Water Dogs in 1983. Her foundation bitch was Ch. Weathervane's Neocles Charo, TT. Charo, in her brief span of five years, produced sixteen puppies in two litters, eight of whom became champions. The most notable was Ch. Neocles Acabado, CD, CGC, TT, TD. Acabado, one of the top PWDs for several years, was always handled by his co-owner, Kathy Conroy Votca. Afong's second foundation bitch was a half-sister to Charo, Ch. Camerell's Neocles Calypso, UD, TT, CGC, WWD. Calypso was co-owned with and trained by Helen Berg. She produced thirteen champions from four litters. "Portuguese Water Dogs have brought me my dearest human friends who share my love for our breed," says Afong, who served on the PWDCA Board for many years. She is now a breeder-judge of PWDs.

Am., South Am., Int., Puerto Rican, Champion of the Americas Ch. La Serene Cordova achieved all these titles by eighteen months of age. Owner-handler-breeder is Dr. Thomas Strain. Allen

Ch. Thor of Dell Mountain, a son of Ch. Charlie de Alvalade, became a popular stud dog, producing multi-champions. He was the foundation stud for Janice Watts (Legado Kennels). Kohler

Ch. Farmion Phlash, CD, CGC, at age 7½, owned by Dr. Linda Fowler, Nautique Kennels. Phlash whelped forty-nine puppies in three litters and was No. 1 Brood Bitch on 1993.

Ch. Neocles Acabado, CD, foundation stud of Neocles Kennels, was co-owned by Letty Afong and Kathy Conroy. John Ashbey

ROUGHRIDER

Because this author wrote the volume *The Uncommon Breeds,* in which I described the Portuguese Water Dog, and because I had also written stories about the breed for canine magazines, telephoning Deyanne Farrell Miller when questions arose, Miller asked me to be her co-author on a definitive book she was planning on the PWD. I answered that I could not undertake such a difficult task without knowing the breed intimately. She suggested I purchase a curly black bitch puppy from her and write as the pup grew up in my home. Almost two years after this conversation, in September 1983, Miller sent me a wavy black male (who turned out to be a curly). She had named him Farmion Geo (*Geo* standing for "geographical placement"), he being the first to be placed in Montana, where my husband, Cyril, and I then resided. This puppy did not like the name Geo and refused to answer to it. He was pleased when we changed his call name to Diver and never failed to answer to the name that fit him.

Diver became a top-winning show dog, the third in the breed and first male to earn the coveted Utility Dog title; he served as the prime model for the character chapter in the book co-authored by Miller and myself, *The Complete Portuguese Water Dog* (1985). Mated to the author's Ch. Camerell's Roughrider Seeley, CDX, five times, Diver was the top sire of champions in the breed until mid-1994, with thirty-four champions. Seeley is still the top-producing PWD bitch, with twenty-one champions. Roughrider has produced many winners for the twenty-two kennels that have been founded with the author's breeding stock.

The top-producing dam of champions in the breed is Ch. Camerell's Roughrider Seeley, CDX, owned by Cyril and Kathryn Braund. Steven Ross

ROVIN

Sheryl Shaker of New Canaan, Connecticut, says, "Calvin (Bittersweet Calvin Big Moo), Rovin's foundation stud dog, was whelped in the last known litter of pure Algarbiorum dogs." These were bred at Helen Roosevelt's Bittersweet Kennel. Remarkably, for the last of something, his pedigree in America was brief. The litter that produced Calvin was whelped on July 4, 1983, the first to be registered with the AKC after the PWD was accepted into AKC's Working Group. I had only sketchy knowledge about the breed when I went to meet Helen Roosevelt and see the puppies. By the end of the visit my head was swimming with medical, historical and anecdotal information about Portuguese Water Dogs.

Shaker has her own theory about why the Algarbiorums were allowed to vanish: "The dogs were very true to the original Standard, including the wording in the FCI 1951 translation of it, 'brawler by nature.' They were tough dogs."

Shaker says that the Algarbiorums seemed to have difficulty producing, litters were small and dams often didn't conceive. Calvin sired two litters for Shaker, producing four champions. One of Calvin's offspring, Rovin's Ribombar of Spindrift, went to Barbara and Ed Whitney's home to live. They had owned his grandfather, Ch. Spindrift Galley, CDX. "As Barbara and Ed prepared to leave with their puppy," says Shaker, "they opened the back of their minivan. There sat an empty crate with a simple engraved plaque, Ch. Spindrift Galley, CDX. They put their new puppy, whom they named Jib, in his grandfather's crate and were on their way. I like to think the Whitneys feel there's still some of Galley living at their house."

SEABREEZE

Karen and Bob Arends of Richmond, Texas, acquired their first PWD in early 1984. Bobo, when grown up, acquired several important titles and was officially known as Int., Am., Mex. Ch. Trezena Benquisto, CD, PC (CD in Mexico). Bobo came from Trezena Kennels, a source of foundation stock that helped many present-day kennels achieve recognition. He possessed the basic type, structure and working attitude the Arends admired in the breed. Their foundation bitch was White Cap Dama of Neocles, Socks, bred by Pam and Jon Schneller of New York (White Cap Kennels), and purchased from Letty Afong. The two dogs—Bobo and Socks—nicked well, and the specific style of the Seabreeze dogs emerged. The Arends children, Luke and Stacey, have played a large part in caring for, training and showing Seabreeze dogs.

SETE MARES

Lorraine Carver's famous show dog and stud, Int., Am. Ch. Sunrider's Diver of Sete Mares POM, ROM (co-owned with Helen Greschel), was first shown

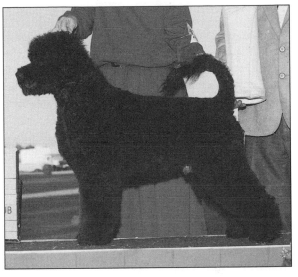

Int., Am. Ch. Sunrider's Diver of Sete Mares, Lorraine Carver's multi-Best in Show dog and the top-winning PWD three years in a row. Kohler

because Carver of Petaluma, California, a professional handler for many years, needed a dog to replace a PWD champion (Special) she had been campaigning. This young dog was soon winning Bests of Breed and Group placings regularly, and so became Carver's new Special. Diver also became a multiple Best in Show winner, always breeder-owner-handled. He set records that should stand for many years.

Carver's daughter, Kathleen Walser, also of Petaluma, California, has co-bred two litters with Carver and is co-breeder of the BIS-winning Ch. Sete Mares Windward Breeze. Another daughter, Lynne Carver, who has won grooming competitions all over the world, also co-owns a champion black wavy male. Carver's other daughter, Lisa Hubbart (Alto Mare Kennels), has done much to promote the breed and helped form the regional Northern California PWDC.

SUNNYHILL

Sunnyhill stems from Barbara Schmit's maiden name, Sonnenberg, meaning "sun over the hill." Schmit, of Longmont, Colorado, began her kennels with a Roughrider, Ch. Roughrider's Renaissance Maya, a champion at eight months in two show weekends. Ch. Sunnyhill Genoa Jib, CD, TT, whelped in 1987 from Maya's only litter, was a top PWDCA dam in 1992. This was also the year that Sunnyhill Kennels was named a top PWDCA kennel. Barbara's other foundation bitch was Ch. Costa Azul Sophie's Choice, CD, TT, CGC, POM, ROM. She was a top PWDCA producing bitch in 1993 and 1994, producing fifteen champions and performance title holders.

TIMBER OAKS

Linda Scheele of Traverse City, Michigan, became interested in the Portuguese Water Dog in 1984, chiefly because of the nonshedding characteristic and the breed's love of water. But not until four years later did the first PWD join her family. She was Lisa, more formally Ch. Eastlake Delilah. Seventeen months later, Ch. Sete Mares Storm Diver (Stormer) arrived. "From these two wonderful foundation bitches," says Scheele, "we have so far produced fifteen homebred champions and counting. We can't imagine what life would be without these people-oriented, intelligent dogs."

TREZENA

It was on February 20, 1976, that the destined-for-fame "M" litter (Farmion Azinhal ex Farmion Defeza) was whelped. Little did Jayne Kenyon of Sewickley, Pennsylvania, realize that from this litter would come dogs who would be the backbone of the breed. Kenyon really didn't want to be a breeder when she purchased Farmion Defeza out of the fourth litter born in the United States; she just wanted a puppy! But since there were so few living PWDs at the time, Deyanne Miller told Kenyon that if she wanted the puppy she would have to breed it at two years, providing it was healthy. Praia, who was born with a short, straight coat, turned out to be an ugly duckling.

Nevertheless, when Praia was old enough, Miller arranged for the stud, Kenyon, giving back one pup for the stud fee plus a second to, as Miller put it, "further the breed." Kenyon decided her kennel name should be Trezena because the litter was whelped in the American bicentennial year, there were thirteen original states, and surviving in the litter were seven males and six females—76!

Pick-of-the-litter PWDs were priced at $500 in 1976, with the better pups in the remainder of the litter going for $350. "Every breeder abided by these prices," recalls Kenyon. "And despite Praia's physical drawbacks, she apparently had designer genes, as from this litter came some of the most important foundation dogs in the country." The best known of these were Trezena Monte Clerico, who went to White Cap Kennels; Trezena Manta Rota, who went to Captree Kennels; and Trezena Meia Praia, who stayed with Kenyon.

WINDWARD

Robin Zaremba of Petoskey, Michigan, who had owned a Great Pyrenees in the early 1980s, was seeking a better obedience-oriented breed and in 1986 spotted an interesting-looking, biddable dog sporting a gorgeous coat. It was a Portuguese Water Dog. In 1987 she purchased a black wavy male, Fozzie, although she wanted a female. Fozzie, although excelling in obedience, suffered from severe hip dysplasia and was euthanized after surgery failed to relieve his pain.

Ch. Sete Mares Windward Breeze, a Best in Show winner, co-owned by handler Virginia Murray and breeders Robin Zaremba and Lorraine Carver. He is shown after winning the top prize at the Oshkosh KC under judge Betty Moore. K. Booth

In late 1988, Zaremba found the special PWD she wanted. It was another male, bred by Katrina Jez (Jewell de Agua Kennels), a grandson of Ch. Farmion Geo, UD. Moose became the breed's first Best in Show and High in Obedience Trial dog—Am., Can. Ch. Jewell De Aguas Windward Lad, CDX, Can. CD, WWD, TT, CGC, PT. Zaremba's foundation bitch is the High in Trial, Am., Can. Ch. Lake Breeze Windward Echo, Am., Can. CD, AWD, TT, CGC, PT. Zaremba also became co-owner of a another BIS dog, Ch. Sete Mares Windward Breeze, who was campaigned in 1995 to be the breed's ninth all-breed BIS winner.

OTHER PRESTIGIOUS KENNELS

No listing of long-time and active kennels would be complete without mentioning Baerbach, owned by Laird Philbrick of Woodinville, Washington; Benhil, owned by Joan C. Bendure of Fairview, Pennsylvania; Fantaseas, owned by Nancy and James Carter of Preston, Maryland; Skyline, owned by Cathy Cates and Charles White of Houston, Texas; C-Water, owned by Roberta and Floyd Corkill of Oceanside, California; Northwind, owned by Jill Gilbert of Golden Valley, Minnesota; Knollcrest, owned by Lew Grello of Newark, Delaware; Beacon Hill, owned by Deborah Gressle of Selden, New York; Charkit, owned by Catherine Hinnant of New Canaan, Connecticut; Seamajik, owned by Helene Kunze of Glen Cove, New York; Starview, owned by Bobbie Kurtz of Desert Hot Springs, California; Captree, owned by Noreen Lowery of Babylon, New York; Windruff, owned by Carol M. Mattingley of

Pottstown, Pennsylvania; Mariner, owned by Cynthia McCullough of Houston, Texas; Scrimshaw, owned by Susan and John McMahon of West Chester, Pennsylvania; Toraq, owned by Rebecca Morin of Orangevale, California; Robel, owned by Michael Nicholas of Darien, Connecticut; Questar, owned by Marilyn Rimmer of La Jolla, California; Regala, owned by Eleanor Dee and Rudy Pierce of Bethel, Pennsylvania; Pinehaven, owned by Beverly Rafferty of Colorado Springs, Colorado; Piedelai, owned by Judith and Richard Seibert of Overgaard, Arizona; Timbermist, owned by Joyce Vanek-Nielsen of Evergreen, Colorado; Robel, owned by Patricia Stuart Volz of Darien, Connecticut; Le-Hi, owned by Jeanette and Joel Ward of Sellersville, Pennsylvania; Galaxy, owned by Janet Warnsdorfer of Elverson, Pennsylvania; Tywater, owned by G. Taylor Watson of McDaniel, Maryland; Spindrift, owned by Barbara and H. Edward Whitney of Smithtown, New York; Del Sur, owned by Lana Woodburn of Erie, Colorado; and Fair Wind, owned by Troy Johnson and Chester Young of Bainbridge Island, Washington.

A complete list of presently active Portuguese Water Dog kennels and owners can be found by directing an inquiry to the PWDCA Corresponding Secretary (see Appendix chapter).

chapter 17

Showing Your Dog

This author was standing at ringside at a dog show just before Portuguese Water Dogs were called to compete. I heard the judge say to the steward, "Now you're going to see a fun breed. These dogs have personality. They wag their tails, have strong bones, look good, and are happy to be examined."

What nice compliments!

It's FUN to show a Portuguese Water Dog.

The dogs who adhere to the Standard float around the ring, because they are balanced, carry their tails correctly and enjoy showing off. They're full of themselves!

While showing dogs is a sport, judging them is very much a subjective art. Regardless of negative remarks heard in the dog fancy, most judges are knowledgeable of the breeds they judge, even though each may interpret the same Standard differently. That's why different dogs win under different judges.

A large percentage of "show dog" owners become lifelong devotees of the sport. The training, disappointments and thrills build with each show entered and make showing a fascinating hobby. Many exhibitors begin an intense study of the breed, then of all breeds, some branching out to become breeders, agents, writers, judges, etc. It's a whole new wonderful world; showing dogs becomes a way of life.

Many exhibitors begin as pet owners. Lou Guthrie and Steven Bean (Rough Seas Kennel) purchased a dog from Roughrider as a pet. Several years later, they decided to show him. He won his championship and returned to Roughrider to sire a litter. I then sent them a puppy, which they campaigned to win several BIS and two BBs at Westminster, where he also won a Group Second, the best a Portuguese Water Dog has done to date at this, the Wimbledon of dog shows.

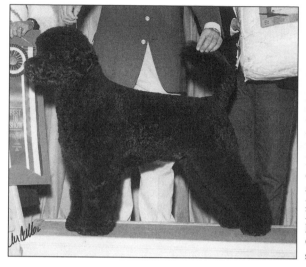

Dr. Lou Guthrie and her husband, Steven Bean, bought a pet dog and later decided to show him. This author bred to him and sent the pick of the litter to his owners. He became Ch. Rough Seas First Buoy, WWD, a Best in Show dog. "Stormy Gremlin" was also twice Best of Breed at the prestigious Westminster Kennel Club show, topping his accomplishment with a Group Second at this great show. Callea

RING PROCEDURE

Ring procedure is fairly simple. Dogs that have not yet become champions (males first, then bitches) enter the ring by classes, gaiting counterclockwise around the ring so the judge can watch them move. Next, the owner or handler poses the dog so the judge can examine it. The judge then compares each dog against the others shown, studying both their stance and movement from the side, front and rear. Finally, after deliberation, the judge awards four ribbons: blue for first prize, red for second, yellow for third and white for fourth.

There are six possible regular classes at all-breed shows. At the larger shows, the puppy classes are divided into two per sex by age (six to nine months and nine to twelve months), followed by a twelve-to-eighteen-month class, Novice, Bred by Exhibitor, American-bred and Open classes. Dogs and bitches are shown separately in these regular classes, vying for a chance to win championship points. Only one male and one bitch from all the classes can win the points. That award is called Winners, and the prize is a purple ribbon.

After the selection of Winners, all defeated first prize winners and the second prize winner from the class that produced the Winners return to the ring to compete for Reserve Winners. This award is signified by a purple-and-white ribbon and is meant to provide a recipient for the points if there was some infraction of the rules or entry irregularity by the Winners, which requires forfeiture of the points.

Following the judging of Reserve Winners Bitch, Winners Dog and Winners Bitch reenter the ring to be compared with the champions being shown for Best of Breed. Sometimes, one of these two class dogs defeats the champions in competition to become Best of Breed. The prize is a purple-and-gold ribbon. Following the judging for Best of Breed, the judge chooses one of the class animals for Best of Winners, signified by a blue-and-white ribbon. In the event that either Winners Dog or Winners Bitch goes Best of Breed, Best of Winners is awarded automatically, and, if a male dog is Best of Breed, the Winners Bitch and any champion bitches present then complete for Best of Opposite Sex. This award is signified by a red-and-white ribbon.

CHAMPIONSHIP REQUIREMENTS

A dog or bitch must win fifteen points at AKC shows to become an American champion. This total must also include at least two wins under two different judges in which the dog won a minimum of three points at each. A win of three, four or five points is termed a major. Points awarded are predetermined by the number of dogs shown in each sex and each breed, with the rating varying by region. The rating is reviewed annually by AKC and is adjusted up or down as conditions warrant. To find the point rating at a given show, consult the catalog for the point rating to see what the win is worth, but be sure to subtract absentees. Complete information is available in the AKC's *Rules Applying to Registration and Dog Shows,* single copies of which are available on request from the American Kennel Club.

SHOW TRAINING

In the show ring, the dog is actually under the judge's scrutiny for less than three minutes. With so little time in which to present a dog's good points to a judge, it's important to learn how.

This is why it's wise to begin your PWD's show ring education as soon as it is settled at your home. Show training is an extension of house training.

Each day, after you have groomed your pup, re-stand it on the grooming table, giving the command "stand." Use the grooming loop if necessary to steady its head with your hand under its muzzle. Remember rule #1: Control of the dog's head means control of the whole dog.

Several times a day, at different places both inside and outside the house, with a show collar and lead attached, stand your pup and offer it treats from your hand. Don't give one if your pup jumps up on you or sits down. Reward only when it does what you ask—stand.

When your pup understands what you want, encourage it to look at you by holding the treat close to your mouth and then lowering it. Move backwards; this teaches the pup to move forward into a better stance. As it learns, help it by placing it into a stand as described above, then reward with the treat.

Practice until the pup can stand watching you without moving its feet. You may want to slide your foot in front of the front paws to prevent it from moving out of position. If it's easier, move a knee instead of a foot to hold the puppy back. Talk to your pup happily throughout the entire session. Have fun!

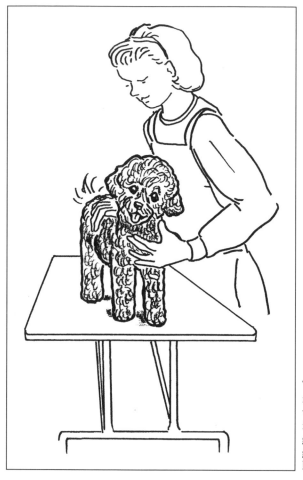

The well-trained show dog must accept examination without moving. Training for this must begin on the grooming table and on the ground during early puppyhood.

Now pose the puppy on the grooming table. To help your dog learn to stand alertly with tail wagging, practice posing many times. Stand the pup so its "show" side—the left—faces away from you. Having placed the show lead high on its neck, hold the lead in your right hand, tightening it when necessary to hold the dog's head high, and fold the remainder of the lead in your right hand so it's out of the way. (In the ring you don't want anything to distract the judge's eye from your dog.)

Now reach over your pup's shoulders with your left hand. Take hold of the left elbow and place the left front leg in the proper position. As you do, shift the dog's front weight to the left paw in one of two ways: (1) Turn the puppy's head slightly to the right. This forces the dog to lean to the left. (2) Lift the right front leg, removing weight from it. The dog will transfer weight to the left paw.

Next, transfer the show lead from your right to left hand. Keep it taut. With your right hand, grasp the right elbow and place the right paw on the ground in the correct balanced position.

Practice placing the left paw correctly. Now, practice placing both front legs correctly without allowing the dog to shift position. Offer a treat while the puppy holds this position. Soon you'll be able to pose your dog precisely and quickly.

When keeping the front legs in place becomes familiar to your puppy, begin posing the back legs. With the slack from the show lead folded in your right hand—the lead held high behind ears for a heads-up position—place the front paws without releasing tension on the show lead, then slide your left hand smoothly along the puppy's back. Praise your pupil for remaining steady. Set the left back leg by taking hold of the left hock, close to the stifle joint. Take hold from between the legs, not on the outside. Lift and place the hock so the dog's leg is perpendicular to the ground. Repeat the procedure with the other rear leg. Make certain the other three legs remain in position.

Praise by rewarding the cooperative youngster with a treat. Place your left arm in front of the chest to prevent breaking position and hold the treat several inches out and up from the dog's head. "Steady, good dog!" The dog will stretch neck and shoulders forward and up. If a rear leg moves, command "stay," and repose.

Practice. Pose the dog on the grooming table, then on the floor. Work several times a day—for only a minute at a time. Always praise the dog highly; at the end of each session, play with the dog.

Now it is time to teach your dog how to walk into a show pose. Your preliminary training has covered the basics. If, in walking the dog into a show pose, it continually moves forward when you want a four-square stance, the dog is confused. Back up your training steps.

To complete the show pose training, your dog must allow you to lift its tail upright so that the tuft falls gracefully over the back. Lift the tail slowly, sliding your hand from under hindquarters to tail tip. Praise as you do. Then relax.

The last step in teaching your dog to pose is for it to motionlessly accept examination. Stand at the puppy's left side. Grasping the upper jaw with your right hand, the lower jaw with your left, raise and lower the lips with your fingers so a judge can examine the bite. As you do, praise and smile. Then slide your hands over muzzle, skull and ears. Slide them over the shoulders, front legs, back, tuck-up, hindquarters and back legs. Praise as you work. Practice. When your dog is comfortable being examined by you, have others examine it in this manner.

Teaching these procedures takes much practice. Some days your dog forgets what is expected. Be patient. Stop if a session ceases being fun. Remember, dogs, like humans, have good and bad days.

The next step is to teach your dog how to move with you. Place the show lead high on its neck, right under the ears. Hold the lead in your left hand, close to your left hip, with barely any slack in it. With elbows against your body, holding the dog a foot away from your left side, its chest even with your left leg, begin walking in a large counter-clockwise circle. In so doing, the dog cannot lag when you turn. As you walk, keep your eye on your dog. You cannot train if you don't watch the dog.

"Zip" lightly when your PWD breaks position. Zipping means making gentle jerks on the show lead. As you zip, chatter exuberantly, "Gee, we're taking a show walk," "This is fun," or words to that effect. Walk briskly. When the dog learns to move beside you in a large, counter-clockwise circle and stays in position on a loose lead, begin turning right, left, and right and left about. Learn not to vary your step when making these turns. As you turn, give a turning signal. Occasionally, give the dog a treat as it turns. When teaching a left turn, move your left arm across your body so your hand leads into the turn. When teaching a right turn, zip lightly on the lead and move your left hand across your body. These hand and lead directions will help the dog learn. In the ring, the judge will check agility in turning, so important in a PWD's original function.

After you practice turning, practice walking slowly. Then practice gaiting at the trot as required in the show ring. Chatter happily as you work, because you want your dog to wag its tail and radiate pleasure. Remember, your dog receives spirit from you.

Remember also, when handling a dog in the show ring, the handler should be as invisible as possible. So practice moving by yourself, making each step smooth and effortless.

Finally, ask others to watch you and your dog perform. Have someone videotape your performance so you can see your mistakes. Then expose your dog to different distractions. Pose and gait him among crowds at shopping centers and at parks. Many will come up to admire your PWD; their attentions contribute to your dog's composure.

When you feel your dog is thoroughly acclimated to show procedures, loosen the lead so your dog learns to move beside you at an arm's distance. In the show ring your dog should be able to gait at full extension so the judge can evaluate its true movement.

CONDITIONING

The final step in developing a winning show dog is physical conditioning. Commence light roadwork (and, if you can, swimming) when your dog is about nine months old. Before that time, muscles are loose and legs often unsteady. Turn your dog out in fields where it can run up and down hills. However, remember a PWD is still a puppy at nine months, so don't overdo. Never put a PWD puppy through strenuous exercise until it's at least fifteen months. Allow muscles to develop naturally.

CONFORMATION CLASSES

We advise all Roughrider puppy owners—show and pet—to take their puppies through a puppy conformation class. Most enroll puppies as young as twelve weeks. However, in this environment your puppy will be exposed to a multitude of bacteria, fungi and parasites. The wise owner makes sure his or her puppy is fully protected before going to class for the first time.

Conformation puppy classes socialize the puppy to people and other dogs as well as teach show ring procedures. The puppy learns to stand and be petted and rubbed (while being examined), then given a delicious treat; it learns to gait with its owner and expect a treat when turning or stopping; it learns to be patient as it waits for a turn at being petted and examined by the teacher. Conformation classes for puppies are also wonderful training classes for new owners learning handling techniques. Instructors are knowledgeable about dogs, can answer most questions and know dates of upcoming matches where owners and their puppies can practice for the formal shows to come.

PROFESSIONAL HANDLERS

If you decide not to handle your own dog for any reason, a professional handler can be hired to act as your agent. The handler will show and probably groom your dog for you. Many prefer to house your dog for at least several days before a show to train it. Like magic, in those few days your dog learns to be a show dog! That's because this is the professional handler's business.

A good handler knows how to treat dogs and how to make them succeed in the ring. A professional handler, even though he or she may win only 50 percent of the time with your dog, will undoubtedly win far more than would a novice handler. Hiring a professional handler (particularly if travel is involved in attending shows) makes showing a dog far less expensive than if the owner does it all. However, because showing one's own dog is enjoyable, many owners would rather "do it themselves." Vicki Stores has shown two of her dogs to their championships. "It has taken me a little longer," she says, "but I wouldn't have relinquished these experiences for anything. It's fun as well as rewarding."

One incentive for breeders to show their dog in the Bred by Exhibitor class is a program initiated by the AKC in May 1996. The AKC now awards special medallions when all points are accumulated in the BBE class to breeder-owners who show a dog to its championship.

If you decide to use a professional handler, inquire into how your PWD will be cared for when away from you. Watch handlers and their techniques at dog shows. Visit and notice how the dogs they show are cared for. Talk to other exhibitors and ask why they chose this or that particular handler. You want your dog in the best hands and care possible, so no trouble is too great.

When showing your dog yourself, display good manners. Thank the judge for any award you receive. When another dog bests yours (and it happens), congratulate the winner. Dress tastefully, remembering you are exhibiting the dog, not yourself or your clothes.

Owner-handler Vicki Storrs says, "It takes a little longer, but owners can show their dogs to their championships." Vicki has shown two of her dogs to both American and Canadian championships. She is shown here with Am., Can. Ch. Roughrider's Cisco Pete, CDX, AWD (Ch. Timbermist's Lancar Flor De Mar, CDX ex Roughrider's Salt Water Taffy). Linda Lindt Studios

The litter sisters Starview's Windstar and Starview's Desert Fantasy (Piccures Do Portago ex Salsa of Sunrider), owned by Bobbe Kurtz, are shown here after winning the Senior Puppy and Bred by Exhibitor classes at Los Encinos KC (California). Mitchell Photography

Beverly Jorgensen (Sun Joy Kennels) handles many of her own dogs and is shown here with Am., Can. Ch. Sun Joy's Guarda O Mar Alto (Ch. Magia Flor de Mar, CGC ex Ch. Sun Joy's Kalinka do Condinho, CD, TT, CGC), placing second in the Working Group at Great Barrington under judge Dorothy Collier. Guardo was also Best of Breed at the 1996 Westminster KC show. Chuck Tatham

Above all, have fun and—win or lose—be a good sport.

Listed here are Best in Show dogs through the end of 1996.

Ch. Charlie de Alvalade
June 30, 1984; August 12, 1984;
November 14, 1985.

Ch. Gozo do Mar
October 18, 1987.

Ch. Timbermist Lancar Flor de Mar
November 1, 1987;
August 21, 1988.

Ch. Sunrider's Diver of Sete Mares
October 29, 1990; May 23, 1993.

Ch. Jewell De Aguas Windward Lad
October 21, 1991.

Ch. Timbermist Sea Kaper Hi Noon
May 24, 1992;
November 20, 1993.

Ch. Rough Sea First Buoy
November 28, 1992;
April 9, 1993.

Ch. Helm's Alee Summertime
January 20, 1993 (Canada).

Ch. Farmion the Bismarck
June 12, 1994.

Ch. Sete Mares Windward Breeze
May 29, 1995.

Ch. Sun Joy Neocles Forma Grande
April 6, 1996.

Ch. Dacher's Monsoon
September 22, 1996.

chapter 18

Obedience Training and the Portuguese Water Dog

Dog obedience training had its formal beginning in Europe in the early 1900s. The first American Kennel Club–sponsored obedience trial was held in 1936, and Obedience, as a dog sport, quickly became popular in the United States. It was recognized that teaching basic obedience exercises to a dog is necessary in helping it adapt and live happily in the human environment. Owner/trainers learned that obedience training established an exceptionally close bond with a dog and was a marvelous tool in developing the dog's full companion animal potential.

Since the Portuguese Water Dog is a working dog, its temperament demands that it be taught basic obedience exercises. A trained PWD is a confident dog. It is in control of himself, responds immediately to commands, and is able to develop its extraordinary potential as a willing, well-adjusted companion animal.

A PWD owner does its pet a disservice if he or she does not enter it in basic obedience classes. Classes help socialize a dog to other dogs and environments, as well as help it learn rules of behavior, making it an asset as a family member. And classes have an advantage over training at home. Dogs learn by observing what other dogs around them do. Many PWDCA member-breeders, including the author, stipulate in their contracts that the owner must follow through with basic obedience class lessons.

Novice exercises teach the dog to heel (walk calmly at a person's left side), sit, stand, lie down and come when called. Advanced classes, Open and Utility, teach it to retrieve, jump over obstacles, use its scenting powers and respond to signals as well as voice commands. A Portuguese Water Dog must respond to basic obedience commands to perform reliably in water work,

Obedience Titled Portuguese Water Dogs
Total Numbers: CD=321; CDX=90; UD=35; (UDX=2)

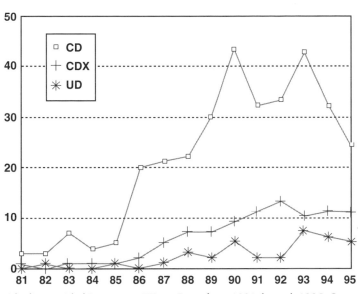

Obedience-titled Portuguese Water Dogs from 1981 through 1995. Courtesy Elsa Sells

Seacatch Xa (Farmion Cabo de Sta. Maria ex Farmion Dalva), owned by Bob (handling) and Ruth Hollander, was the first of the breed to earn a Companion Dog title and the first to achieve a highest-scoring PWD in Trial. Out of a possible 200 perfect score, Prince earned 198½. The trial was held at the Riverhead KC on March 28, 1982. Prince was also the first dog his owner had trained in obedience. Bushman

Tracking and Agility—three other enjoyable dog sports, especially for owners and Porties.

Newcomers to the breed often ask about PWD trainability. These dogs are quick to learn and often become star pupils in beginning obedience classes. But they get bored when instruction becomes repetitive. That's why motivational games, like retrieving, should be taught. Varying drill work with retrieving keeps a PWD continuously motivated.

Motivation, after all, is a very important thing in this world. Without the right kind, no human or animal would be doing anything!

So we teach the dog by motivating it to act as we require. Know, however, that dogs are initially motivated by physical senses, most notably internal muscle (kinesthetic) and organic senses, as well as by the senses of touch, smell, hearing, sight and taste, and also by temperature. While there are many ways to motivate dogs, three positive motivators are play, praise and food.

PLAY RETRIEVE MOTIVATION

Play motivation is designed to introduce your dog to work, as well as to foster a continuing desire to do so until work becomes forged into its memory. Since PWDs love to carry things in their mouths, we begin to train by appealing, in play, to those carrying instincts. Because it is useful to have dogs retrieve (as well as carry), we teach retrieving via play exercises. Force break after the dog advances in training.

NOTE: Force breaking is insisting the dog do something. It's teaching reliability. For instance, training a dog to relieve itself outside instead of in the house is a form of force breaking. In force breaking retrieving, we insist the dog take the object we want it to take. You cannot force break "retrieving" an object; you can only force break pickup of an object. Once reliable pickup is instilled, the dog becomes a willing retriever.

HOW TO TEACH PLAY RETRIEVE

Take out your play-training toy, preferably a training dummy or boat bumper. The dummy is more versatile than a ball. It is equipped with a short loop on one end through which a rope can be attached to make throwing easier. The dummy can also be dragged along the ground on a long line; furthermore, it is easily seen wherever it lands. Dummies are made in several different sizes, in both cloth and plastic, and in various colors. An hour before you start your game, give the dummy to your dog and let the dog examine and play with it.

Begin the game by attaching the dog's training collar (a slip collar, often called a choke collar) and leash. You are going to use its leash as a directional guide, not a line with which to pull or choke it by tightening the collar. Say to the dog in a highly excited voice, "Come on, let's have some fun!"

Ch. Farmion Geo, UD, the first male and the third in the breed to earn a UD Utility title, was owned and trained by the author. Diver was also a noted winner and one of the breed's top stud dogs. Courtesy Stuart White

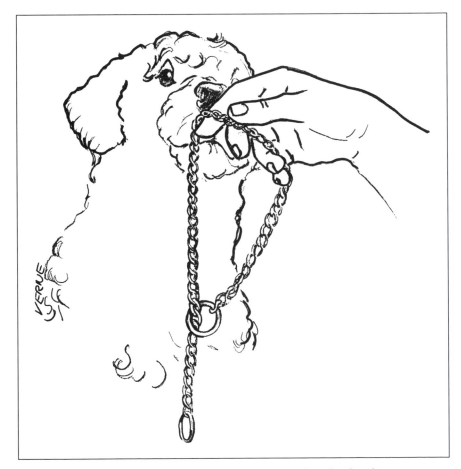

Begin the game by attaching the training collar over your dog's head in this manner.

Then enthusiastically swing or wave the dummy in front of it. Throw it. As you throw, exclaim "Take it," happily. (You may prefer to use another command, like "Get it" or "Fetch." Just be consistent.)

NOTE: When dogs play, their voices are high pitched. So use high tones when encouraging a dog. If it becomes tense and doesn't want to have anything to do with the dummy after you've endeavored to entice it four or five times, praise the dog, then put the dummy away until the next session.

REMEMBER: You must teach the dog how to play your way. Some dogs become nervous at the beginning of play if a leash is attached. This is natural. They're fearful because they don't know what to expect. Study your dog in play. Observe how different canine play body movements are from human body movements. Be patient. Your dog will learn. After all, during each session you are stimulating it by reawakening its inherited chase instinct.

Ninety percent of all dog training is done on leash, so it's important to teach your dog to play with you on leash. Think of the leash as a textbook. It may take one to fifteen sessions for the dog to want to grab the dummy while it's on leash. Keep at the game in very short (two-minute) sessions and continue to be highly enthusiastic whether it participates or not.

REMEMBER: If you think your dog is stubborn and that is why it refuses after a certain number of sessions, think again. I wrote in my training book *(The Second 10 Weeks,* Denlinger, 1983): "As you teach retrieving, you'll discover the enormous quality and quantity of canine stubbornness. In primordial life, stubbornness is an instinctive reaction—it translates to being bold, stout, relentless, brave, determined—qualities we admire in the Portuguese Water Dog. *Stubbornness in nature is grace under duress.* Therefore, you mustn't allow the dog's great stubbornness to dismay you. Accept it as a challenge; as a behavior pattern to control." Puppies, in particular, prove this in their initial burst of puppy self-will. Because PWDs are so bright, self-will must be sensibly and dynamically channeled for dogs to become willing, responsive workers.

When your dog does begin to reach out for the toy, allow it to grab and shake the toy. Get hold of the other end, but don't play tug of war. That's a game your dog can win at, and you don't want it to win. (Tug of war teaches aggressiveness.) If it doesn't want to drop the dummy, take it gently from the dog. Then, instantly, with a high-pitched encouraging voice, toss it several feet in front of you. As you toss, encourage the pickup: "Take it, take it, Oh good dog, take it!" Do whatever you have to—wave the toy around in circles, or keep it close and wriggle it back and forth on the ground in front of you. Keep moving the dummy as you continue to encourage. At some point, the dog will rush to grab, attack or at least nose it. If all it does is nose it, praise to the skies. Your dog is advancing in its classwork!

When, finally, its mouth closes over the dummy, call the dog back to you. Run backwards if that gets it moving towards you. Grin at it happily!

Encourage. The dog is on leash and cannot run off; nevertheless, coax it back. Never pull or haul it back. If you do, it will freeze in its tracks, drop the dummy and refuse to play. If it comes in to you but insists on holding the dummy tightly, praise and take it from the dog in one of two ways: (1) Place your left hand over the top of its muzzle and exert pressure just behind the canine teeth. Lift the muzzle and extract the toy; or (2) Offer it the treat you have been carrying in your pocket. The dog will drop the dummy. Pick it up. Don't fret that your dog drops it instead of delivering it to hand. Give it some freedom of expression in learning phases; it will deliver the dummy to hand when it learns responsible retrieving. If you feel this initial success is ample for this session, stop. If your dog is jumping with eagerness to see what comes next, repeat the exercise and then put the dummy away. The rule of thumb is to always end a game at the height of the dog's enjoyment of it. This keeps you in control.

REMEMBER: After the initial introduction, play retrieving toys are given to the dog only during play motivation exercises; otherwise, it will learn to chew them.

Once your dog is retrieving happily and consistently, vary the play pattern. While running, drag the dummy along the ground behind you at the end of a long line. Once the dog pounces, praise. Motivate a double-fast return by using two dummies. Throw the second one in back of you or out at the side as the dog returns to you with the first. Don't take the dog off leash until it's consistent and finds your game fun. You want to teach your dog to work independently before you take it off leash. When it is off leash, motivate it to retrieve by throwing the dummy progressively further. Keep your voice highly excited. Run with your dog as it dashes to get the dummy. Gradually introduce other toys, such as balls and dumbbells.

Verne Foster of New Hampshire has trained three PWDs, winning, along the way, seven High in Trials and a *Dog World* award for earning three obedience titles in one year. She trained the first PWD to win a Utility Dog Excellent title and a dog who won a PWDCA National Specialty High Combined (Open and Utility). Foster, who also is the talented artist who has enhanced this book with her wonderful drawings, says, "Play retrieve is good. But what happens if the dog doesn't feel like playing that game? I play eight to ten different games with my dogs. When they tire of one, I use another to motivate."

When you and your dog have learned to play together *your* way, it's time to start basic obedience. You can teach initial basics at home. You have already begun the sit, down, stand and stay exercises on the grooming table. We'll better instill the sit, down and stay exercises here, as well as add the whistle recall. Then you'll be ready to start classes.

First, find a secluded outdoor area. Make sure the ground is even, and if the weather is warm, practice in the shade if possible. Do not instruct near the dog's toilet area or where there are distractions. If you begin training during

Katrina Jez works with Am., Can. Ch. Belcarra's Pescador, CGC, JWD, to perfect his retrieving skills.

Kim Beach uses hand as well as voice commands to Roughrider's Diamond Tuxedo (Ch. Roughrider's Adventure, CD ex Ch. Roughrider's Fancy That, CD) for the Down exercise. Courtesy Jim Beach

the winter months, wear warm clothes. Your PWD wears its warm clothes, and inclement weather doesn't (and shouldn't) bother him.

SESSIONS

Instruction sessions for puppies should never last more than several minutes and for older dogs, no longer than five minutes. You can accomplish more in five minutes or less if every second consists of quality instruction. That's why it's wise to take a minute beforehand to write down and/or practice by yourself what you're endeavoring to teach.

It's excellent if you have time to give two sessions a day; however, if your sessions cannot be consistent, limit training to one session daily. As the dog understands what you want of it and thus develops confidence in its growing skills, it will be willing to spend more time performing them. Be certain you make each training session enjoyable. If you're depressed or weary, don't train. The PWD is extremely sensitive to its owner's mood, and PWDs respond with eagerness in a happy and energetic training session.

Sit Exercise

PRIME MOTIVATION: You are going to motivate your dog with its TOUCH and FEEL senses. Command: Sit.

How to Teach:

Step 1. With collar and leash attached, holding the loop end of the leash in your right hand with slack as it extends to the dog, guide (with the leash) your dog to your left side. You want its skull even with your hip. Its muzzle should be inches forward of your leg. If the dog is wary of what you are doing, laugh and tell it, "Hey, you're going to learn how to sit." Then sit it. How?

Step 2. Stroke the dog with your left hand lovingly from the front of its muzzle to the top of its head, soothing it; then slide your left hand down its back, saying a drawn-out "Sit Good Dog" as you do, exerting slight pressure against its back. Your right hand is now under its chin. Lift its chin with your hand so that in order to balance itself, the dog will slide into the sit. As you lift the chin, begin stroking its underside.

REMEMBER: Touch and feel are forms of praise.

Step 3. As your dog completes the sit, not after, but *during,* praise verbally.

WARNING: Do not repeat the sit command. If you start repeating a command, you will teach the dog to react to a command slowly. The dog will begin to wait for the fourth or tenth command and will never gain reliability.

REMEMBER: If you cannot enforce a command the first time given, don't give it.

NOTE: Some owners find this rule difficult to adhere to. When visiting friends and rightfully proud of the manners they are teaching their puppy, they like to show how nicely their puppy sits. The puppy, not understanding the command when given in a strange place, does not sit with the first command. So the owners repeat and repeat the command until finally, the puppy, still slightly puzzled yet endeavoring to please, sits. The owners smile proudly. Believe it or not, the fact that a command is repeated and repeated is remembered by the puppy. It then later takes a great deal of retraining to initiate prompt command responses.

Step 4. Repeat the sit exercise several times. If you praise too highly, your puppy will become overly excited and jump out of position. This exercise is therefore teaching you the correct amount of praise you can give your dog while retaining its attention.

FINAL TOUCH: Play retrieve.

Second session: Identical to first.

Third session: You will add dimension to the sit exercise, which enables your dog to better understand what you want it to do.

Sit and Stay Exercise

PRIME MOTIVATION: TOUCH/FEEL.

Command taught: Stay.

How to Teach:

Step 1. Place your dog on a sit beside you (as described earlier). If it sits without your asking, reward it with praise.

Step 2. With the palm of your right hand facing your dog, your palm in front of its eyes, with the leash in your left hand, command, "Stay," and move one step in front of it. Do not move two steps, one only. To instill reliability, we move away from the dog slowly—by inches, not feet. To gain control of its head, tighten the collar by zipping the leash up (not sideways). Release the pressure as soon as the dog is back in place.

REMEMBER: Control of a dog's head is control of the dog.

Step 3. Remain in this position thirty seconds. If the dog moves, zip the leash upward, making it feel the collar tightening.

REMEMBER: Dogs are initially motivated by physical rather than mental senses.

Step 4. Return to the dog, but do not immediately release and praise. Vary the time before returning and before releasing and praising. Sometimes, remain away thirty seconds, other times a minute or more. This teaches the dog not to help out by anticipating. Then, as you release, praise. Practice this exercise three to four times. End the training session.

FINAL TOUCH: Play games.

NOTE: At each session, increase the distance you go from your dog on the stay exercise. However, do so gradually. At the end of six days, you should not be farther away than the end of the six-foot leash.

REMEMBER: Training reliability when working at a distance is done in inches, not feet.

Believe it or not, if you take it slow and easy, within several months you will be able to command your dog to "sit" when you are twenty feet away and it will obey. You will not be able to do this if you repeat commands or expect too much from the dog too quickly. Because PWDs long to be close to their owners at all times, teach your dog to accept distance between you slowly—in every exercise.

PROGRESS ACHIEVED

Your dog has not yet fully learned the commands "Sit" or "Stay," although you may think it has. It needs several weeks of daily practice for these commands to become reliably implanted in its mind. After several more weeks of training, the dog has to be taught to perform the exercise whenever and wherever asked. This is called proofing. When proofing an exercise, you take the dog to a variety of at least five places and train it. As with all training, this process is done on a gradual basis.

Down and Sit, from Down Exercise

PRIME MOTIVATION: TOUCH/FEEL.

Command taught: Down.

How to Teach:

Step 1. Place your dog on a sit/stay beside you.

Step 2. Remembering to keep its head even with your hip, kneel beside it, your knees facing front. Do not turn toward it with the lower half of your body. To teach it to lie down straight, you must keep your body line straight.

Step 3. As in teaching the sit exercise, pat the dog's muzzle and head, then, turning only your upper torso towards it, extend your left hand down its back, stopping right behind its shoulder blades. Exert pressure with your left thumb and forefinger behind the shoulder blade. A dog will never fail to relax and go down with pressure in this particular spot. Command pleasantly, "Down." If you initially have trouble finding this spot, lift the dog's front legs straight forward with your right arm and hand, your left arm straight down its back, and with your left elbow exert pressure on the lower back. You cannot do this if you turn your elbow toward you. You must extend it straight down the dog's back. Once the dog is down, keep it there while praising softly but not allowing it to get up.

REMEMBER: The down exercise is a difficult one for many dogs to learn and accept, since it requires submission. However, the pressure mark method right behind the dog's shoulder relaxes nerves and muscles (kinesthetic senses), making the exercise easier for dogs of all temperament to accept.

Step 3. Since you already introduced your dog to the Stay command during the previous week, once you have secured the dog in the Down position, command "Stay" as you stand up and move a half-step away. Why not a full step? Again, the Down exercise may be difficult to teach some dogs because of their dominance instincts. You must stay close to press the dog down again immediately, if necessary. Return to the dog. Praise while it is down. Release. Praise again.

Step 4. Repeat. Stand up, telling the dog, as it is jumping back up onto its feet, "Sit." Place the dog on a Sit, if necessary. Praise.

NOTE: The Sit, coming up from the Down position, is a new exercise to the dog. The physical movements of sitting from a Down position are completely different from those of a dog taught to sit from the standing position.

CORRECTION RULE

Never correct, only replace, a dog when it is learning. You defeat the purpose of training if you correct. Place the dog in the correct position and praise while repositioning it, thus letting it understand it is now doing the exercise correctly. You must remember, a dog's thinking process is different from ours.

FINAL TOUCH: Play retrieve.

For the remaining days of the second week, practice (1) the Sit from the Stand; (2) the Sit Stay, with you progressing to the end of the leash; (3) the Down from the Sit; (4) the Down/Stay, with you progressing to the end of the leash; (5) the Sit from the Down; and (6) play retrieving and/or other play motivation games.

This is not a book dedicated to obedience training, per se; however, you have now been given ample instruction on how to start training and how to enjoy these sessions with your dog. If you have introduced your dog to whistle recalls (see chapters 9 and 13), your dog responds immediately when you call it, and you have the basics of the recall exercise.

You are now ready to enter beginning dog obedience classes. The other basics, along with practice of those above, will be taught there. The Stand and Come exercises are taught with prime motivators of taste. Heeling is also initially taught with the taste, touch and feel senses.

REMEMBER: Portuguese Water Dogs are active dogs. They move fast, so you must learn to move quickly in all training.

You must also be continually one step ahead of the dog in thinking. An example of this necessity comes from obedience trainer Bill Harkins, who says of his own dog: "Buddy (Ch. Le-Hi's Cute as a Button, CD, TT) would get bored if we did an exercise more than three times in a row. He would anticipate the exercise before I gave him the command and do it, but halfheartedly. I had to keep him off guard by mixing up the exercises, never doing the same one twice in a row. This developed great concentration on Buddy's part, and helped him keep an up attitude.

"Although food played a part in Buddy's training, his main motivation came from praise. Before he was two, he achieved his Companion Dog title in three straight trials, with scores which earned him a *Dog World* award."

Because there are many different dog training philosophies, dog owners need to investigate methods and classes, just as they need to thoroughly research a breed before getting a dog. The library is the best place to start. There are excellent books on dog training, so read as many as you can. If your library has a short supply, go to a bookstore, and buy and study several. Then look in your area newspaper and in the Yellow Pages of your telephone book for obedience training centers and attend several, watching classes in action.

Heeling is initially taught using the senses of taste, touch, hearing and sight.

Having done your homework, you'll understand what's happening as you watch the instructor and dogs in session. Attend dog shows and watch dogs and owners in the obedience rings carefully.

In formal obedience trials, the dog is tested and scored in the exercises required at its class level with its handler. When a dog qualifies at three different obedience trials, it earns a title. It becomes a Companion Dog (CD) after it has completed the requirements for the Novice class; a Companion Dog Excellent (CDX) title after completing the requirements for the Open

Ch. Le-Hi's Cute as a Button, CD, TT (Daker do Condinho ex Brinmar's Put'n On the Ritz), owned and trained by Bill Harkins, earned a *Dog World* award for achieving his Companion Dog title in three straight shows with scores of 195.5, 196.6 and 198. Ashbey Photo

class; and a Utility Dog (UD) title after completing the requirements for the Utility class. The titles are progressive. It may take four to five years for some dogs to advance from a CD title to a UD title. Some never make the grade; the exercises become more difficult in each succeeding class. Once the UD title is earned, a dog can continue to compete. The next title is a Utility Dog Excellent (UDX). The AKC's highest obedience title is the Obedience Trial Champion (OTCh.). It is won according to a point schedule determined by the number of dogs competing in each class.

Katrina Jez of Jewell De Agua Kennels, says, "PWDs work for attention— any kind, good or bad. Remember that when your urge is to chase a dog who has your favorite shoe in his mouth. Teach him that coming close to you or delivering something to you is really one of the best things in life."

Peggy Wireman, who has two High in Trial PWDs as well as a High in Specialty Trial dog, said in an obedience article (*The Courier*, May–June 1994): "When I first began dog training, food was not used at all. I trained with the old method of corrections and praise. The bad part was that corrections were given before the dog even understood what he was doing. Therefore, by the time the dog learned what he was supposed to do, he did not enjoy it and worked only to avoid the correction. Gradually I have introduced food as a reward along with praise. I now show the dog what I want by helping him do it right and rewarding with praise and food. It is only when the dog knows what is expected and refuses to do it, must a correction be given, followed immediately with praise when he is doing what you want."

The only triple-titled Utility Portuguese Water Dog, U-UD Ch. Pickwick's Port of Edmonds, CD, CDX, UD, Canadian OTCh., UD, also hunts with his owner Vern Olsen. Olsen says: "The PWD needs confidence and that only comes from the owner in tone of voice and body language. The PWD is a very smart dog with a strong will—hence respect for your PWD is a big plus in obedience. Always keep your dog on leash with food in your pocket and hand. Everyone needs correction (that's why the leash) and everyone needs motivation (that's why the food). My motto is tons of praise; lots of patience. The PWD is a complete dog that can do anything!—with the proper guidance and patience."

Verne Foster says, "Once I've made a correction in training, it is over with. Most PWDs become stressed if allowed to dwell on the mistake or if they see you are upset. Each dog handles stress in a different way. There are both positive and negative stressing dogs. A negative-stresser is one who shuts down and appears depressed. The positive-stresser is one who becomes more active but stops thinking and just moves, jumps, spins, etc. Although all dogs

Ch. Pickwick's Port of Edmond's, CGC, AWD, Am., Can., and UKC UD (Camerell's Mr. Pickwick ex Ch. Marmais's Belo Um) is the most titled working dog in the breed as of mid-1996. Port, who earned all his AKC titles in 1993, thus becoming eligible for a *Dog World* award, also hunts doves, ducks and pheasants for owner Verne Olsen.

can exhibit both, whichever comes out most during training and showing is the category which fits your dog. There seem to be more PWD negative than positive stressers in the obedience ring. At a show a dog who will happily maintain his attention on you in the chaos outside the ring will likely be less stressed when he gets into the ring. That's why it is important to teach a dog how to play with you."

Owners will find that training a PWD is challenging as they learn how a dog thinks and how it reacts to training. It's also fun and often becomes an addictive hobby. Believe me, there are high rewards and high pleasures as one hones one's dog's companion animal skills with the dog developing a great sense of pride in its accomplishments.

Listed below are the names of dogs, owners and the year titles were awarded them, through 1995, for the most advanced obedience titles: Companion Dog Excellent (CDX), Utility Dog (UD) and Utility Dog Excellent (UDX). For complete rules and titles, see the AKC's *Obedience Regulations*.

COMPANION DOG EXCELLENT TITLES

DOG	OWNER	YEAR
Birchbrook's Mariner Miguel	K. Taylor	1985
Ch. Camerell's Jupiter Pluvius	Jean Robinson	1986
Ch. Keel Beleza	Pam Schneller	1986
Captree's Jib of Actondale	N. Lowery/S. Mejais	1987
Ch. Camerell's Roughrider Seeley	Kathryn Braund	1988
Eastlake's Christmas Past	D. & R. Zaremba	1988
White Cap Corinthian	L. Webb	1988
Actondale's Salty Sailor	G. Dorsman	1989
Ch. Farmion Homeward Bound	K. & M. Braiman	1989
Glacier Winds Domino	R. Zaremba/R. Pinney	1989
Ch. Regala's Dockside Good N Plenty	P. Wireman/E. Pierce	1989
Roughrider's Dona Maria	R. & W. White	1989
Ch. Spindrift Galley	B. & E. Whitney	1989

DOG	OWNER	YEAR
Bamerell's Call Me Cooper	A. Axford	1990
Ch. Neocles Coral Sea Treasure	C. McCullough	1990
Rockmere's Joaquim de Agua	R. & N. Griswald	1990
Ch. Roughrider's Divers Cascade	C. & V. Kramer	1990
Ch. Aabest Mr. T Dedemon	E. Allen	1991
Ch. Rebento Dita	P. Stevens	1991
Regala's Feliz Huellas	E. Kimberly	1991
Ch. Anacoves La Primera Samba	C. Cates/C. White	1992
Ch. Aqua Lama's Dulcinea	D. Zorn/A. Vanek	1992
Brinmar's Little Miss Liberty	P. Marshall	1992
Fantaseas Baleboss	C. Reimer	1992
Ch. Neocles Beata Brio	L. Afong	1992
Ch. Roughrider's Montana Sky Sail	S. & D. Lawrence	1992
Seatail's Avante Maria	Michelle Feins	1992
Ch. Timbermist Lancar Flor De Mar	J. Vanek-Nielsen	1992
Ch. De Leão's Master Blaster	S. & R. Marshall	1993
Halcyon's Harmony	T. Hutchinson	1993
Ch. Neocles Destiny of Mariner	C. McCullough/J. Madderra	1993
Ch. Regala's Daboomer of Tailwind	B. Matheis	1993
Roughrider Nina Carmenita	M. Warriner	1993
Ch. Sunnyhill's McKinley Moondance	S. Malick/B. Schmit	1993
Windjammer Meia Noite Mariner	M. Collier	1993
Windward's Preto Magic	L. & J. Seymore	1993

DOG	OWNER	YEAR
Ch. Highsea Sunnyhill's Quequo Man	D. Kaplan/B. Schmit	1994
Ch. Jewell De Aguas Windward Lad	R. Zaremba	1994
Ch. Neocles Facil Figaro	G. & M. Troll	1994
Ch. Neocles Fulgar of Brio	L. Lewis	1994
Ch. Roughrider Isabela Ensopada	J. Adams	1994
Ch. Sanddollar's Majik Blitzen II	J. Roland	1994
Ch. Alto Mare Candura	L. Hubbart	1995
Alto Mare Jocoso De Sete Mare	M. Tassey/L. Carver	1995
Ch. Cutwater's Knight Errant	L. Thompson/J. Harding	1995
Deblyn Aezia Preto	E. & D. Durant	1995
Ch. Downeast Diego De Armada	C. Noyes/S. Dostie	1995
Ch. Janota's Cabre De Sorta	P. Wireman/J. Babbitt	1995
Ch. Le-Hi's Dockside Dory	C. & R. Devlin	1995
Le-Hi's Shear Image	K. & D. Buehrer	1995
Maritimo Ebbtide Tyler	N. Wentworth	1995
Maritimo Fielle Castagna	B. Zand	1995
Ch. Neocles Ganhador of Mooridge	A. Moore/L. Afong	1995
Questar's Little Dipper	G. Zuckerman	1995
Regala's Optical Illusion	L. Davis	1995
Regala's Takes Two to Tango	J. Heater	1995
Robel Tazmanian Devil	C. & K. Chapman	1995
Ch. Roughrider's Cisco Pete	E. & V. Storrs	1995
Ch. Rovin's Ribombar of Spindrift	B. Whitney	1995

UTILITY DOG TITLES

DOG	OWNER	YEAR
Spindrift Kedge	B. & E. Whitney	1982
Ch. Spindrift Genoa	B. & E. Whitney	1985
Ch. Camerell's Delta Dawn	Lynn Bondurant	1986
Ch. Farmion Geo	Kathryn Braund	1987
Ch. Baybrite's Algazzara	S. Dostie	1988
Roughrider's Galley Mate	B. & C. Friedrich	1988
Whalekey's Brigantine	V. Foster	1988
Ch. Camerell's Neocles Calypso	H. Berg	1989
Ch. Roughrider's First Skipper	B. & C. Freidrich	1989
Ch. Camerell's Delta Clipper	V. Foster	1990
My Sonnet From the Portuguese	M. Foster	1990
Ch. Neocles Foutshouse Astro	N. & J. Fouts/L. Afong	1990
Ch. Timbermist Blackjack Scuba	G. Clark/J. Vanek-Nielsen	1990
Ch. Trezena Meia Bela	G. Dorsman	1990
High Seas Blue Boy	E. Jaskowski	1991
Ch. Piedelai Brut De Paolo	E. Jaskowski	1991
McShoer's Lucky Clover	J. Porowski/L. Shoop	1992
Ch. White Cap Hurricane Warning	J. & G. Martin	1992
Ch. Azul Rebentacão's Alegre	D. Wacker	1993
Ch. Foutshouse Stars N' Stripes	N. & J. Fouts	1993
Ch. Hunter's Franks Raisin Cain	P. Heinzleman	1993
Piedelai Arpeggio Raffee	K. Wood/J. Seibert	1993

DOG	OWNER	YEAR
Ch. Regala's Daboomer of Tailwind	B. Matheis	1993
Ch. Roughrider's Manhattan	D. Haddock	1993
Ch. Roughrider's Reba Donzi	V. & C. Robinson	1993
Ch. Timbermist Aqua Lama Pipin' Hot	G. Clark/ J. Vanek-Nielsen	1993
Ch. Camerell's Buccaneer Beaver	B. & B. Franklin	1994
Rune's Chocolate Polliwog	R. Bartholoma/J. Spaid	1994
Ch. Alto Mares Gambol N Man	E. Verkozen/L. Hubbart	1994
Ch. Marinheira Flor De Mar	J. & H. Gilbert	1994
Ch. Neocles Anrique	D. & L. Jackson	1994
Ch. Pickwick's Port Of Edmonds	V. Olson/S. Helsel	1994
Ch. White Cap Fancy That	L. Reilly/B.Schneller	1994
Ch. Azul Rebentacão's Acostavel	M. Lauterjung	1995
Farmion Nobska II	J. Williams	1995
Farmion Obrigada II	L. Thompson	1995
Jewell De Agua Anjo	K. Jez/S. Cheney	1995
Seabreeze Clara Bee	S. & J. Bradley	1995
Ch. Sete Mares Sohappy Shana-Dawn	P. Bartholomew/L. Carver	1995

UTILITY DOG EXCELLENT TITLES

DOG	OWNER	YEAR
Ch. Alto Mares Gambol N Man	E. Verkozen/L. Hubbart	1994
Ch. Camerell's Delta Clipper	V. Foster	1994

c h a p t e r   1 9

Water Work

To earn a water trial title is the dream of many Portuguese Water Dog owners, since the breed is renowned for swimming and diving. Several hundred PWDs have earned Water titles since the sport was formally initiated by the parent club in 1991.

Of course, some PWDs like the water better than others. Acquainting dogs born during the spring to the water is usually no problem. Some dogs enjoy venturing into the water the moment they are introduced to it; others are wary, particularly if there are waves. The best way to introduce your dog to water is to go into it with it, keeping the dog next to the shore until it gains confidence, all the while encouraging it to get its feet wet. By all means, keep its collar and leash on. They give the dog added confidence. Be sure to give it plenty of encouragement and praise as you wade through the water. Walk back on shore for a few minutes, then repeat the lesson. Most puppies and older dogs will begin splashing about in the water, enjoying the experience. Some require incentives, such as sticks or dummies thrown into the water for them to fetch. Usually the introduction to water releases an instinctive desire to retrieve.

Owners of puppies born during the winter aren't always able to introduce their dogs to water until the next summer. However, despite the chill of winter, you can successfully introduce the PWD puppy to water. Your bathtub is an excellent place to start. Fill it with three to four inches of tepid water and place several floating toys that a puppy can grab. Once it finds pleasure in scooting about in the tepid water, introduce treats that it can first snatch from your hand at the top of the water, then grab from underwater, holding them in your hand a half-inch farther down during each succeeding bathtub session.

Deborah Lee Miller-Riley's expression shows the thrill of having her dogs earn Water Trial titles. Ashbey

Let's look back at how American PWDCA Water Trials began. The year was 1989; the place was New York City; the event, the annual meeting of the PWDCA. One comparatively new member, Deborah Lee Miller-Riley, was sitting listening attentively to member comments. Those about the show dogs and the health problems went over her head. Then she heard Herbert Miller, Jr. speaking with someone about water tests. The conversation intrigued her.

Miller mentioned it was one of his late wife Deyanne's fervent wishes to have the PWDCA form a water test of some kind. Committees had tentatively inquired into producing a Water Trial—they even had tried to write one similar to a Newfoundland Water Trial, but little had been accomplished.

Miller-Riley went home that night wondering what she could do to further an activity based upon the breed's working heritage.

Mathew Riley assists an eight-week-old puppy in its first water excursion. Courtesy Verne Foster

In these two pictures, Ch. Cequella's Count Sonny Bubba (Ch. Le-Hi Madeira Lancer ex Ch. Le-Hi Permanent Wave), owned by John and Lois Proniewski, shows the Portie's ancient heritage. Introduced to water as a puppy, Bubba waits for his ball to be thrown, then dives dramatically into the pool after it, fetching it from the bottom. Courtesy John Proniewski

"I knew," Miller-Riley said, "I would enjoy that kind of activity. I was an inexperienced trainer still dragging my PWD around an obedience training class. I wanted to do more with my dog." Then she laughed. "What did I know about training a dog for purposeful water work!"

However, she decided she was going to do something about it. She belonged to the regional club in Connecticut, the Fairfield County PWD Club (later renamed the Nutmeg PWD Club), which had been founded by Deyanne Miller. In honor of Miller, she decided she would do something about getting a water test for the PWD. Miller-Riley read every book she could find about water retrievers. She also contacted a member of the Newfoundland Dog Club of America, Elaine Lehr, author of a water-training book for Newfoundlands. Lehr urged her to move forward with her project, but to create tasks unique to PWDs, not to Newfoundlands. Lehr even visited the regional club and conducted a water-training workshop.

On July 16, 1989, the Fairfield club sponsored a Water Trial with certificates for those dogs that were able to perform a set of tasks in the water. Miller-Riley says, "My dog, Badge (Ch. Aquaries A Amparo, CD), earned his first acknowledgment for water work and received a certificate for Junior Water Dog from our regional club. I shall always treasure that certificate."

Within months, Miller-Riley was contacted by Kathy Olsen-Monroe, who belonged to the regional club called the Twin Cities PWDC. She, with another club member, Peggy Thomas, was initiating a water trial for their club and were looking for information. The three met later that year, and with the obedience expertise of Verne Foster, formulated the first Water Tests, which, in 1991, were accepted by the PWDCA.

The first tests were an immediate success; although revisions have been made, the basic tests reflect the hard work Miller-Riley, Olsen-Monroe and Thomas put into formulating them.

And the response of PWD owners to the tests is remarkable; they work as a team in their dedication to preserve the breed's water function. It's a sport in which owner and dog are a team (as in obedience), with training conducted year-round since 90 percent of it can be done on land. PWD regional clubs hold water seminars and water workshops, attracting more and more owners to the exciting and fulfilling sport. Growing numbers of owners are participating, because they find joy training their dogs in work almost lost with the near extinction of the breed.

If earning a water trial title with your PWD is one of your dreams, you can successfully accomplish it. Renee Reiherzer did. And she did it with a ten-year-old dog! Reiherzer, of De Leão Kennels, had wanted to earn a water title with Sardio, Ch. Ilara Sardio, but didn't have the opportunity to fulfill that dream until 1995 when her regional club (Valley of the Dogs PWDC) decided to host a water work weekend seminar. Although the seminar was held just a week prior to the closest water trial, Reiherzer realized this might be her only chance to earn a title for her dog. She says, "At Sardi's age, a

Ch. Anacove's La Primera Samba, CDX, Agility Dog (AD), Courier Water Dog (CWD) (Int., Am., Puerto Rican, South American Ch., Champion of the Americas White Cap Capitão do Monab, CD, TT ex Ch. Camerell's Delta Dawn, UD), demonstrates his eagerness to retrieve for his owner, Charles White. White, a PWDCA Water Trial judge, and his wife, Cathy Cates, are breeders associated with the Skyline prefix. Courtesy Charles White

dog's vigor and abilities can wane. But the instructing and the camaraderie at the seminar spurred me on. I was fairly confident Sardi could learn the water exercises, because the foundation had been laid in the past. He was obedient and he could swim.

"When one competes with an older dog," Reiherzer continues, "you have to watch how the dog reacts to unusual stresses. Our drive to the trial site took nine hours and when we arrived the temperature hovered near 100 degrees. I kept a close eye on him for signs of heat stress and kept him in the water or shade as much as possible. Then, even though I had carefully read the rules, there were points I hadn't understood. I anticipated the judge's commands in my eagerness to send Sardi on an exercise before I was supposed to send him. We failed."

Reiherzer continues: "Thank goodness, the regional club of Chicago put on a two-day trial. I had entered both days. We passed the test the second day. It was ten days before Sardi's tenth birthday when he earned the right to add AWD (Apprentice Water Dog) to his name. Sardi proved he could do the work he was meant to do. He also proved you can teach an old dog and—tougher yet—an old owner new tricks."

In PWDCA Water Trials there are one certificate and four titles to be earned. The first, a Certificate test (Junior Water Dog Certificate, JWD), is an easy test with the dog retrieving an object from under the water, riding on a moving boat with its owner and proving its swimming ability by swimming a short distance. The title tests—Apprentice Water Dog (AWD), Working Water Dog (WWD), Courier Water Dog (CWD) and Courier Water Dog Excellent (CWDX)—progress in difficulty, but all demonstrate water teamwork between owner and dog. Water Trial manuals can be purchased from secretaries of regional clubs sanctioned by the national club. (See Appendix for further information.)

Renee Reiherzer is encouraging her dog, Sardi, to pick up the wiffle ball from the lake bottom, an exercise required for the Apprentice Water Dog title.

Listed below are the names of dogs who have earned the two advanced water titles through the year 1995. To earn the Working Water Dog (WWD) title, dogs perform in the water several useful retrieving tasks, demonstrating teamwork with their owners. They retrieve a gear bag, a dummy from off a boat and multiple articles from the water and execute blind retrieves. To earn the Courier Water Dog (CWD) title, dogs must demonstrate their proficiency in performing difficult water tasks—a blind retrieve of a floating line, double retrieves from a boat, retrieval of a fishing net and retrieves following multiple directions, exercises that reflect the breed's historical value as a fisherman's helper. To earn the Courier Water Dog Excellent (CWDX) title, dog and handler have to qualify two more times at the CWD level. The list below notes the most advanced title each dog has earned.

WORKING WATER DOGS (WWD)

Dog's Name	Owner(s)
Ch. Afamado do Vale Negro	C. White/B. Rafferty/C. Molinari
Ch. Alto Mares Gambol N Man UDX CGC	E. Verkozen
Amendoa de Agua Pe	K. Fitzgerald
Ch. Aquaries A Amparo CD	D. L. Miller-Riley
Ch. Aquaries Bebe Por Moleiro	D. L. Miller-Riley
Ch. Augustine's Seagram's Seven CD	L. & L. Reinhart
Ch. Beira-Mar Barqueiro CD	R. Crosse/S. Burke
Brinmar's Portofino at Hi Tide	T. Burns
Ch. Camerell's Neocles Calypso UD	H. Berg
Ch. Cutwater's Knight Errant CD	L. Thompson
Cutwater Trafalgar Square	B. & V. Stoddard
Dacher's Just in Time CD	S. & L. D'Augusta
Ch. Fausto Bom Porto of Abeja CD	C. Reif
Ch. Glad Tidings Do Mar CD	K. & D. Olson
Ch. Helms Alee Restora's Neptune's Car	K. Monroe/J. Forsythe
Hunter's Great Gadabout	C. Gadd
Hytyd Moondance	J. Murray

WORKING WATER DOGS (WWD)

Dog's Name	Owner(s)
Jewell De Agua Anjo UD	K. Jez
Ch. Jewell de Agua's Windward Lad CDX	R. Zaremba
Knollkrest Kalypso Dancer	P. Marshall
Ch. Mariner Aldanza Cha Cha TD	M.J. & G. Dill
Ch. Maritimo's Helluva Brisa	R. & J. Kraus
Ch. Mooridge Blue Navigator	T. & M. Jennings
Ch. Neocles Achado of Mariner CD	S. Waltrip/L. Afong
Ch. Neocles Coral Sea Treasure CDX TDX	C. McCullough/J. Madderra
Northwind's Bolina	L. McDermott
Ch. Peja Aslan Amaral CD	J. Janes
Ch. Pennrico's Polly Wolly Doodle	R. Garcia
Ch. Pickwick's Port of Edmonds UD	V. Olson
Ch. Regala's Da Boomer of Tailwind CDX TDX	B. Mattheis
Regala's Navarro O'Cruzado NA	M. Harvey/M. Jackson
Restora's Dear Abby	J. & D. Miller/K. Olson
Restora's Don Pedro	J. & C. Kremer/E. Jaskowski
Ch. Robel First Lady	M. Dominguez/M. Lowman
AM/CAN Ch. Roughriders Cisco Pete CDX	E. & V. Storrs
Ch. Sandral Aurora Beldade	R. Birkholz
Seatail's Bosco da Gama CD	L. Hertzog
Ch. Seawatch Lady Godiver	M.K. & J. Schroeder
Ch. Sete Mares Sohappy Shanna-Dawn UD	P. Bartholomew/L. Carver
Stone Hollow's Borrasco CD	R. Garcia

Ch. Timbermist Lancar Flor de Mar CDX	J. Vanek-Nielsen
Ch. Whalers Cove Tobias CD	R. & J. Kraus

COURIER WATER DOGS (CWD)

Dog's Name	Owner(s)
Ch. Agua Lama Dulcinea CDX TDX	D. A. Zorn
Ch. Anacove's La Primera Samba CDX	C. White/C. Cates
Camerell's Buccaneer Beaver TD CDX	B. & B. Franklin

Ch. Roughrider's Reba Donzi, UD, CWD (Ch. Farmion Geo, UD ex Ch. Camerell's Roughrider Seeley, CDX), owned by Vicki and Charles Robinson, models the type of harness PWDs must wear when competing in PWDCA Water Trials.

Ch. Camerell's Buccaneer Beaver, UD, CWD (Ch. Le-Hi's Madeira Lancer ex Ch. Camerell's Delta Dawn, UD), owned by B. and B. Franklin, was the first Portuguese Water Dog to earn a Courier Water Dog title. Ashbey

COURIER WATER DOGS (CWD)

Dog's Name	Owner(s)
Ch. Camerell's Delta Clipper UD	V. Foster
Driftwood Little Surfer Girl CD	A. Haynie
Farmion Obrigada II UD	L. Thompson
Ch. High Seas Blue Boy UDTX	E. Jaskowski
Ch. Hunter's Franks Raisin Cain UD	P. Heinzleman
Ch. Marinheira Flor de Mar UDX	J. & H. Gilbert
My Sonnet from the Portuguese UD	M. Foster
Ch. Neocles Brisa of Peja CD	P. L. Thomas
U-CD Ch. Neocles Destiny of Mariner CDX TDX	J. Madderra/C. McCullough
Pennrico Alegria Diva	B. Bekker
Ch. Piedeli Brut De Paola UDTX	E. Jaskowski
Restora's Don Pedro	J. & C. Kremer
Ch. Roughrider's Reba Donzi UD	C. & V. Robinson
Sagres Do Vale Negro	R. Hirsch
Seatail's Aspirador CD AD	M.A. & B. McGunigle
Ch. Sun Joy's Flor Por Moleiro CD	D. Miller/B. Jorgensen

chapter 20

Performance Sports

AGILITY

Agility is an obstacle-course dog sport that makes for thrilling moments for all who watch or participate. Having the time of their lives, dogs jump over jumps, climb up and down ramps, crawl through tunnels and weave through poles, while being directed over and under and around and through by their owners—all against a time clock.

Another plus for the sport since its official inception in England in 1980 is that it's a great confidence builder and temperament stabilizer for dogs, young and old. Although fun, it's nonetheless a challenging team effort by owner and dog.

Variations of the original English rules soon swept the United States, and a number of clubs formed, such as the North American Dog Agility Committee (NADAC), United States Dog Agility Association (USDAA) and National Club for Dog Agility (NCDA), which is linked to the United Kennel Club. The American Kennel Club has also added Agility to its program of performance events.

The titles given by the existing clubs vary, but because participation is so rewarding, most devotees seek titles from more than one club even though the programs differ. Newcomers, puppies and adults, are introduced to all obstacles gradually, and Portuguese Water Dogs take to Agility like they take to water. The AKC Agility regulations rightfully say, "Agility results in a better rounded, conditioned dog, provides good basic training for search and rescue dogs, demonstrates good training and citizenship and has excellent spectator appeal."

The sport has become so popular that most classes have waiting lists and most Agility events have entry limits. AKC Agility Trials award the following

This photograph was taken at the exact moment Camerell's Call Me Cooper, CDX, AWD, MAD (Trezena Urso ex Ch. Natale do Mar), finished his Master Agility Dog title from the United States Dog Agility Association (USDAA). Cooper, owned by Alaina Alford-Moore, was nine years old at the time. Courtesy 4U2C Photography

Camerell's Mirror Image (Ch. Camerell's Duel at Diablo ex Ch. Camerell's Might E Minnie), owned by Alaina Axford-Moore, competing.

titles: Novice Agility (NA), Open Agility (OA), Agility Excellent (AX) and Master Agility Excellent (MX).

Charles (Bud) Kramer was one of the first Americans to see the sport's exciting potential. He initiated the NCDA program, providing a national Agility club for those interested in the sport and to help generate enthusiasm among all participants regardless of club affiliation. An official transfer of his NCDA program was made January 1, 1995, when the United Kennel Club, the second largest dog registry in the world, took the NCDA into its ever-expanding performance sports program. Kramer explains the differences in tests by the Agility clubs:

Conceptually, there are only two types of dog Agility. One stresses speed, while the other stresses accuracy in negotiating a greater variety of obstacles. The USDAA and AKC Agility programs emphasize speed in negotiating the courses, especially at the higher test levels. The NCDA/UKC program places less importance on speed, but uses the basis for scoring on additional obstacles plus a higher level of accuracy in advanced tests. I believe each of the two basic concepts serves a distinct purpose, and as such, will continue to expand. There is no doubt in my mind that Agility will eventually become the No. 1 dog performance event.

Kramer adds, "All organizations conduct trials under their own regulations, which exhibit various degrees of differences. One of the main differences between the NADAC and USDAA programs involves jump heights. The world registry, Federation Cynologique Internationale (FCI), has established regulations, but these apparently are used only at international competitions. Otherwise, trials are held under the regulations adopted by each member country's clubs."

How active will the Portuguese Water Dog be in this sport? Kramer says, "Certainly, the so-called 'obedience breeds' have made the biggest impact on the sport. The PWD is well adapted to this kind of activity. They are strong, fast and agile and love the sport."

Alaina Axford-Moore says, "In my opinion Agility is the most fun you can have with your dog. I purchased a three-month-old puppy, Camerell's Call Me Cooper (Cooper), in April, 1987. Five months later I enrolled him in an Agility workshop, sponsored by a local obedience club. 'Bud' Kramer was the guest speaker/instructor of the workshop. He used Cooper as a demonstration dog and Cooper seemed a natural. I was so encouraged that I attended all the workshops the local obedience club offered for the following two years."

The USDAA held a regional qualifying test in West Chester, Pennsylvania, in 1989, which Axford-Moore entered with Cooper. Much to her surprise, he qualified for the national competition to be held in Houston, Texas, later that year. Excited, she practiced with Cooper daily and when the date arrived, flew with him to Houston. They passed the first round, then the second and qualified for the finals, with Cooper placing eighth in the country.

Moore says, "I was hooked!"

Because there weren't any Agility clubs in her area, Moore founded one, the Keystone Agility Club, Inc., of Norristown, Pennsylvania, serving as its president for five years. In 1990, Cooper became the first dog in the United States to earn a USDAA Agility Dog title. His spectacular accomplishments include finishing third in the country at the Pedigree Grand Prix of Dog Agility in 1992 and completing his Master Agility Excellent (MX) title at age nine years in March 1996.

Ch. Camerell's Delta Clipper, UDX, CWD, performing the weave poles and bar jumping Agility exercises. Clipper is owned by Verne Foster

"Owning a Portuguese Water Dog," says Moore, "has certainly changed my life. My husband and I currently own three PWDs, Cooper, Ditto and Tatum. I now teach Agility and obedience classes and I am a licensed USDAA judge."

The most difficult title to earn in the USDAA format is Master Agility Dog (MAD). At the middle of 1996, four PWDs have earned the right to add this title to their name. They are:

Ch. Camerell's Call Me Cooper, CDX, AWD, MAD	Alaina Axford-Moore
Ch. Cutwater's Knight Errant, CD, WWD	Lynnmarie & Tom Thompson
Farmion Obrigada II, UD, CWD, MAD	Lynnmarie & Tom Thompson
Seatails Aspirator, CD, MAD*	MaryAnn & Brian McGunigle

TRACKING

Tracking is an extension of obedience work, and to be a successful tracker, a dog must be under the control of its owner at all times. The dog's sense of smell is so different from that of humans that we have no conception of the remarkable scenting abilities dogs possess. In the sport, the owner uses the dog's scenting ability to search for objects. Owners must rely on the dog's exquisite scenting abilities to recognize and follow the track laid. AKC's *Obedience Regulations* lists the rules.

At present, there are three titles dogs can earn in tracking: Tracking Dog (TD), Tracking Dog Excellent (TDX) and Variable Surface Tracker (VST), open to dogs with a TD or TDX title. This third title is eminently suited to contemporary tracking dogs, most of whom live in urban environments. A VST title would include tracking on different surfaces, such as asphalt, concrete and sand, with the dogs tracking on playgrounds, city streets and even staircases (rather than on open fields, as required for the TD and TDX titles).

Trezena Meia Bela earned the first Tracking title for PWDs on September 23, 1984. Bela was not quite eight months old at the time. Her owner, Virginia Dorsman, an obedience instructor, began tracking Bela at just eight weeks old. Dorsman says, "I began Bela's lessons in the basement; she found things I hid in a fun-and-games manner. At twelve weeks I started training her in the yard, using tracking flags."

Seatails Aspirator (Webster) earned his first USDAA title on May 27, 1995. In late April 1996, he earned his MAD title, the first dog of any breed to have accomplished this.

While Tracking titles should be easy for PWDs to earn considering their exquisite sense of smell, as noted by the listing below, too few Tracking titles have been earned as this book goes to press. In the listing below of dogs who have earned tracking titles through 1995, dogs earning a TDX title are not included among the TDs.

TRACKING DOG TITLES—TD

Dog's Name	Owner's Name	Year
Ch. Camerell's Jupiter Pluvius	Jean Robinson	1986
White Cap Corinthian	Lillabeth Webb	1986
Ch. Rebento Dita	Paula Stevens	1987
Ch. Roughrider's First Skipper	Barbara & Carl Friedrich	1987
Roughrider's Galley Mate	Barbara & Carl Friedrich	1987
Roughrider's Violeta	Jean & William Robinson	1987
Camerell's Amadeus	Ruth Giuffria	1988
Lake Breeze Amadeus Gimpy	B. & J. Rissman	1989
White Cap High Sea Xebec	C. Winkler/H. Dyson	1989
High Seas Blue Boy	Eileen Jaskowski	1991
Ch. Camerell's Buccaneer Beaver	B. & B. Franklin	1992
Ch. Camerell's Escamillo	Ruth Giuffria	1992
Ch. Mariner Aldanza Cha Cha	G. & M. Dill/C. McCullough	1993
Regala's Takes Two to Tango	Joan Heater	1993
Ch. Mariner Bait N Switch River Run	Cathy Winkler	1994
Roughrider Nina Carmenita	Margaret Warriner	1994
Seabreeze Nimble McDivot	Michael Caisse/K. Arends	1994
Ch. Riverrun Bet Ur Bottom Dollar	Cathy & Michael Winkler	1995

TRACKING DOG EXCELLENT TITLE—TDX

Dog's Name	Owner's Name	Year
Ch. Trezena Meia Bela	Virginia Dorsman	1985
Actondale's Salty Sailor	Virginia Dorsman	1987
Ch. Regala's Daboomer of Tailwind	Barbara Matheis	1990
Ch. Neocles Coral Sea Treasure	J. Madderra/C. McCullough	1991
Ch. Piedelai Brut De Paolo	Eileen Jaskowski	1991
Ch. Aqua Lama's Dulcinea	D. Zorn/A. Vanek	1992
High Seas Blue Boy	Eileen Jaskowski	1992
Ch. Neocles Destiny of Mariner	C. McCullough/J. Madderra	1992
White Cap High Sea Xebec	C. Winkler/H. Dyson	1995

chapter 21

Portuguese Water Dogs in Other Countries

CANADA

The Portuguese Water Dog Club of Canada was formed in 1993 with recognition accorded by the Canadian Kennel Club (CKC) shortly thereafter. Nine directors assist Club officers in supplying services to members. These include a newsletter providing information about health, education and training; it also describes upcoming events, as well as relating anecdotes about members' dogs. The Club sponsors a yearly supported entry at the Credit Valley Kennel & Obedience Club, the largest dog show in Canada, held at the Skydome in Toronto, Ontario. At the end of 1995, the Club had more than fifty members, most of whom resided in the Ontario area. The Club began expanding its education program to fanciers in other provinces, a difficult task given the vastness of the country. Many import dogs from the United States, because the few PWDCC breeders have long waiting lists for puppies. Club members also support many U.S. regional and national Club events. Current PWDCC member breeders are Barbara Floch, Cosmos Kennels (Milton, Ontario); Leona Ives, Aliana Kennels (Niagara Falls, Ontario); and Cathy Sockett (Orillia, Ontario).

Further information can be obtained from PWDCC Director Heather L. Evans, 33 Glen Manor Drive, Toronto, Ontario, M4E 2X4, Canada.

ENGLAND

Miss Patricia Jones of Wellknowe Kennels, Cartmel PWDs, Cambria, who judged Sweepstakes at the PWDCA National Specialty in 1995, says, "There were about 350 registered PWDs in Great Britain in 1995, with only approximately forty-five shown. To my knowledge, there are not any health problems with most of the dogs living to great ages. Temperaments are usually good—with a very small percentage being shy. I have only seen one dog show aggression towards another, and this was at a very busy show. The Lion clip is the standard trim in Great Britain. As we do not have a Retriever clip, pet buyers, who do not like the clipped parts of the show dogs, therefore, fortunately, do not buy a 'cute puppy.'"

The Portuguese Water Dog first arrived in Great Britain in the 1950s. The original imports died out, and the ancestors of the present British population were imported in 1979 and 1980, with one pair going to Trish Gilpin and one pair to Paddy Holbrook O'Hara. Gilpin's pair were to start the Glenwhin line, but the male was sterile, and so the bitch, Balalaika, was mated to Devil de Alvalade. Imports from Sally Starte of Portugal followed.

Paddy Holbrook O'Hara imported Eveil and Dana de Alvalade. After a short while she imparted them to Miss Pat Jones, and so began the Cartmel line. The first litter bred at Cartmel contained Cartmel The Fisherman, who was the first of the breed to be exhibited at Crufts in the Any Variety (AV) class in 1984. However, it wasn't until 1989 that the PWD would have its own classes; this was at the National Working Breeds Championship Show. In 1991 the PWD began to be exhibited at Crufts.

British breeders include Ruth and David Bussell (Brigantia); Cheryl Ducket (Coparit); Nigel Barrow (Elmley); Jayne Johns (Gemsons); Trish Gilpin (Glenwhin); Carol Queen (Grandways); Rachael Reddin (Rarjo); Sue Tweedie (Rysalka); and Patricia Jones (Cartmel).

Direct inquiries regarding Portuguese Water Dogs in England may be made to the Secretary, PWD Club of Great Britain, c/o The Kennel Club, 1 Charges Street, Piccadilly, London, W1Y 8AB.

FINLAND

The first Portuguese Water Dogs arrived in Finland in 1990. At the end of 1996 there were approximately 200 Portuguese Water Dogs in Finland, the breed fast rising in popularity. The national PWD club in Finland, established in 1995, is named *Vesikoirat r.y.*, the name meaning "water dogs." At the present time, two other breeds are also sponsored by the Vesikoirat r.y: the Spanish and Italian Water Dogs.

Direct inquiries to the chairperson of the club, Mrs. Taru Hentola, Temppelikatu 19 D 77, 00100 Helsinki, Finland.

PORTUGAL

Augusto Guimaraes of De Gifford Kennels comments on the Cão de Agua of today: "The dogs in the Algarve are not small but well built. The males about twenty-two inches tall, even more. Bitches are, of course, smaller—nineteen

Glenwhin Cafezinho at Gemson (Ch. Batel de Alvalade ex Josefiog de Azambuja), owned by Jayne Johns (UK). Courtesy David Calton

Grandways Fire Water at Gemson (Glenwhin Cafezinho at Gemson ex Elmley Muddy Water at Grandways), owned by Jayne Johns (UK). Courtesy Luther

to twenty inches tall. The families Algarbiorum and de Alvalade/Vale Negro have nothing in common, although some sources claim they are alike."

The first dog Carla Molinari owned after she began her Vale Negro Kennels in 1980 was Ch. Arriba de Alvalade (Ch. Yole de Alvalade ex Ch. Truta de Alvalade). She then imported two bitches from Sig Orselli of Italy. They were Ch. Bamba del Bragozzo (brown) and Kira (black), both sired by Ch. ZumZum de Alvalade. Ch. Arriba de Alvalade and Ch. Truta sired Baluarte de Alvalade, later sent to Sonja Santos, a PWDCA member of Hampton Bays, New York. Baluarte became a well-known American champion and popular stud.

Molinari also obtained Ch. Makuti, sired by Ch. Yole de Alvalade. "Makuti," says Molinari, "established the type this kennel is known for, namely broad heads and heavy bones." Two of his daughters, Margarida and Hortense do Zoo De Lisboa, became important additions to Molinari's breeding program. Cherna Reliant, whom Deyanne Farrell Miller sent to Portugal for a period of time, sired Portuguese/Spanish/French/ International Ch. Juba Do Vale Negro and his daughter Portuguese/Spanish Ch. Lisboa Do Vale Negro.

Molinari says, "In more recent years we have used a UK import from the original Alvalade lines, Cartmel do Vale Negro, and recently from the breeding of Cacau's granddaughter Ch. Lontra do Vale Negro to Am., Port Ch. Pinehaven's On the Town (Best of Breed and Best in Show at the 1992 PWDCA Specialty) produced our two younger champions: Ch. Al-Taje Do Vale Negro and Ch. Al-Gharb Do Vale Negro."

The following kennels in Portugal bred at least two litters in 1994: (1) National Kennels run by the government and located in Olhão, Algarve; (2) Val Do Zebro, run by the Navy, Escola De Fuzileiros, Val Do Zebro, Barreiro; (3) Vale Negro, Carla Molinari; (4) Canil Das Avencas, Eurice Rodrigues; (5) Cerrado Do Rio, Arnaldo Capela; (6) Casa Serra De Agua, Teresa Guedes; (7) Monte Da Catula, M. Lodato Faria; (8) Quinta Da Victoria, Francisco Sousa; (9) Canil Do Caique, Miguel Ferreira; (10) Canil Do Seixal, Odete Duarte; (11) De Gifford, Augusto Guimaraes; (12) White Tower, João Pedroso Fernandes.

Inquiries on Portugal's PWD clubs and breeders may be directed to Augusto Guimaraes, Past and Honorary President of the Clube Do Cão De Companhia De Portugal. His address is Casa Val De Areal, Qta Da Marinha, 2750 Cascais, Portugal.

The first ophthalmology (CERF) clinic held in Portugal took place in 1994. These participants are (from left) Dr. James Clinton of the United States and Dr. Neiva Rorreiaand and Augusto Guimaraes, of Portugal. Of the 120 Portuguese dogs tested, 27 were PWDs. Americans who helped make this clinic possible were Lewis Grello, Suzanne Garcia, Susan McMahon, Art and Martha Stern, Barbara Paul, Robin Valliant, Carol Mattingly, Sandra Sayboldt, Beverly Jorgensen, William and Mary Harkins, Judy Ferland, and Darryll and Jeanne Rylatt.

Ch. Cacau do Vale Negro (Ch. Mare do Vale Negro ex Margarida do Zoo de Lisboa). Courtesy Carla Molinari

Ebano do Vale Negro, owned by T. Hanslev, has amassed many distinctions in dog shows on the European continent. His titles include International, Austrian, Dutch, Danish and Swedish championships, Bundesieger (Germany), Winner at Amsterdam, World Winner 1993–1995 and European Winner 1993, 1995. Courtesy Carla Molinari

SWEDEN

The name of the Swedish Portuguese Water Dog Club is *Sallskapet for Portugisisk Vattenhund*. Direct inquiries to the chairperson of the club, Mrs. Luise Ekenflycht, Edebo Prastgard, S-76391 Hallstavik, Sweden.

Appendix: Resources for Information

When requesting information by mail from the following sources, always enclose a self-addressed stamped envelope (SASE).

CHAPTER 2, THE PORTUGUESE WATER DOG IN AMERICA: THE EARLY YEARS

PWDCA Directory of Dogs

Jody Van Loan

99 Maple Avenue

Greenwich, CT 06830

Fax: 203-661-9347

PWDCA Health Registry

Mrs. Howard C. Babbitt

P.O. Box 74, 1153 Rt. #47

Dennisville, NJ 08214

Fax: 609-861-5402

The Courier

Kathryn Braund, Editor

824B Rhoades Road

Winlock, WA 98596

Fax: 360-785-0212

CHAPTER 9, REARING THE PUPPY

Information on microchips or tattoos: The American Kennel Club (AKC) manages a database for all microchip and tattoo organizations and assists in recovering a lost pet. Help is available on a twenty-four hour basis. Contact:

AKC Companion Animal Recovery

5580 Centerview Drive, Suite 250

Raleigh, NC 27606-3394

Tel: 1-800-252-7894; Fax: 919-233-1290; E-mail: found@akc.org

CHAPTER 10, GROOMING THE PORTUGUESE WATER DOG

Dog equipment supply catalog houses

Cherrybrook

Route 57, Box 15

Broadway, NJ 08808

Tel: 1-800-524-0820

Doctors Foster & Smith

2253 Air Park Road

Rhinelander, WI 54501

Tel: 1-800-826-7206 (24 hours)

J-B Wholesale Pet Supplies, Inc.

5 Raritan Road

Oakland, NJ 07436

Tel: 1-800-526-0388

Pet Warehouse

P.O. Box 310

Xenia, OH 45385

Fax: 1-800-513-1913

R.C. Steele

1989 Transit Way, Box 910

Brockport, NY 14420

Tel: 1-800-872-3773

Video: *Grooming the Portuguese Water Dog,* by Judith G. Seibert

P.O. Box 2062

Overgaard, AZ 85933

Tel: 520-535-3540

CHAPTER 12, WHELPING PORTUGUESE WATER DOG PUPPIES

Acidophilus. A biological product containing lactobacillus cultures. Acidophilus helps kill harmful bacteria in the stomach. It is particularly useful after a dog has been on antibiotics for infections (antibiotics can kill good as well as harmful bacteria). Use it also for an acute case of diarrhea caused by bacterial infections. This product can be purchased at drugstores.

Duprin. A respiratory aid used by veterinarians for treating newborns with excess fluid in their lungs.

Pedialyte. From the makers of Similac, a solution of water, dextrose, potassium citrate, sodium chloride and sodium citrate used in puppy milk formulas for excellent oral electrolyte maintenance. It is used by veterinarians for treating fluid loss in puppies due to diarrhea and vomiting, as it quickly restores lost fluids and minerals.

CHAPTER 14, HEALTH

What's The Diagnosis, by Race Foster, DVM, and Marty Smith, DVM (1995), Howell Book House, 1633 Broadway, New York, NY 10019. Written in lay terms, this book helps dog owners when their pet has health problems and offers an excellent understanding of common canine disorders.

The Consumer's Guide to Dog Food, by Liz Palika (1996), Howell Book House, 1633 Broadway, New York, NY, 10019. This excellent paperback book tells dog owners everything they could want to know about dog food and how to choose the right food for a particular dog.

CHAPTER 16, AMERICAN BREEDERS OF THE PORTUGUESE WATER DOG

PWDCA Corresponding Secretary

Jody Van Loan

99 Maple Avenue

Greenwich, CT 06830

Fax: 203-661-9347

CHAPTER 17, SHOWING YOUR DOG

Rules and Regulations Applying to Registration and Dog Shows

The American Kennel Club

5580 Centerview Drive, #200

Raleigh, NC 27606-3390

(Single copies are free. Additional copies are $1.00 per copy.)

CHAPTER 18, OBEDIENCE TRAINING AND THE PORTU-GUESE WATER DOG

Dog Obedience Training Manuals, Volume I and II, The First and Second Ten Weeks, by Kathryn Braund (Denlingers, 1983, 1984), are available from Alpine Publishers, 225 S. Madison Avenue, Loveland, CO 80537. Fax: 970-667-9157.

Getting a Head Start in Obedience with Verne Foster, video (1992), is available from Professional Production Services, 25302 Branchaster, Farmington Hills, MI 48336-1637.

AKC Obedience Regulations is available from The American Kennel Club, 5580 Centerview Drive, #200, Raleigh, NC 27606-3390. Single copies are free. Additional copies are $1.00 per copy.

CHAPTER 19, WATER WORK

PWDCA Water Trial Manual

   c/o Cheryl Smith (Mrs. David)

   116 Teresita Way

   Los Gatos, CA 95032

   Fax: 408-358-3003

CHAPTER 20, PERFORMANCE SPORTS

AKC Regulations for Agility Trials

   The American Kennel Club

   5580 Centerview Drive, #200

   Raleigh, NC 27606-3390

   Single copies are free. Additional copies are $1.00 per copy.

AKC Tracking Regulations

   (Address and copy cost as above.)

References

Algarve Water Dog, Silveira Santana.

Animals, Men and Myths, Richard Lewinsohn, 1954.

Caes De Racas Portuguesas...Uma Boa Escolha (Portuguese Dog Breeds...A Fine School!), Clube Portugues De Canicultura.

Caes Portugueses (Chiens Portugais), Lisbon, Portugal, 1955.

Cão de Agua Portugues, Estalão da Raca, Dr. Frederico M. Pinto Soares, Prof. Dr. Manuel Fernandes Marques, 1938.

Canine Reproduction, Phyllis A. Holst MS, DVM, 1985.

Dogs in Britain, Clifford L.B. Hubbard, 1948.

Dogs of the World, Dr. Erich Schneider-Leyer, 1972.

Dogs: Their History and Development, Volume 1, Edward C. Ash (1927).

Facts About the Portuguese Water Dog (Um Pouco de Historia Sobre A Historia Do Cão de Agua Portuguese), Dr. Maria Ana Marques, 1981.

Genetics for Dog Breeders, Frederick B. Hutt, 1979.

Genetics for Dog Breeders, Roy Robinson, F.I. Biol., 1990.

How to Breed Dogs, Leon F. Whitney, DVM, 1971.

Livro Portugues De Origens (LPO), 1946 through 1982.

Medical and Genetic Aspects of Purebred Dogs, Veterinary Medicine Publishing Company, 1983.

Of Englishe Dogges, Dr. Caius, 1570.

Official Standard of the Spanish Poodle, FCI.

Origin of the Weimaraner, Deutsche Waidwerk, No. 19, Robert Fries.

Os Pescadores, Raul Brandão, 1932.

Portuguese Dictionary, Algarve, 1938.

Practical Dog Breeding and Genetics, London, Eleanor Frankling, 1974.

Standards for the Portuguese Water Dog, 2nd Edition, Frederico Pinto Soares and Manuel Fernandes Marques, 1951.

The American Book of the Dog, G. O. Shields, 1891.

The Art and Science of Judging Dogs, Curtis and Thelma Brown, 1976.

The Classic Encyclopedia of the Dog, Vero Shaw, 1881.

The Dog in Action, Lyon McDowell, 1970.

The Inheritance of Coat Color in Dogs, Clarence C. Little, Sc.D., 1957.

The Joy of Breeding Your Own Show Dog, Ann Serane, 1980.

The Marvels of Animal Behavior, National Geographic Society, 1972.

The National Geographic Book of Dogs, 1958.

The New Complete Labrador Retriever, Helen Warwick, 1986.

The New Complete Newfoundland, Margaret Booth Chern, 1975.

The Observer's Book of Dogs, Clifford L.B. Hubbard, 1945.

The Sportsman's Cabinet, William Taplin, 1803.

The Sportsman's Repository, John Scott, 1831.

The Standard Book of Dog Breeding, A New Look, Dr. Alvin Grossman, 1992.

"The Water Dog," by Prof. Manuel Fernandes Marques, *Magazine of Veterinary Medicine,* Lisbon, Portugal, 1938.

The Water Dog, Customs of Fishermen and Techniques of Fishing, Margarida Ribeiro. Lisbon, Portugal, 1974.

The World of Dogs, Josephine Z. Rine, 1944.

The World of Dogs, Josephine Z. Rine, 1965.

Working Dogs of the World, Clifford L.B. Hubbard, 1947.

World Book, 1968.

Voyage of the Armada, David Howarth, 1981.